T0295657

'Demaria makes a timely and important contribution to political ecology, demonstrating that neither the political economy nor materiality can be considered as "context" since they are always already co-constituted. The book's rich analysis exposes how the politics around social metabolism is intrinsically linked to the struggle against exploitation, dispossession, and contamination'.

—Maria Kaika, University of Amsterdam, author of *City of flows: Modernity, nature, and the city* and co-editor of *Turning up the Heat: Urban Political Ecology for a Climate Emergency*, with Keil, Mandler and Tzaninis

'This book delves deeply into unseen aspects of poverty in India, discusses the environmentalism of the poor, and clarifies the debates on the so-called circular economy. We know that the industrial economy is entropic. This book is a major contribution to research on the economy of the Entropocene'.

—Joan Martinez Alier, Universitat Autònoma de Barcelona, and author of *Environmentalism of the Poor*

'Based on more than ten years of field experience and two case studies in India, Federico Demaria provides a perceptive and compelling exploration of the power relations at the heart of recycling in the global South. His detailed discussion of the conflicts that exist in the recycling sector, both locally and globally, not only highlights social, political, and institutional dynamics but sensitively tells the story of informal recyclers, or waste pickers, whom he identifies as important environmental workers. Ultimately, Demaria makes an impassioned plea for a fair and just evaluation of the contribution made by waste pickers who stand at the front line of climate change resilience.'

—Libby McDonald, Lecturer and Inclusive Economies Lead; Massachusetts Institute of Technology, Boston, D-Lab

'How can we "repoliticize waste metabolism beyond techno-managerial solutions"? What are the global and urban "social relations of recycling"? What are the key concepts to understand the recycling scape and the processes of dispossession waste pickers are subject to? Under what conditions can informal waste pickers be meaningfully engaged in complex systems such as circular and green economies? We need to critically engage with the debates on sustainability, alternative models for the economy, and development and explore in depth the room for waste pickers inclusion in such systems—and this is what precisely the book *The Political Ecology of Informal Waste Recyclers in India: Circular Economy, Green Jobs, and Poverty* does. Drawing from many cases but particularly from the Delhi waste conflict around privatization of waste and introduction of incineration, the book traces back the struggles of workers and allies and makes a powerful call for the recognition of the crucial role informal waste workers make to the environment and the economy. The book makes a critical contribution to the growing knowledge of waste pickers by studying not only through a poignant narrative of conflicts and struggles but also by introducing key concepts for understanding the threats and the struggles for resistance. As Paulo Freire said: "Knowledge emerges only through invention and re-invention, through the restless, impatient, continuing, hopeful inquiry human beings pursue in the world, with the world, and with each other"'.

—**Sonia Dias**, Women in Informal Employment Globalizing and Organizing (WIEGO)

The Political Ecology of Informal Waste Recyclers in India

Circular Economy, Green Jobs, and Poverty

FEDERICO DEMARIA

*Associate Professor of Ecological Economics and Political Ecology,
Department of Economic History, Institutions, Politics and World
Economy, University of Barcelona (Spain); Senior Researcher, Institute
of Environmental Science and Technology, Autonomous University of
Barcelona (Spain); and Visiting Fellow, International Institute of
Social Studies (The Hague, Netherlands)*

OXFORD
UNIVERSITY PRESS

Great Clarendon Street, Oxford, OX2 6DP,
United Kingdom

Oxford University Press is a department of the University of Oxford.
It furthers the University's objective of excellence in research, scholarship,
and education by publishing worldwide. Oxford is a registered trade mark of
Oxford University Press in the UK and in certain other countries

© Federico Demaria 2023

The moral rights of the author have been asserted

First Edition published in 2023

All rights reserved. No part of this publication may be reproduced, stored in
a retrieval system, or transmitted, in any form or by any means, without the
prior permission in writing of Oxford University Press, or as expressly permitted
by law, by licence or under terms agreed with the appropriate reprographics
rights organization. Enquiries concerning reproduction outside the scope of the
above should be sent to the Rights Department, Oxford University Press, at the
address above

You must not circulate this work in any other form
and you must impose this same condition on any acquirer

Published in the United States of America by Oxford University Press
198 Madison Avenue, New York, NY 10016, United States of America

British Library Cataloguing in Publication Data

Data available

Library of Congress Control Number: 2023930679

ISBN 978-0-19-286905-0

DOI: 10.1093/oso/9780192869050.001.0001

Links to third party websites are provided by Oxford in good faith and
for information only. Oxford disclaims any responsibility for the materials
contained in any third party website referenced in this work.

To the waste recyclers of the world,
to which I belong, since the ideas discussed here are also
the result of recycling.

Foreword

In this book, Federico Demaria discusses a world issue through case studies in India. In particular, he looks at solid waste disposal conflicts that are related to recycling. We could say that he discusses the social and political dimensions of the circular economy. Recycling tends to be always seen as positive, but what are its social and environmental costs? Are we ready to use slaves and pollute local ecosystems in order to close a little the circularity gap?

The industrial economy is not circular, it is increasingly entropic. Energy from the photosynthesis of the distant past, fossil fuels, is burned and dissipated. Even without further economic growth the industrial economy would need new supplies of energy and materials extracted from the 'commodity frontiers', producing also more waste (including excessive amounts of greenhouse gases). Therefore, new ecological distribution conflicts (EDCs) arise all the time. Such EDCs are often 'valuation contests' displaying incommensurable plural values. There are many examples of such conflicts in the Atlas of Environmental Justice (EJAtlas. org), for instance on the mining of coal, iron ore, and bauxite in India. There are conflicts on extraction of materials, on their transport and on the disposal of waste. Climate change is arguably the largest waste disposal conflict given the excessive production of carbon dioxide. Also the pollution of water is a waste disposal conflict.

The concept of 'circular economy' implies that material resources could be increasingly sourced from within the economy, reducing environmental impact by increasing the reuse and recycling of materials. The aim would be to minimize waste and move towards a closed-loop economy. However, this socio-technical 'imaginary' has no relation to reality as revealed by biophysical, metabolic analysis. There is an enormous 'circularity rift' that looks more like an abyss than a bridgeable gap. The industrial economy is not circular, it is entropic. There is a huge 'metabolic gap' between the 'fresh' material input and the recycled material input into the economy. At the world level, the first is about 92 Gt (gigatons or billion tons) per year (including the energy carriers, excluding water) and the second about 8 Gt. Let us assume that the world economy grows slowly and merely doubles the material input requirement in 70 years. Of the material input of 200 Gt let us assume that 100 Gt are recycled. An enormous improvement in the recycling rate from 8% to 50%, and however still a small increase (from 92 Gt to 100 Gt) in the 'fresh' material input required every year. If less than 10% of materials are recycled, where do the other 90% come from? My answer is: from the new commodity extraction frontiers and also to some extent from customary sources. Thus aluminium may come to some extent from recycling, it may come from bauxite from old mines which are used more intensively, or it may very likely come from new bauxite mines.

There is a new collective initiative for the historical study of 'commodity frontiers' and also a new journal with this title (https://commodi tyfrontiers.com/journal/). This concept (Moore, 2000) is becoming ever more relevant. The industrial economy marches all the time to the extraction frontiers in search of materials and it also travels to the waste disposal frontiers. The waste is sometimes deposited anywhere (solid or liquid waste, or GHG, greenhouse gases), and sometimes a small part of it is economically valued again by recyclers, or in controversial REDD schemes for 'capturing' carbon dioxide (Demaria and Schindler, 2015). Both the expanding commodity extraction frontiers and the waste disposal frontiers are often inhabited by humans and certainly by other species. Hence the growth in the number of conflicts over the use of the environment, and as a response the growing strength of the environmental justice movement.

In my 2002 book *The Environmentalism of the Poor*, I discussed indicators of urban unsustainability as indicators of social conflict. The ecological view of cities, today well known, has roots in the chemistry and physics of the nineteenth century, as when Justus von Liebig lamented the loss of nutrients in cities which did not return to the soil. Before the Athens Charter and Le Corbusier's influence, the ecological view was influential in urban planning, most significantly in Patrick Geddes' work, and later in the work of Lewis Mumford in the United States and Radhakamal Mukerjee, a self-described social ecologist, in India. Geddes was a biologist and urban planner. Writing to Mumford from Calcutta on 31 August 1918, he had made one main point regarding ecological city planning. In his City Report for Indore he wanted to break with the conventional drainage of 'all to the Sewer' replaced by 'all to the Soil'. Today, we would refer to this as closing a little the 'circularity gap'. Shiv Visvanathan powerfully asserted that today's Gandhi would not be so uniquely concerned with the virtues of the rural village.

> Gandhi would make ... the scavenger the paradigmatic figure of modern urban India ... Gandhi argued that waste has not been fully thought through by city science ... sewage rather than becoming a source of pollution would become a source of life and work. The classic example of city sewage use was Calcutta. This much maligned city uses its sewage to grow the finest vegetables ... By focusing on waste, the city sciences of today can recover an agricultural view of the world.
>
> (Visvanathan, 1997: 234–235)

Federico Demaria doesn't discuss such scavenging but he discusses deeply, after many years of fieldwork in both cases, the informal recyclers of both industrial and urban solid waste, namely shipbreaking at Alang and recycling in Delhi. I have known Federico for over 15 years already, he came to ICTA at the Autonomous University of Barcelona after studying economics in Bologna and in Paris, already interested in degrowth of the economy but without experience outside Europe. After securing a doctoral fellowship he went on his own to Alang in Gujarat to research shipbreaking and metal recycling, not an easy place for a first contact with India. He came back safely to Barcelona. Already struck by attraction to India, he went back to Delhi and lived with urban recyclers and cooperated with their trade union, All India Kabadi Mazdoor Mahasangh (AIKMM). Armed with these deep personal experiences and with some concepts from ecological economics and political ecology, he wrote several articles and a doctoral thesis, which he has now converted into this readable book. It is a monograph on India but the topic is relevant also for the rest of the world.

Joan Martinez-Alier
Emeritus Professor, Institute of Environmental Science and Technology, Autonomous University of Barcelona (Spain). His most well-known books are *Ecology and Economics* (1984), *Environmentalism of the Poor* (2005), *Land, Water, Air and Freedom* (2023). He has been awarded the Balzan Prize in 2020.

Preface

Since I was a teenager I have always been concerned with justice. Being born in a conservative small village in the Alps of the northwest of Italy did not make political engagement too easy. The Catholic Church was the only site for community activities. Thanks to my older brother Daniele, and Radio Flash (an historical anarchist radio from Torino), I was introduced in the late 1990s to the anti-globalization movement. I was then lucky enough to obtain a scholarship for the United World College of the Adriatic where I finished my high school, but more importantly expanded my horizons. It was there that I started to study economics, which then convinced me to learn and practise development economics. However, the years spent in Bologna (Italy) for my undergraduate degree in political economy, rather than shedding some light, confused me a lot. The more I studied economics, the more I was disappointed with it. This triggered an intellectual search that brought me to degrowth, ecological economics, and political ecology. I spent one year in Paris with Allain Caillé, an economic anthropologist and leader of the MAUSS group (Anti-utilitarian Movement in the Social Sciences), and then went to the Autonomous University of Barcelona to study ecological economics and political ecology with Joan Martinez-Alier and his team. I didn't expect at the time that Barcelona would become my new home.

How I became interested in waste, I don't exactly know and might have to be found in my subconscious, to be explored in other instances, for instance with psychoanalysis. The initial idea for this book was given to me by Joan Martinez-Alier. Back in 2008 he asked if I was interested in doing some research on shipbreaking in India. The interest for waste pickers came from my friend Juan David Uribe, a post-industrial designer from Colombia who had worked with *recicladores* in Medellin. In 2009 I started my PhD thesis, on which this book is based, that I defended in 2017.

The perspective to work with some of the most impoverished social groups in one of the most impoverished countries in the world, like India, attracted me because of my original interest about development. What I have learned about development, in India and elsewhere, is not entirely explained in this book. The critique to development and the alternatives to it has been my other research interest. In particular, the degrowth movement and debate has been where I have engaged the most. This should explain why it took me so long to actually finish this book. The rest of the story is what I narrate in this book. In a nutshell, I argue that the struggles of informal recyclers constitute an attempt to re-politicize waste metabolism beyond techno-managerial solutions by fostering counter-hegemonic discourses and praxis.

What are the main theoretical contributions of this book? Political ecology understands every ecological issue as a political one. It aims at politicizing environmental issues. To this end, there are fundamental questions to be addressed: Who has access to the environment? How and by whom is it managed? How are environmental goods and bads distributed? How is nature socially constructed? How and by whom are new socio-natures and spaces produced? Who benefits and who loses? Accordingly, along these lines, my research in general, and this book in particular, aims to inform theory on how environments are shaped, politicized, and contested. This book contributes to our understanding of social metabolism in general (the use of energy and materials within the economy), and waste in social metabolism in particular. First, I examine the relationship between social metabolism and conflict, looking from a situated political ecology perspective, at how differences in the structure and nature of particular social metabolisms create different conflict dynamics. Second, I shed light on an often forgotten but very important part of social metabolism which is the informal recycling of waste. I evaluate the contribution of informal recycling, and I investigate how power influences the social relations of production (or recycling), and how these shift costs to informal recyclers. Then, I make a case for the recognition of the important contribution of informal recyclers in making social metabolism more circular, and I call for due compensation of the services they provide, instead of a dispossession from their means of production, and a shifting of social costs of enterprises and consumers to them. The latter is what I call accumulation by contamination. The case studies help to explain what I mean with this new concept, and how it differs from accumulation by dispossession (famously introduced by the geographer David Harvey). In the postface, I will contextualize this book in my broader intellectual project that could be seen as a contribution to a global political economy of environment and development.

Acknowledgements

First and foremost, I acknowledge the recyclers, both the ones that spent time with me, and the ones that would have liked to, but were not allowed and sometimes even threatened. I owe to them what I have understood about the informal recycling sector (and beyond) that is here explained. This is also true of the many activists that supported me throughout my journey, in particular Shashi Bhushan (AIKMM), Gopal Krishna (Toxic Watch Alliance), Dharmesh Shah and Neil Tangri (GAIA), Lucia Fernandez (Global Alliance of Wastepickers, WIEGO), Kaveri Gill, Dunu Roy (Hazard Centre), Ravi Agarwal (Toxic Links), Madhumita Dutta (Corporate Accountability Desk), and Nityanand Jayaraman (Vettiver Koottamaippu).

Second, I acknowledge the help received by colleagues, students and friends, at the Institute of Environmental Science and Technology (ICTA) at the Autonomous University of Barcelona (UAB), Research & Degrowth (R&D), University of Barcelona (UN), Centre for Studies in Science Policy (CSSP) at the Jawaharlal Nehru University (JNU), International Institute of Social Studies (ISS) and elsewhere. In particular, Giorgos Kallis for his intellectual clarity; Joan Martinez Alier for his guidance; David Harvey for his encouragement; Seth Schindler who has been an incredible research mate in Delhi; my good friend Giacomo D'Alisa with whom I have grown intellectually and personally for the last 10 years; my researcher assistants D. & D. and Prerna Nair; my coach Amalia because her guidance during the late stage of writing this book helped me to overcome my mental barriers; last, but not the least, Brototi Roy for the copy editing. I also want to thank for support and constructive comments on previous drafts of the manuscript Deepak Malghan, Ignasi Puig Ventosa, John O'Neill, Julien Francois Gerber, Christos Zografos, Giuseppe Munda, Richard Christian, Isabelle Anguelovsky, Arturo Escobar, Melanie Samson, Lucia Fernandez, Rohan D'Souza, and the three anonymous reviewers at Oxford University Press. Since so many people have participated in this research project, I have chosen to use the subject pronoun 'we'. In particular, the ideas about accumulation by contamination presented in Section 2.4 were developed with Giacomo D'Alisa. Moreover, Chapter 4 is co-authored with Seth Schindler, with whom we also formulated the concept of waste-based commodity frontiers discussed in Chapter 6.

Third, I am thankful for the support from all staff at Oxford University Press, in particular the editors Moutushi Mukherjee, Chandrima Chatterjee, and Dhiraj Pandey.

Fourth, I am grateful to my partner, son, and extended family for their support.

Fifth, I acknowledge support from the Serra Hunter programme, the Maria de Maeztu Unit of Excellence ICTA UAB (CEX2019-0940-M), the FP7 European project EJOLT (Environmental Justice Organizations, Liabilities and Trade), the European Research Council (ERC) projects EnvJustice (GA695446), led by Joan Martinez Alier, and PROSPERA (GA947713), led by Mario Pansera; and last, but not least, the Global Alliance of Wastepickers and the NGO Women in Informal Employment: Globalizing and Organizing (WIEGO).

Contents

1
Introduction

Waste Is Increasingly a Site of Social Conflict

1.1 Why This Book: The Research Questions

Smithu and Akbar never met but they could have been brothers. Both were born in rural villages of India, just like more than half of the country´s population. Their families depended on subsistence agriculture in two of the poorest states of India, Jharkhand and Bihar respectively. However, they did not own enough land to obtain a decent livelihood. They migrated in search of better opportunities. Smithu now spends his days cutting down the large metal structures of ships with a torch on the beaches of Alang, Gujarat, some 1,800 km away from home. Meanwhile, Akbar goes door-to-door collecting recyclable waste in a neighbourhood of Delhi on his tricycle rickshaw with a cart. Both are a part and parcel of the informal recycling sector. Both have found themselves obliged to work in dangerous conditions, risking their lives for about US$100 per month. Both are involved in an everyday struggle to survive and hopefully improve the working and living conditions for them and their families. They are brothers in the struggle, together with other millions of informal waste recyclers around the world. Here, we narrate their story in an attempt to contribute to their struggle—making the invisible visible.

Informal waste recyclers are those people who collect and segregate recyclable waste, in order to sell it to make a livelihood. Urbanization has seen an increase in the consumption of recyclable materials, such as plastic, paper, and metals and that has led to an increasing number of informal waste recyclers. People that are living out of other people's waste are predominantly present in low-income countries, but on the rise also in high-income ones due to increasing inequalities and urbanization.[1]

---

[1] For example, see this recent article about informal recyclers in Barcelona (Spain), that features our own research by Stephen Burgen published in *The Guardian* and titled 'Chariots of

The Political Ecology of Informal Waste Recyclers in India. Federico Demaria, Oxford University Press.
© Federico Demaria 2023. DOI: 10.1093/oso/9780192869050.003.0001

There are no reliable estimates of the number of people engaged in waste picking or of its economic and environmental impact. According to the International Labour Organization (ILO, 2013), the informal recycling sector is a way of making a living for 19 million to 24 million people in the Global South. Similarly, the World Bank estimates that at least 1% of the urban population in low- and middle-income countries works in this sector (Medina, 2008). This means at least 30 million people worldwide, and this number is on the rise. These are workers exclusively dedicated to collecting, separating, and selling recyclable materials from municipal solid waste. Apart from municipal solid waste, there are also other important streams of recyclable waste, such as e-waste or shipbreaking, which also employ millions of recyclers. Despite the recognition of the existence of millions of informal recyclers, they have been neither properly investigated nor taken into account in formal waste management policies. We argue for an urgent need for better understanding of the informal recycling sector, so as to improve waste management under economic, social, and environmental criteria. Calls for integrating the informal recycling sector into the formal waste management systems have mainly gone unheard. Improving our understanding of this sector is a first essential step if we intend to improve their conditions and the sustainability of the economy.

The informal economy relates to 'economic activities by workers and economic units that are—in law or in practice—not covered or insufficiently covered by formal arrangements' (ILO, 2003). It plays an important role in the overall economy of a country. In fact, for many countries across the globe, the informal sector employs more persons than the formal one (ILO, 2012). For instance, in India, the proportion of persons employed in the informal economy is more than 80%. The neoliberal restructuring of the global economy and wide-ranging policy reforms have not resulted in the disappearance of this sector, which continues to rapidly expand. Whereas the sector provides livelihood to a large number of so-called low skilled labour, there are concerns related to wage disparities

steel: Barcelona's hidden army of scrap recyclers. 23 March 2021. Available at https://www.theg uardian.com/global-development/2021/mar/23/chariots-steel-barcelonas-hidden-migrant-army-scrap-recyclers (Accessed 28 October 2021).

between formal and informal sector workers, and the lack of any kind of work or social security (Harriss-White and Sinha, 2007).

The informal recycling sector in low-income countries is part and parcel of this economy. In the twenty-first-century metropolis, it is a sophisticated web of waste workers who manage to autonomously make a living and achieve high recycling rates, in the range from 20% to 50% (Wilson et al., 2009). In fact, contrary to what many people think, waste picking does not only take place at the landfill, or randomly in the streets of cities. In many cities, informal recyclers (commonly called waste pickers) carry out door-to-door collection and separation of waste, while municipalities often do not have in place any effective formal recycling program. The working conditions are normally precarious, unhealthy, and dangerous. They operate in hostile social environments and are vulnerable to exploitation by middlemen. Because the recycling industry demands large volumes of materials that are processed (sorted, baled, crushed, or granulated) it does not buy directly from individual recyclers. Instead, middlemen purchase recyclables recovered by recyclers, and then sell them to the industry. This intermediation places them at the bottom of the recycling value chain, leading to further exploitation. In fact, from a standard economics point of view, the informal recycling sector resembles many of the characteristics of a free market where recyclers are mere price takers.

Lacking social recognition, recyclers are much looked down on as beggars, criminals, drug addicts, and alcoholics. Instead, a recycler is a person who salvages reusable or recyclable materials thrown away by others to sell it and obtain a livelihood. They are (waste) workers in search of a source of livelihood, in the absence of other employment opportunities. The factors that push people into informal recycling are fundamentally economic. Many belong to vulnerable groups: recent migrants, the unemployed, the disabled, women, children, and the elderly. For the urban poor in developing countries, informal waste recycling is a common way to earn income.

Studies suggest that when organized and supported, waste picking can spur grassroots investment by poor people, create jobs, reduce poverty, save municipalities money, improve industrial competitiveness, conserve natural resources, and protect the environment (Medina, 2008; Samson, 2009, 2020). Recyclers have self-organized in different ways to overcome these barriers, from local groups in the form of associations and unions, to national and international networks.[2] The collective business model includes micro-enterprises, cooperatives, and public-private partnerships. Working in collectives improves their bargaining power with public authorities and business, potentially leading to more efficient recycling and more effective poverty reduction.

Different names are used in different languages and regions of the world, such as waste picker, scavenger, rag picker in English, 拾荒 in Chinese, *recicladores*, *pepenadores* or *cartoneros* in Spanish, *chiffonier* in French, and *riciclatore*, *rigattiere*, *cenciaiolo*, or *straccivendolo* in Italian. In English other names include reclaimer, informal resource recoverer, binner, recycler, poacher, and salvager. We propose to use the term 'informal waste recyclers', or simply recyclers, because it seems to us the one that more accurately describes their activity and the most respectful one. In fact, as we will argue, recyclers play in society the role carried out by decomposers in natural ecosystems. The obvious difference lies in the fact that, while nature is based on cyclical processes, industrial societies are characterized by linear processes, where only a small percentage is actually recycled (Haas et al., 2015). In biology, despite the fundamental role played out by decomposers, they have been historically underestimated in comparison to other biological organisms higher in the food chain. The same could be said for recyclers in human societies. This is the gap that this book attempts to fill. By evaluating recyclers' contribution to waste management, we argue that they should gain social recognition and be compensated for their services.

The exact figures of global waste production are unknown. The World Bank (2012) estimated that in 2012 the global average generation of municipal waste was about 1.2 kg per person per day. In the same year, the urban population generated about 1.3 bn tonnes, which is expected to almost double by 2025. India alone in 2016 generated about 62 mn tonnes of waste. However, according to estimations by Marín-Beltrán et al. (2022), in our article titled 'Scientists' Warning Against the Society of Waste' and based mostly on data retrieved from Krausmann et al. (2018)

---

[2] Formed in 2008, the Global Alliance of Waste Pickers is a networking process among thousands of waste picker organizations with groups in more than 28 countries covering mainly Latin America, Asia, and Africa. See: http://globalrec.org/

and Haas et al. (2020), the world generates at least 23.5 Gt of solid waste (including both industrial and municipal) annually. This value is 10 times higher than reported by The World Bank (Kaza et al., 2018)—which only includes municipal solid waste, and does not consider, for example, losses from minerals other than metals—but it is as the 20 Gt reported by Krausmann et al. (2018). While municipal waste generated in lower-income countries is mostly composed by food and greens, 51% of the waste generated by high-income countries is dry waste, including plastic, paper, metal, and glass (Kaza et al., 2018).

Peak waste does not seem to be happening soon, as long as affluence and urban populations are on the rise. These figures are significant for the social, environmental, and economic complexities related to its management. For instance, the twenty-first-century metropolis in the Global South, given both its high population density and large surface, finds it difficult to find the space to dispose of its waste and increasingly reverts to waste incineration. However, municipal solid waste is just a small percentage of the overall waste produced, probably less than 10%, in terms of weight (EEA, 2000). Worldwide, there are very few comprehensive statistics about industrial waste, despite it often being hazardous. The lack of reliable data sets constitutes the first barrier for public authorities in their attempt to carry out integrated waste management, which implies simultaneous strategies to reduce waste generation that include reusing, recycling, and composting, and implementing disposal methods that reduce harm to the environment. A material assessment of the global economy can be used to argue that currently the aggregate recycling rate is only about 6%, compared to the total material input (processed materials) (Haas et al., 2015). In this book, we will focus on the 'social relations of recycling,'[3] which are the social relations that recyclers must enter into in order to survive, to produce, and to reproduce their means of life. To this end, from the perspective of situated political ecology, and based on extensive field work lasting a decade, the book discusses two case studies

---

[3] Here, we suggest a parallelism with the Marxist concept of social 'relations of production', which means the sum total of social relationships that people must enter into in order to survive, to produce, and to reproduce their means of life. These are specific to a certain mode of production, meaning the constitutive characteristic of a society or social formation, based on the socio-economic system predominant within it.

in India about both global and urban relations: ship breaking in Alang-Sosiya, and solid waste management in Delhi.

Waste is by definition refuse, the unwanted. However, since it is produced, it generates problems, and something needs to be done about it. The questions related to its management are not merely technical; what, how, where, and by whom become intrinsically political questions. Waste is a site of social conflict. The costs related to its generation and management are often shifted from those with more power to those with less. Most visible to ordinary citizens is the opposition faced by local waste treatment and disposal facilities, such as incinerators and landfills (Pellow, 2007). In China, opposition to incinerators sometimes turns violent.[4] In high-income countries, this opposition together with the rising management costs has given way to a rapidly changing and lucrative trade, global in nature, in which waste flows towards developing countries or poorer areas of developed countries (Pearson, 1987; McKee, 1996). The case of Naples and its region Campania in Italy is probably among the most emblematic (D'Alisa et al., 2010), together with the Somali pirates, some of whom are self-declared coast guards against the dumping of toxic waste (and illegal fishing).[5] Moreover, there is also a shift from waste-as-externality to waste-as-resource, driven by new waste-based commodity frontiers (Schindler and Demaria, 2020). In a special issue, co-edited by Seth Schindler and myself, and tellingly titled 'Garbage is Gold', we argue that in fact there is a long history of realizing value from waste. The papers in the collection demonstrate that attempts to reconfigure socio-metabolic systems in order to create, enhance, and capture value from waste continue to take place around the world. How do these attempts happen? What are the driving forces? Are they contested? These are the issues which this book highlights, focusing on the two case studies: shipbreaking and Delhi's waste conflict. Similar processes happen elsewhere. In Bogota, Colombia, the Mayor Gustavo Petro was removed after his attempt to implement a Zero Garbage programme that would have reverted the privatization of the waste management

<hr/>

[4] The Economist. Keep the fires burning. 25 April 2015. Available at: http://www.econom ist.com/news/china/21649540-waste-incinerators-rile-public-are-much-better-landfill-keep-fires-burning (Accessed on 20 March 2017).
[5] See EjAltas (2014) Somalia toxic waste dumping, Somalia. Available at: https://ejatlas.org/conflict/somalia-toxic-waste-dumping-somalia (Accessed on 15 March 2017).

system and formally integrated thousands of informal recyclers.[6] The Environmental Justice Atlas, that is the world's largest inventory of environmental conflicts, reports a few hundred cases of social mobilizations related to waste management (see ejatlas.org). No one knows how many such contestations exist worldwide, but there is no doubt that waste is conflictive. It is a question of justice, to be more precise of environmental justice. Political ecology investigates who loses and who wins from the processes that lead to these contestations. Conflicts, in fact, give visibility to the contradictions between capital accumulation and life reproduction. This is why studying them is so important. They are like a lighthouse in the dark.

The world is producing more and more waste, with serious health and environmental consequences. In urban areas, domestic waste is accumulating fast and landfills fill up quickly. Public authorities are trying to manage this problem in new ways. In the Global South these tend to involve private corporations and expensive technology rather than waste pickers. This policy shift towards realizing value from waste is limiting waste pickers' access to recyclable materials. This is happening despite the fact that waste pickers are responsible for a very high percentage of recycling.

Side-lining informal recyclers is leading to conflicts. Our Barcelona Research Group on Informal Recyclers[7] has been tracking them, in collaboration with researchers and activists from EnvJustice (envjustice. org), the Global Alliance of Waste Pickers (globalrec.org), and Women in Informal Employment: Globalizing and Organizing (WIEGO). Together, we documented more than 100 socio-environmental conflicts in cities of the Global South (Africa, Asia, and Latin America) related to waste pickers. They can be consulted by visiting the thematic map 'Waste pickers under threat', which includes a 1,000-word description for each of them, along with coded variables on the environmental, health, and

[6] Costanza Vieria. Zero Garbage Plan Tied to Fate of Ousted Bogotá Mayor. IPS News. 13 December 2013, http://www.ipsnews.net/2013/12/zero-garbage-plan-tied-fate-ousted-bogota-mayor/ (Accessed on 20 March 2017).
[7] The Barcelona Research Group on Informal Recyclers, founded and coordinated by myself, has counted contributions from Nina Clausager, Max Stoisser, Marcos Todt, Rickie Cleere, Benjamin Irvine, Chandni Dwarkasing, Laia Guardiola, Valeria Calvas, Javier Lujan Gutierrez, Daniele Vico, Julian Porras, Anna Karin Giannotta, Michael Rendon, and Josep Espluga Trenc, with the support of Lucía Fernández Gabard and Federico Parra (WIEGO-GlobalRec).

socio-economic impacts, the social actors and their forms of mobilization, and the outcomes of the conflicts (available by clicking on the conflict sheet; see https://ejatlas.org/featured/wastepickers).[8]

Historically, waste pickers have been confronted with dangerous
working conditions, social marginalization, and persecution. The map
shows how this precarious situation is getting worse. In the past decade,
threats to waste picker livelihoods in the Global South has been intensified by shifts in public policy towards realizing value from waste at the
benefit of private corporations. A preliminary analysis of the 100 conflicts suggests that threats seem to have taken three main forms: incineration, privatization, and urban space restrictions.

First, incineration technologies get large public subsidies, for example
as emissions reduction projects from the Clean Development Mechanism
of the Kyoto Protocol. The first incinerator in Africa was built in Ethiopia
in 2018 with Chinese investment and Danish technology. National bans
on incineration are being challenged from the Philippines to Mexico. But
research shows that recycling is always preferable to burning.[9] This is true
both socially in terms of the livelihoods of waste pickers as well as environmentally for CO_2 emissions and risks of air pollution. As we will
discuss in detail in Chapter 4, in Delhi waste pickers and residents have
allied against incineration.

Second, in the case of privatization, corporations have become increasingly interested in waste as a resource. For example in Johannesburg
(South Africa), the Genesis landfill was privatized and waste pickers
were violently evicted. Formal criteria for contracting municipal waste
management services that are being put in place end up excluding waste
pickers, for example in Egypt and Ghana. The closure of problematic
landfills has often led to the simple shifting of environmental damage in
places like Belém and Rio de Janeiro (Brazil) as well.

---

[8] See our article published at *The Conversation* and titled 'How waste pickers in the global
South are being sidelined by new policies'. Available at https://theconversation.com/how-waste-
pickers-in-the-global-south-are-being-sidelined-by-new-policies-132521 (Accessed on 23
October 2021).

[9] The main reasons why recycling is better than incineration are (1) it saves energy; (2) it is
more profitable; (3) it creates more job; and (4) it is more flexible and dynamic. See https://zero
wasteeurope.eu/2017/09/4-reasons-why-recycling-is-better-than-incineration/ (Accessed on
18 October 2022).

Third, restrictions in urban space can affect waste pickers, and their livelihoods. An example is the prohibition of animal or human-drawn vehicles. Such examples can be seen in Porto Alegre (Brazil) and Montevideo (Uruguay). Another example is the installation of 'anti-poor', 'smart' containers in Buenos Aires (Argentina) and Bogota (Colombia). And, in the name of modern, beautiful and hygienic city centres, waste pickers are denied access to certain urban areas, like in Phnom Penh (Cambodia).

Informal recyclers are increasingly taking action to oppose policies that exclude them from their source of livelihood. The main areas of focus are social rights and formal inclusion into municipal waste management. They also organize to make their environmental services visible, fight discrimination, and empower their communities. This is happening mostly in Latin American countries. But it's also happening in South Africa and India, among others. The Global Alliance of Waste Pickers, supported by the nongovernmental organization Women in Informal Employment: Globalizing and Organizing (WIEGO), works with organizations in more than 28 countries. Their aim is to include waste pickers in decision-making, improve their working conditions, develop their capacity, and achieve recognition for their work. Civil society groups have also formed a network in the Global Alliance for Incinerator Alternatives (GAIA). Recognition of the contribution that waste pickers make is growing in some countries. But the vast majority still face social marginalization, highly unsuitable working and living conditions, and most recently a global trend of capital accumulation through realizing value from waste that threatens to deprive them completely of their livelihood. In reaction, informal recyclers fight for social and environmental justice.

In this book, we focus on two case studies in India about the social relations of recycling. They are related to two different geographical scales: global and urban. The first, shipbreaking, is related to shipping, the key infrastructure of global trade. The second, Delhi's waste metabolism, exemplifies the processes just mentioned in other twenty-first-century metropolises of the Global South. We use these case studies to contribute to the further understanding of the ways societies' metabolism (that is the flows of energy and materials) works and changes. More precisely we want to shed light on the relationship between social metabolism and political economy, or else materiality, power relations, and social conflicts, with a focus on waste.

First, and in line with previous research on social metabolism and ecological distribution conflicts (Martinez-Alier, 2002; Temper et al., 2018; Scheidel et al., 2018), we want to follow a situated political ecology perspective and explain how differences in the structure and nature of particular social metabolisms create different conflict dynamics. Social metabolism leads to environmental conflicts, but how and what type of metabolism, when and where?

Second, we want to shed light on an often forgotten but very important final component of global and urban social metabolism: the informal recycling of waste. We want to evaluate quantitatively and qualitatively the contribution of informal recycling to a local ecological economy, investigating the power relations that govern the production and disposal of waste, and explaining why and how these shift costs to informal recyclers. Then, we intend to build a case for the recognition of the important contribution of informal recyclers in making social metabolism more circular, and we call for a recognition and due compensation of the services they provide, instead of a dispossession from their means of production, and a shifting of social costs of enterprises and consumers to them and other vulnerable social groups.

The research questions are as follows:

(1) How and why does the metabolism of waste cause social conflicts, where and under what conditions?

Our main argument will be that metabolism causes conflicts because it involves the dispossession of resources and/or a shifting of costs. Waste is unwanted and there is a tendency to shift its costs from those who have more power to those who have less. We investigate two cases at two different geographical scales, and different types of waste: first, shipbreaking, where the metabolism of a global infrastructure shifts the costs to very localized communities; and second, waste metabolism in a twenty-first-century metropolis which simultaneously shifts costs to the urban residents, and dispossesses recyclers of the access to recyclable waste.

(2) How do capitalist dynamics and power relations shape waste metabolisms unevenly?

Apart from the materiality, we should understand the political economy of these processes, be they at the global or urban level. This can help to clarify why the metabolism changes in the way it does, so as to determine its driving forces. We discuss the concept of capital accumulation by dispossession, and argue that there is an additional strategy that needs more attention, which could be called 'lower costs of output' via cost-shifting, namely capital accumulation by contamination.

(3) What is the role of informal recyclers in the metabolism of waste? How and under what conditions might their work and contribution be valued and compensated? How do power relations reduce them to invisible subjects? How do they resist and attempt to transform their role in waste metabolism?

We will look at the power relations in recycling. Waste recyclers are invisible for both waste studies and public policy. Their struggle, sometimes in alliance with other actors, aims to transform this situation.

1.2 How This Book Was Made: The Methods

From the perspective of situated political ecology, we aimed at a research that was theoretically broad but empirically situated. This was meant to expand the range of local experiences and, in doing so, inform theory on how environments are shaped, politicized, and contested.

We have carried out extensive field work in India from 2009 to 2019, with several visits summing up to more than two years. Data from interviews, official documents, direct and participant observation have been combined using the case study research methodology (Yin, 2003). Semi-structured, in-depth interviews, and focus groups were conducted in English, most of the time with the help of local translators (mainly in Hindi but also in other Indian languages, like Gujarati and Bengali). Interviewees were selected to represent a broad spectrum of interests and knowledge, using both random and snowball sampling methods. We combined qualitative and quantitative methods. In each chapter, we further present in details the methods, while here we only intend to give an overall evaluation.

For shipbreaking, we carried out field work from April to July 2009. The access of researchers to the industry site is strictly regulated and workers' freedom of expression is limited. This was a major challenge which, in the end, we were able to partially overcome thanks to a local guide and a translator, a lot of patience, and perseverance. During our stay, we never felt that our personal security was at risk. However, our guide and translator were threatened after we left, and we decided not to go back. Their names are kept confidential.

In Delhi, I have been a visiting researcher at the Centre for Studies in Science Policy, Jawaharlal Nehru University, under the guidance of environmental historian and political ecologist Rohan D'Souza. We collaborated very closely with the waste pickers union AIKMM (All India Kabadi Mazdoor Mahasangh). We used to live at their headquarters, a tiny office in East Delhi, that allowed us to draw interesting insights. The research design and implementation, especially for the last chapter, was developed together with them. We established a close relationship with both waste pickers and junk dealers, and accompanied them regularly throughout their working days. At times, we were helped by a research assistant. We also kept regular relations with local experts, both scholars and activists, among others Gopal Krishna (Toxic Watch Alliance), Kaveri Gill, Dunu Roy (Hazard Centre), and Ravi Agarwal (Toxic Links). We also collaborated with the Global Alliance of Waste Pickers, and took part in their 2012 Global Strategic Workshop in Pune, South India.

One of the major limitations was our inability to speak the local languages linked to the fact of being a foreigner. Our appearance, as white foreigner, did not easily allow for camouflaging, which was a major problem in Alang and Sosiya. We partially overcame the language barrier with the help of local translators, but this made at times communication with interviewees rather difficult. We shall also admit that there were cultural barriers, and at times we were not able to evaluate properly different situations. We are grateful for two major characteristics of the Indian culture: (1) the fact that it is mainly a patient (if not peaceful) one; and (2) a great sense of hospitality. One aspect that was of help, is that we kept visiting the different sites regularly, for several years. This helped us to build some kind of trust because it showed that we were truly interested. In the case of Delhi, we actively took part in the AIKMM activities, supporting them at times. In this case, we developed a reciprocal relation. They helped us to understand their sector, and we tried to help them, for example with drafting texts in English (such as flyers, press releases, funding application, and letters to the authorities).

Last, in this book there is no pretence of objectivity. We normally take a position that is explicit, but with the intention of it being a critical and informed one.

1.3 What This Book Is About: A Preview of the Chapters

The book is structured as follows. We introduce the theoretical framework (Chapter 2), and then the two case studies: shipbreaking in Alang-Sosiya (Chapter 3) and waste management in Delhi (Chapters 4 and 5). In Chapter 6, we draw some conclusions.

Chapter 2. Theoretical Framework: Ecological Economics, Political Ecology, and Waste Studies

Chapter 2 provides the theoretical framework explaining, first, how the contribution is situated in the common ground between three fields: ecological economics, political ecology, and waste studies; and second, the main theoretical contribution, namely the concept of capital accumulation by contamination. First, ecological economics provides a framework to understand the relationship between the environment and the economy, with concepts such as social metabolism (that is the flows of energy and materials), and cost-shifting (VS externalities). Second, political ecology brings into the picture the political dimension, or else the power relations. The focus is on ecological distribution conflicts, born out of an unequal distribution of benefits and burdens, due to an uneven distribution of power. Third, it contextualizes the case studies within waste studies explaining why waste management, and in particular recycling, has been chosen to be the focus of this book. In particular, it proposes to extend the metaphor of metabolism between biology and economics, and view waste recyclers in societies playing out a role similar to decomposers in natural ecosystems. Last, the chapter explores key political economy concepts (such as capitalism, and capital accumulation), that allows me to introduce the new concept of capital accumulation by contamination, and explains how it differs from the one of accumulation by dispossession. This is defined as the process by which capitalism socializes costs, through successful cost-shifting, which degrades the means of existence, and bodies of human beings (as well as of other species) in order to find new possibilities for capital valorization. This will be of help to clarify what are the driving forces which influence the way social metabolism changes.

Chapter 3. Shipbreaking in Alang: A Conflict Against Capital Accumulation by Contamination

Chapter 3 investigates the management of ocean-going ships as waste. The shipping industry constitutes a key element in the infrastructure of the world's social metabolism. In fact, more than 80% of international trade in goods by volume is carried by sea. Ocean-going ships are owned and used for their trade by developed countries but are often demolished, together with their toxic materials, in developing countries. Ship breaking is the process of dismantling an obsolete vessel's structure for scrapping or disposal. The Alang-Sosiya yard in India, one of the world's largest shipbreaking yards, is studied with particular attention to toxic waste management. Ship owners and ship breakers obtain large profits dumping the environmental costs on workers, local farmers, and fishers. The latter see their means of existence and bodies degraded, at the economic benefit of the former. This unequal distribution of benefits and burdens, due to an international and national uneven distribution of power, has led to an ecological distribution conflict. This is exemplified by the controversy at the Indian Supreme Court in 2006 over the dismantling of the ocean liner *Blue Lady*, that shows how the different languages of valuation expressed by different social groups clashed and how a language that expresses sustainability as monetary benefit at the national scale, dominated. Shipbreaking in the developing world is not

just an externality but a successful case of cost-shifting, or else, capital accumulation by contamination. In this case, capital accumulation by contamination takes place thanks to the indirect profits due to saved costs
(i.e. indirect subsidies).

Chapter 4. Delhi's Waste Conflict: An Unlikely Alliance Against Capital Accumulation by Dispossession and Contamination

Chapter 4 investigates the struggles related to municipal solid waste management in Delhi, the capital of India. We focus on a conflict that has
erupted as authorities have progressively privatized the city's solid waste
management system in response to an increase in the volume and metabolic density of waste, as well as a change in its composition. Authorities
have embraced waste-to-energy incinerators hoping it would be a magic
bullet, but encountered opposition from those who lose from this policy
shift. Workers in the informal waste sector fear that these changes
threaten their access to waste, while middle-class residents oppose waste-
to-energy incinerators because of their deleterious impact on ambient
air quality. The Delhi waste conflict shows resistance against both capital accumulation by dispossession (recyclers are dispossessed of their
livelihood source, namely recyclable waste), and capital accumulation
by contamination (environmental costs are shifted to urban residents).
The chapter narrates the emergence of an unlikely alliance between these
groups, whose politics opposes the production of a waste-based commodity frontier within the city, as well as the imposition of exposure to
waste on an everyday basis. Recent scholarship on the materiality of cities
has been criticized by critical urban scholars for being overly descriptive
and failing to account for political economy. The chapter argues that in
order to understand cities in the Global South whose metabolisms are
subject to fierce contestations, it is necessary to incorporate materialist
and critical perspectives. It concludes that the materiality and political
economy of cities are co-constituted, and contestations over the configuration of urban metabolisms span these spheres as people struggle to
realize situated urban political ecologies.

Chapter 5. Informal Waste Recyclers and their Environmental Services: A Case for Recognition and Capital De-Accumulation

Informal waste recyclers are those people that segregate and collect recyclable waste, in order to sell them to make a livelihood. Despite the informal recycling sector employing about 1% of the urban population in developing countries, their contribution to waste management has neither been evaluated nor compensated. This chapter fills this gap. First, it provides an assessment of the current available data set on waste management in Delhi, leading to a first approximate estimation of recycling rates. It also discusses a taxonomy of informal recyclers based on their means of transport and their area of collection, as well as how their absolute number can be estimated. Second, it suggests a new methodology to evaluate their contribution. This aims to reliably estimate how much they recycle, what type of materials, and how much they earn. To this end, data for 100 informal recyclers for one year were collected from junk dealers' ledgers. Results show that in Delhi informal recyclers collect approximately 50 kg of recyclable material per day, mostly plastic and paper (60% and 30% of their income, respectively), but also metals, hair, and organic materials. They earn roughly 8,000 Indian Rupees per month (about US$125). This is close to the minimum wage, but as recyclers themselves claim, public authorities should compensate them for their services. The chapter develops two policy proposals that suggests a monthly payment for collection as well as recycling services, respectively 4,200 Rupees (about US$65), and 1,500 Rupees (US$25). This would increase informal recyclers' monthly income to US$215.

Chapter 6. Conclusions: How Environments Are Shaped, Politicized, and Contested

We conclude by showing how the case studies provide a new understanding to the three research questions mentioned above. In particular, we show how they present a range of experiences to inform theory on how environments are shaped, politicized, and contested. We shed light on the relationship between social metabolism and conflicts, with a focus on recycling and looking from a situated political ecology perspective. First, a situated understanding of waste shows that there is a complex relationship between its materiality and political economy; they are co-constituted and produce different socio-metabolic configurations. Ultimately, the co-evolution of materiality and political economy (including social and institutional dynamics) shapes metabolisms and as a result political opportunities are fostered and foreclosed. Changes in the social metabolism are mediated by the social, economic, and institutional logics at play. They ultimately lead to socio-metabolic reconfigurations which, in turn, eventually lead to ecological distribution conflicts. People struggle to defend, or realize, desirable situated urban political ecologies. Second, we show that examining the political economy of these processes, be it at the global or city level, can help to clarify why the metabolism changes in the way it does, meaning its driving forces. In particular, we argue that capital accumulation takes place at waste-based commodity frontiers through extra-economic means, namely both dispossession and contamination. Third, we attempt to investigate the social relations of recycling, which means the social relationships that recyclers must enter into in order to survive, to produce, and to reproduce their means of life. These are inherently intertwined with the waste metabolism. We suggest that recyclers play in human societies a similar role to the decomposers in natural ecosystems. Then, we evaluate the contribution of informal recycling and call for a due compensation of recyclers' waste management and environmental services, instead of a dispossession from their means of production, and a shifting of social costs of enterprises and consumers to them, and other vulnerable social groups. The struggles of recyclers constitute an attempt to re-politicize waste metabolism beyond techno-managerial solutions by fostering counter-hegemonic discourses and praxis.

2

Theoretical Framework

Ecological Economics, Political Ecology, and Waste Studies

Our contribution is situated at the interface of three fields: ecological economics, political ecology, and waste studies (see Figure 2.1).

First, *ecological economics* provides a framework to understand the relationship between the environment and the economy. After explaining the origins of this approach, we present the concept of *social metabolism* that examines the energy and material flows within the economy. From this perspective, waste is seen as an unavoidable feature of production due to thermodynamics. We then briefly review how ecological economics has investigated both waste in general, and recycling in particular. This helps to understand the roots of waste generation and the complexities related to its recycling. Last, we put emphasis on the fact that the social and environmental costs emerging out of the metabolic flows are not accounted for in the balance sheets of enterprises, but instead are shifted to third persons. This is what is called *cost-shifting*, and differs from what environmental economists mistakenly call externalities.

Second, *political ecology* brings into the picture the political dimension, or rather the power relations. After outlining the different ways in which it is understood, we focus on *ecological distribution conflicts*. These social conflicts are born out of an unequal distribution of benefits and burdens, due to an uneven international and national distribution of *power*. We discuss both the roots of these conflicts, as well as the different languages of valuation in which they are expressed.

Third, we contextualize our case studies within *waste studies* explaining why waste management, and in particular recycling, has been chosen to be the focus of this book. We start by discussing different definitions and categories of waste, both in general and in particular in Indian

The Political Ecology of Informal Waste Recyclers in India. Federico Demaria, Oxford University Press.
© Federico Demaria 2023. DOI: 10.1093/oso/9780192869050.003.0002

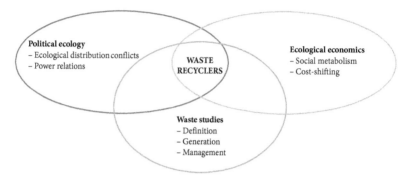

Figure 2.1 The theoretical framework.

legislation. Then, we discuss *waste generation* at the global level, in particular in India. This is followed by a discussion of the functional elements of *waste management*. Last, we propose to extend the metaphor of metabolism between biology and economics, and view waste recyclers in societies playing out a role similar to *decomposers* in natural ecosystems.

We call for both ecological economics and political ecology to pay more attention to waste recyclers because (1) they contribute to improving the sustainability of waste metabolism, and (2) they are involved in ecological distribution conflicts.

2.1 Ecological Economics

Ecological economics (hereafter EE) is a transdisciplinary field that aims to improve and expand economic theory to integrate the earth's natural systems, but also human values, health, and well-being. In conventional economics, the primary goal is to increase the goods and services produced by humans; the gross domestic product (GDP) is a national measure of the total value of goods and services produced annually, in monetary terms. Conventional economics assumes that ever-increasing GDP is desirable, possible, and that everyone benefits from it. EE takes a different stand. In a nutshell, it addresses the current conflict between positive economic growth and negative environmental consequences (Spash, 1999).

Martinez Alier (1987) provides a history of the early attempts to introduce energy analysis into economic thinking. European conceptual founders include Nicholas Georgescu-Roegen (1971), K. William Kapp (1950), and Karl Polanyi (1944). Costanza (1989), right after the ecological economics community was founded in Barcelona in the late 1980s, argued that EE is concerned with 'the relationships between ecosystems and economic systems'. These relationships, he argued, are where the problems with sustainability will be located, problems that at that time were not covered by any existing disciplines.

A decade later, EE has become a broader 'science of sustainability' (Dodds, 1997). Exactly what sustainability means has been contested. However, there is a consensus that EE stands for strong sustainability, the idea that there are certain functions that the environment performs that cannot be duplicated by humans. This is diametrically opposed to the weak sustainability perspective of Environmental Economics. EE also stands for the weak comparability of values, implying incommensurability of values (Martinez Alier et al., 1998). EE has also been called an 'economics for sustainable development' (Soderbaum, 2004). Issues debated cover a wide range such as resilience and evolution in socio-ecological systems, the metabolism of society, trade and globalization, income growth and environmental impacts, environmental sustainability and social welfare (Martinez Alier and Røpke, 2008).

Røpke (2004 and 2005) provides a history of EE as a field of research outlining its characteristic cognitive features at the time of its birth, and how it has then been influenced by broader social factors and shaped by the inflow and outflow of different researchers. Røpke (2005) argues that central topics include: (1) the roots of the field, such as the relation between the environment and growth, trade and/or technology;[1] (2) the scale issue deriving from the embeddedness of the economy in nature, including the resilience perspective (i.e. 'the calculations in nature', such as social metabolism); (3) valuation and decision-making (e.g.

---

[1] This included a series of debates on controversial issues such as the questions of: substitution between natural and man-made capital, growth and the environment, trade and the environment, technological change, quality of life, the view of nature.

cost-shifting);[2] and (4) some of the tensions that emerge, concerning in particular, but not only, the relationship with neoclassical economics.

Despite hopes about dematerialization, industrial economies based on economic growth constantly need to extract and process new resources (energy and materials), that—sooner or later—because of thermo-dynamics, will end up as waste. The system is therefore deemed to en-counter limits to growth, not only for its inputs (e.g. peak oil), but also in relation to the assimilative capacity of its sinks, or ecosystems (e.g. climate change). In this book, we are concerned with this second set of limits. Hereafter we present and discuss some of the central issues de-bated in EE that are of relevance for this book: social metabolism, waste and recycling, and cost-shifting, the last being the least explored in recent developments in the field.

2.1.1 Social Metabolism

Sustainability depends largely upon the interactions of humans with bio-geochemical cycles, having thus an intrinsically biophysical component that needs to be understood. Similar to how biologists study the metab-olism of living organisms, ecological economists and industrial ecolo-gists study the metabolism of societies (Fischer-Kowalski and Hüttler, 1999; Fischer-Kowalski and Haberl, 2015). The biological analogy grew out of the observation that biological systems—that is organisms, but also higher-level systems such as ecosystems and socio-economic systems, that is human societies, economies, companies and households—depend on a continuous throughput of energy and materials in order to main-tain their internal structure (Fischer-Kowalski and Haberl, 1993). So, so-cial metabolism is understood as the manner in which human societies organize their ever-growing exchanges of energy and materials with the environment (Fischer-Kowalski, 1997), or else, the energy and material flows within the economy. It refers to the processes of appropriation,

---

[2] This includes a series of debates on social structures and institutions, the motivations and behaviour of human beings, values and their incommensurability, social processes of change as evolutionary and dynamic, social change as characterized by conflict rather than harmony, so the existence of power and privilege are at the centre of interest.

transformation, and disposal of material and energy by society in order to maintain and evolve (Scheidel and Sorman, 2012).

Different schools of thought have developed different accounting methods aiming to quantify material inputs and outputs, and capture the biophysical processes that result in relation to economic and societal processes, as resources are assembled and transformed, and waste is produced. These empirical analyses of the biophysical structure of economies are based upon a number of standardized accounting methods (Gerber and Scheidel, 2018). Most notably, the Vienna school focuses on the quantification of energy and material flows (material and energy flow accounting, MEFA), and the Barcelona school looks at the relationship between the flows and fund, that is, the agents that transform input flows into outflows, while preserving their own identity (e.g. multi-scale integrated analysis of societal and ecosystem metabolism, MuSIASEM). Different approaches lead to different metabolic indicators, like the material intensity/efficiency of our economies or the energy input per hour of labour.[3] In this book, we will not carry out a detailed accounting (mainly because of a lack of reliable data), but we will mobilize its conceptualization and apply it to the informal recycling sector.

Different societies have distinctive metabolisms. Compare, for instance, hunter-gatherer, subsistence agriculture or industrial societies, and the many forms within these broad categories. They sometimes coexist and surely evolve over time. Their metabolism can be characterized by both their *material dimension*, that is, the amount and composition of materials and energy they consume, as well as by their *immaterial dimension*, that is, their political economy and the institutions of society that define their sources, type of extraction, distribution and disposal models of materials and energy across the members of a society.

Here we propose to use the term 'socio-metabolic configurations' to refer to both material and immaterial dimensions of society's metabolism (Demaria and Schindler, 2015). For instance, as discussed later in Chapter 4, the metabolization of waste in Delhi (India) has to do with

---

[3] Beyond MEFA and MuSIASEM, further methods related to the concept of Social Metabolism include life cycle analysis (LCA), life cycle inventory (LCI) and life cycle impact assessment (LCIA), input-output analysis (IOA), the human appropriation of net primary productivity (HANPP), energy return on energy input (EROI) and Virtual Water, as well as related concepts such as ecological rucksacks (Weisz, 2006).

the production, throughput, and processing of waste. The materiality relates to the quantity, composition and calorific value of waste. The political economy has to do with how, where, and by whom it is managed (private, public, or informal sectors; recycling, incineration, or landfill, etc.) (2015). To understand the sustainability and dynamics of social metabolism, one must not only look into the quantification of metabolic flows, but also into the power relations that shape the reconfiguration of metabolism(s), that is, the political economy. Ultimately, the co-evolution of materiality and political economy, including social and institutional dynamics, shapes and transforms metabolisms and as a result political opportunities are fostered and foreclosed.

As we will argue below, ecological distribution conflicts do not only emerge out of an increase in the volume of social metabolism (i.e. increased extraction of materials; Martinez Alier, 2002), but also out of socio-metabolic re-configurations. In this sense, the first objective of this book is to explore the relations between social metabolism and environmental conflicts. We intend to investigate what metabolisms, how, when, and where they lead to environmental conflicts and why. The focus is on waste.

2.1.2   Waste and Recycling in Ecological Economics

If waste is undesirable, why don't we just avoid it? Mainstream economists consider waste as an externality, due to a market failure that could be internalized in theory. Instead, for ecological economists waste is an unavoidable feature of production due to thermodynamics (Baumgartner, 2002). As Georgescu Roegen explained: 'given the entropic nature of the economic process, waste is an output just as unavoidable as the input of natural resources' (Georgescu-Roegen, 1975: 357). Waste outputs are an unavoidable by-product in the industrial production of desired goods and services. The quantity of waste generated depends upon the degree of (in)efficiency with which these processes are operated, although there is a thermodynamic minimum required. If our society intends to operate within sustainable levels of metabolism, Baumgartner (2002) suggests that the following rules should apply:

(1) Do not use material fuels as a source of exergy,[4] but only sunlight.

(2) Keep matter in closed cycles, that is, heat should be the only waste.

(3) Carry out all transformations with thermodynamic efficiency.

Thermodynamics is a purely descriptive science, while sustainability is a normative one since it involves value statements. Therefore, in relation to waste, ecological economics has also considered the following aspects: (1) Different attitudes towards waste (Bisson, 2002), including throughout history (Winiwarter, 2002); (2) Ecological economic valuations of waste, including life cycle assessment, cost-benefit analysis (CBA) and multicriteria evaluation (Powell et al., 2002); (3) Waste law (Wilkinson, 2002); and (4) The classification of waste—municipal, toxic, and nuclear (Barata, 2002; Adeola, 2002; Proops, 2002). Defining waste can be a very contentious issue, which involves waste for whom, where, and when? What is waste for someone can be a resource for someone else.

The issue that interests us here, recycling, has been explored in EE, both in its theoretical dimension, as well as in its practical implementation. The former has taken the shape of a long controversy regarding whether the entropy law applies only to energy, or does it also extend to material resources (to be precise, matter of macroscopic scale). Georgescu-Roegen introduced the fourth law of thermodynamics stating that complete recycling of matter is impossible. The purpose was to substantiate his initial claim that not only energy resources, but also material resources, are subject to general and irreversible physical degradation when put to use in economic activity. In addition, he introduced the term 'material entropy' to describe this physical degradation of material resources.

Leaving aside the details of this debate involving physicists and ecological economists, we can simplify by saying that energy cannot be recycled, and materials can be only up to a certain extent. The possibility of a complete and perpetual recycling of all material resources, in fact, is a theoretical one since it would require a significant amount of energy, time, and information (Ayres, 1999; Craig, 2001). Despite the

---

[4] Exergy is a thermodynamic concept. It is defined as the maximum useful work which can be extracted from a system as it reversibly comes into equilibrium with its environment. In other words, it is the capacity of energy to do physical work, or else that it is available to be used. After the system and surroundings reach equilibrium, the exergy is zero. Determining exergy was also the first goal of thermodynamics.

theoretical possibility of complete recycling, there is a practical impossibility (Bianciardi et al., 1996).

The practical dimension has been explored by ecological economists looking at issues such as analysis of the environmental effects of recycling, for example, CO_2 emissions (Nakamura, 1999); cost analysis of recycling compared to other waste management options (Nakamura and Kondo, 2006), household behaviour investigating individual motivation, for example the importance of social norms (Berglund, 2006; Abbott et al., 2013; Alpízar and Gsottbauer, 2015; Ari and Yilmaz, 2016), the cycle of specific materials in certain areas, like copper in Europe or aluminium in the United States, estimating their recycling efficiency (Bertram et al., 2002; Chen and Graedel, 2012); the effectiveness and efficiency of different public policies, such as quantity-based pricing for waste collection services and recycling programs (Bohara et al., 2007; Ulli-Beer et al., 2007; Usui, 2008; Abbott et al., 2011). The study of recycling in EE has been characterized by a focus on high-income countries, formal waste management systems and municipal but not industrial solid waste. The informal recycling sector, to which we want to draw attention in this book, has been ignored up until now. It is surprising that the few studies concerned with recycling in middle-income countries, like Costa Rica and Turkey, do not even mention the existence of the informal recycling sector (Alpízar and Gsottbauer, 2015; Ari and Yilmaz, 2016). There are only two exceptions where waste picking is mentioned but it is certainly not the focus of the analysis. The first is a paper that explores the possible connections between the green economy and the informal economy in South Africa (Smit and Musango, 2015). The second is a paper revisiting 'Environmentalism of the Poor' and arguing that 'waste pickers contest the expropriation of waste by commercial firms and incineration often disguised as "energy valorization", as this expropriation jeopardizes their livelihoods. [...] In Delhi, middle income residents support the plight of recyclers of waste against the possible creation of waste-to-energy plants' (Schindler et al., 2012).

In conclusion, there seems to be a mismatch in EE between the theoretical and practical dimensions. While the former focuses on the macro picture, that is, the possibility of complete recycling, the latter focuses on the micro one, that is, proving that recycling rates are low, exploring why this is the case and how it could be improved. EE, when discussing recycling in practice, doesn't seem to take into account the overall socio-economic structure, and limits itself to incremental improvements that do not necessarily lead to the sustainability of waste metabolism per se. This leads us to argue that the recycling sector, despite its important role in social metabolism, has not been properly investigated by EE and lacks a theoretical framework. This is the gap that we intend to fill with this book, paying particular attention to the informal sector.

In the following section, we argue that externalities are preferably seen not as market failures but as cost-shifting to future generations, to the poor and to other species. This will help us to link ecological economics with political ecology. Mainstream economists would argue that if the price for pollution or the extraction of resources is zero, then it is a market failure. Instead, here we argue that this fact signals uneven power relations, and therefore it is intrinsically political.

2.1.3 Cost-Shifting, Not Externalities

EE generally rejects using the term 'externalities' from conventional economics, and proposes instead the term cost-shifting (Kapp, 1963). Spash (2010) has argued that externality theory wrongly assumes environmental and social problems are minor aberrations in an otherwise perfectly functioning economic system. Internalizing the odd externality does nothing to address the structural systemic problem and fails to recognize the all-pervasive nature of these so-called externalities. In fact, from a business point of view, externalities are not so much market failures but cost-shifting successes (1963). In this sense, the modern business enterprise operates on the basis of shifting costs onto others as normal practice to make profits.

K. William Kapp (1910–1976) has been a leading institutional economist and one of the influential figures of ecological economics (Martinez Alier, 1987). Before his seminal work, social science frameworks were formulated without referring directly to environmental issues. At the time, he was an exception with his very early application of an institutional perspective to environmental issues, including ideas of pervasive and systemic 'externalities', basic uncertainty and interdependencies of environmental and social systems—ideas basically in accordance with the foundational premise of ecological economics (Røpke, 2005).

His most well-known work and the one that concerns us here is *The Social Cost of Private Enterprise* (1950), later extended and republished in 1963. Kapp highlighted the shortcomings of the market system and was particularly concerned with social costs, meaning any costs incurred by business activity which falls, at any point in time, upon third persons or the community at large and is not therefore accounted for by business accounting. He critiqued modern welfare economics and went on to explain social costs and thus enable society to create a social system that is free of them. The book is a 'detailed study of the manner in which private enterprise under conditions of unregulated competition tends to give rise to social costs which are not accounted for in entrepreneurial outlays but instead are shifted to and borne by third persons and the community as a whole' (Kapp, 1963: XXIX). This conception arose from a critique of externalities, what he called 'external diseconomies', in relation to Marshall's concept of external economies. Elsewhere, Kapp explained that 'the term "external" refers to the fact that the diseconomies (costs) or economies (savings or benefits) are outside the frame of reference which serves as the foundation of micro-economic cost analysis, namely entrepreneurial costs' (Kapp, 2011: 273).

Kapp rejected such terminology as it suggests that such costs are accidental and infrequent. Instead, he agreed with neoclassical economists that social costs are a form of non-market interdependencies, but underlined that 'the output of a firm is not independent of its ability to shift part of its costs to other sectors of the economy or to the individual' (Kapp, 1963: XXV). It is instead strictly dependent on it, meaning that cost-shifting is not a minor aberration but a regular practice used by business enterprise to make profits. Rather than being external to the (market) system, environmental damages are in reality a normal part of business practice, despite their absence from its accounting books. Thus, the problem is inside the system, not outside it.

Further, Kapp argued that 'uncompensated costs are both pervasive—the rule rather than the exception—and systemic—predictable and widespread rather than incidental' (Swaney and Evers, 1989: 8). On these lines, later on, Martinez Alier and O'Connor (1999) argued that externalities should be seen not as market failures (e.g. the failure of the price system to indicate environmental impacts), but as cost-shifting successes which depend on power relations. Reality is far from the realms of perfect competition where no cost escapes the market's accounting and all market participants are price takers (having no economic power). Externalities by private activities were (and are) seen by welfare economists, such as Arthur C. Pigou (1920), as 'exceptions' that can be remedied within the framework of private enterprise. Instead, for Kapp, these social costs are major, typical and regular occurrences. In his view, 'despite the shift in the balance of power, the main body of neoclassical value theory has continued to regard social losses as accidental and exceptional cases or as minor disturbances'.

Social costs are 'external' and 'non-economic' in character, but to be defined as such they should present two characteristics: first, it must be possible to avoid them; second, they must be part of the course of productive activities and be shifted to third persons or the community at large. For example, water or air pollution caused by industrial activities are social costs, but not damages from an earthquake.

Kapp was highly concerned that social costs were not sufficiently recognized in society. He therefore argued in favour of the importance of their assessment and quantification at the same time that called for prudence on their monetization (i.e. cost-benefit analysis, CBA) and warned not to make a fetish of precision and measurement. In his view, social costs and social benefits could not be measured in money terms because they are extra-market phenomena. For instance, social benefits are public goods (non-rival) and therefore have no market values. For this reason, externalities could not be internalized by a Pigovian tax or through Coasian bargaining (a negotiation between impactors and impactees).

For Kapp, the remediation of social costs remains a political issue as he explained that 'society must be prepared to translate social costs into private costs by political action'. In fact, he continued indicating that 'The history of economic and social legislation as well as economic history could well be written as the history of the success or failure to make sure that private interests are not pursued at the cost of collective interests' (Kapp, 1963: 45). He therefore explicitly recognized the conflictive nature of social cost remediation, and its relation with power, as the 'political history of the last 150 years can be interpreted as a revolt of large masses of people (including small business) against social costs […] an integral part of the gradual access to political power by groups formerly excluded from such power'. Where, on the one hand, 'pressure groups and vested interests have been able to distort and abuse the legitimate struggles for a more equal distribution of social costs, to the detriment of society'. However, on the other hand, a counter-movement (in Polanyi's terms) arises with 'the emergence of an "anti-capitalist" mentality and an intense quest for greater security by large masses of people who have to bear the brunt of the social losses of rapid change'.

Kapp went even further and noted that social costs, such as water and air pollution, 'do much more than shift some of the costs of production to people living outside of a given area. They create a new physical environment for man.' In the words of today's political ecology, social costs create a new socio-nature (Swyngedouw, 2004). Kapp, highlighting the uncertainty associated with it, continued arguing that 'instead of the natural environment in which man has lived for centuries, the permanent revolution of technology has created a man-made environment the full implications of which, for human health and human survival, are far from being fully understood. We are only at the threshold of the realization that his man-made environment may be exceedingly detrimental to all life on this planet'. In other words, the industrial revolution has disrupted the 'natural balance' defined as the 'delicate system of interrelationship between the land and its vegetative cover'.

In conclusion, Kapp's concept of cost-shifting suggests, contrary to neoclassical economics, that capitalism contains an intrinsic tendency to reduce costs, not only through improved management or technology, but also through any other means available, including deliberate shifting of costs to less powerful social groups (e.g. the workers), the environment, or society at large (Swaney, 2006). This is what led Kapp to conclude that 'capitalism must be regarded as an economy of unpaid costs', and what we will propose to call **Accumulation by contamination**. We will argue that unfair ecological distribution is inherent to capitalism, and this represents a major driving force leading to conflicts. Political ecology in turn, discussed in the following section, provides a good vantage point to explain the conflictive power relations that are at the heart of cost-shifting.

2.2 Political Ecology

Political ecology (hereafter PE) is the study of the relationships between political, economic, and social factors with environmental issues and changes.[5] To be more precise, PE is at the confluence between ecologically rooted social science and the principles of political economy. It explicitly aims to represent an alternative to apolitical ecologies (Forsyth, 2008). PE understands every ecological issue as a political one. Politics has to do with the distribution of power and resources within a given group, community, and society; within and across generations. According to Wikipedia,[6] 'the academic community of PE offers a wide range of studies integrating ecological social sciences with political economy (Peet and Watts 1996, p. 6) in topics such as degradation and marginalization, environmental conflict, conservation and control, environmental identities and social movements (Robbins, 2004, p. 14)'. Scholars in PE are drawn from a variety of academic disciplines, including geography, anthropology, development studies, political science, sociology, forestry, and environmental history.

The origins of the field in the 1970s and 1980s was a result of the development of radical development geography and cultural ecology (Bryant, 1998: 80).[7] Historically, PE has focused on phenomena in and affecting the developing world; since the field's inception, 'research has sought primarily to understand the political dynamics surrounding material and discursive struggles over the environment in the third world' (Bryant, 1998: 89). Since the 1980s, political ecology came to mean a combination of 'the concerns of ecology and a broadly defined political economy' (Blaikie and Brookfield, 1987: 17), the latter understood as a concern with effects 'on people, as well as on their productive activities, of on-going changes within society at local and global levels' (1987: 21). This strand of political ecology had the advantage of seeing land management and environmental degradation (or sustainability) in terms of how political economy shapes the ability to manage resources (through forms

---

[5] Political ecology. Available at: http://environment-ecology.com/political-ecology/407-politi cal-ecology.html (Accessed on 23 February 2017).

[6] See https://en.wikipedia.org/wiki/Political_ecology (Accessed on 30 September 2021).

[7] Political ecology. Available at: http://environment-ecology.com/political-ecology/407-politi cal-ecology.html (Accessed on 30 September 2021).

of access and control, of exploitation), and through the lens of cognition (one person's accumulation is another person's degradation). But in other respects it was demonstrably weak, it often had an outdated notion of ecology and it was often remarkably silent on the politics of political ecology as well as on gender. From the 1990s onwards, these weaknesses have been overcome. For example, a number of studies address the question of politics, focusing especially on patterns of resistance and struggles over access to and control over the environment (notably with the debate on environmental justice) and how politics as policy is discursively constructed (Neumann, 1998; Martinez Alier, 2002). More recently, there has been a proliferation of studies on the political ecology of cities, commodities and of forms of green rule and subject formation (Agrawal, 2005; Heynen, Kaika and Swyngedouw, 2006; Swyngedouw, 2004) and violence (Peluso and Watts, 2001). For example, the concept of 'urban metabolism' has now become central to critical explorations of urban nature (Heynen, Kaika, and Swyngedouw, 2006). However, the focus of political ecology remains the dialectical relations between nature and society that the early studies identified.

PE's broad scope and interdisciplinary nature lends itself to multiple definitions and understandings. However, common assumptions across the field give it relevance. According to Tom Bauler, Bryant and Bailey (1997) have developed three fundamental assumptions in practising PE.[8]

(1) 'Costs and benefits associated with environmental change are distributed unequally. Changes in the environment do not affect society in a homogenous way: political, social, and economic differences account for uneven distribution of costs and benefits. Political power plays an important role in such inequalities.'

(2) 'This unequal distribution inevitably reinforces or reduces existing social and economic inequalities. In this assumption, political ecology runs into inherent political economies as any change in environmental conditions must affect the political and economic status quo (Bryant and Bailey, 1997, p. 28)'.

---

[8] See the entry on political ecology by Tom Bauler at the EJOLT Glossary. Available at: http://www.ejolt.org/2013/02/political-ecology/ (Accessed on 30 September 2021).

(3) 'The unequal distribution of costs and benefits and the reinforcing or reducing of pre-existing inequalities holds political implications in terms of the altered power relationships that are produced'.

This understanding resonates with the definition given by Martinez Alier (2002): PE is the study of ecological distribution conflicts, meaning the study of conflicts on the access to natural resources and services and on the burdens of pollution or other environmental impacts that arise because of unequal property rights and inequalities of power and income among humans (both international and internal to each state).

In addition, PE attempts to provide critiques as well as alternatives in the interplay of the environment and political, economic, and social factors. Robbins asserts that the discipline has a 'normative understanding that there are very likely better, less coercive, less exploitative, and more sustainable ways of doing things' (2004: 12). PE does not aim to necessarily generate policies, like environmental politics does, but to understand the phenomenon and eventually engage with social mobilization.

One could identify different school of thoughts within PE, like feminist political ecology or urban political ecology. This book draws from, and is meant to contribute to, the 'Barcelona School of Political Ecology' (Villamayor and Muradian, 2023). This is a distinctive type of PE, different from that of Anglo-Saxon geographers or anthropologists. Giorgos Kallis has outlined the following characteristics (Personal communication, 2016):

—The study of conflicts not just for the academic sake of studying them, but because we want to give voice to those involved and bring their own theories and concepts to academia;
—The book that environmentalists are those who are poor and have a small metabolism, and not the post-materialist rich with their huge metabolisms;
—Criticizing capitalism and its unquenchable metabolism, but not only always engaging also with the potential and conditions for transformative alternatives (degrowth, alternative economies, commons, post-extractivism, etc.);

—An eclectic use of theory (from Gramsci to Kapp to Polanyi etc.), again not for the sake of using theory, but because we want to explain conflicts, and empower political alternatives.

Along these lines, this book is meant to contribute to a better understanding of the relations between social metabolism and environmental conflicts. For this purpose, in the following section, we review the literature on ecological distribution conflicts, paying particular attention to both the roots of these conflicts and how they are expressed in the political arena.

2.2.1 Ecological Distribution Conflicts

According to Conde and Martinez-Alier[9]: 'The definition of political ecology as the study of Ecological Distribution Conflicts (hereafter EDCs), refers to conflicts over access and control of natural resources. The term EDCs was introduced by two economists, Joan Martinez-Alier and Martin O'Connor (1996), to describe social conflicts born from the unfair access to natural resources and the unjust burdens of pollution. Environmental benefits and costs are distributed in a way that causes conflicts. The terms socio-environmental conflict, environmental conflict or EDC are interchangeable'.

Joan Martinez-Alier and Martin O'Connor (1996), trained as economists, were making an extension from political economy as the study of 'economic distribution conflicts' about class distribution of wealth, income and assets (e.g. conflicts between capital and labour—profits vs. salaries—, or on prices between sellers and buyers of commodities, or on the interest rate to be paid by debtors to creditors) to the field of ecology (Martinez Alier, 2002). Later, Escobar (2008) introduced the concept of cultural distribution conflicts, considering those ontological conflicts that manifest themselves in the relative power, or powerlessness accorded to various knowledges and cultural processes. The three typologies of

---

[9] See the entry on Ecological Distributions Conflicts by Marta Conde and Joan Martinez-Alier at the EJOLT Glossary. Available at: http://www.ejolt.org/2016/04/ecological-distribution-conflicts/ (Accessed on 11 January 2022).

conflict (cultural, ecological, and economic) are intertwined, but the idea is that often there is a prevalent cause. The term EDCs stresses the idea that the unequal or unfair distribution of environmental goods and bads is not always coterminous with 'economic distribution' as, for instance, rents paid for by tenant farmers to landlords, or the international terms of trade of a national economy, or claims for higher wages from mining unions opposing company owners.

There are local as well as global ecological distribution conflicts; whilst many of them occur between the Global South and the Global North (a Canadian or Chinese mining company operating in Brazil), there are also many local conflicts within a short commodity chain (e.g. on local sand and gravel extraction for a nearby cement factory) (Martinez Alier, 2002). From a social metabolic perspective one can classify EDCs through the stages of a commodity chain; conflicts can take place during the extraction of energy carriers or other materials, transportation and production of goods, or in the final disposal of waste. The Environmental Justice Atlas documents and catalogues EDCs (ejatlas.org).

Research on EDCs links up with several concepts in ecological economics, political ecology and related disciplines; for instance, the ecological debt and ecologically unequal exchange between the North and the South, the acknowledgement of environmental liabilities; also social ecofeminism that highlights gender in the study of environmental impacts and activism (Agarwal, 1992), the notion of environmental justice, a term originating in the United States and linked to the struggle against 'environmental racism' (Bullard, 1993), and the environmentalism of the poor and the indigenous (Guha and Martinez Alier, 1997). Here we want to discuss more in detail first, the roots of EDCs, and second, the issue of valuation, or else, the value of nature.

2.2.1.1 The roots of ecological distribution conflicts (EDCs)

The movement to accumulate capital by expanding the frontiers of capitalism is resisted by a counter-movement (as Karl Polanyi explained in *The Great Transformation* in 1944) to protect nature and humans. In environmental conflicts, the protagonists are not labour unions or nature conservation societies. They are Environmental Justice Organizations (EJOs), indigenous groups, citizens and peasant groups, and women activists. They deploy their own values against the logic of profit making.

Ecological distribution conflicts refer to struggles over the burdens of pollution or over the sacrifices made to extract resources, and they arise from social asymmetries in the distribution of political and economic power, property rights, and income (Martinez Alier and O'Connor, 1996). The roots of the conflicts lie not only in failures of governance and in maladapted institutions, or in inadequate pricing but in the appetite of the world economy for inputs coming from the commodity frontiers, and the resulting release of waste to the sinks, well beyond their assimilative capacity (Martinez Alier et al., 2010). Most notably, Martinez-Alier (2002) has been argued that ecological distribution conflicts emerge from the expansion of social metabolism where powerful actors shift the costs to vulnerable ones (Martinez Alier, 2002). Metabolic processes are governed by regimes that determine the social relations of production, division of labour, distribution of resources, and ultimately produce what Swyngedouw calls 'socio-nature' (Heynen et al., 2006; Swyngedouw and Heynen, 2003). However, the open question is what drives the expansion and changes of metabolism that, in turn, drives environmental conflicts? Martinez Alier et al., (2010) has been argued that it is economic and population growth. But then, what is it that drives such growth? For Marxists, the expansion of the economy is due to the need to compensate the 'decreasing marginal profits' and takes place with two complementary commodification strategies: expansion (e.g. spatial fix) and deepening (e.g. search for new markets) (Harvey, 2003). In relation to the latter, in the discussion of this book, we will argue that contamination, meant as cost-shifting, is a strategy that needs more attention, apart from capital accumulation by dispossession. We will propose that it is capital accumulation that has to be seen as the principal driving force of social metabolism, which brings up questions of political economy.

2.2.1.2 The value of nature

EDCs emerge out of socio-metabolic re-configurations, and therefore are often of material origins. However, they are expressed in terms of valuation languages, meaning the vocalization of disputes about values, and shaped by cultural discourses. As discussed in social movement theory, diagnosing a problem turns out to be a very contentious process, where the different actors try to affirm and impose their interpretative frame to the detriment of representations proposed by the others (Snow et al.,

1986). The construction of reality is inextricably linked to asymmetries of power (Della Porta and Diani, 2006). In this sense, EDCs can be compared to cultural distribution conflicts that arise from the differences in effective power associated with particular meanings and practices.

'Ecological distribution conflicts' is a term for collective claims against environmental injustices. For instance, a factory may be polluting the river (which belongs to nobody or belongs to a community that manages the river). The same happens with climate change, causing perhaps sea level rise. Yet this damage is not valued in the market and those impacted are not compensated for it. Unfair ecological distribution is inherent to capitalism, defined by Kapp (1963) as a system of cost-shifting, and leads to conflicts. PE, together with EE, advocates the acceptance of different valuation languages to understand such conflicts and the need to take them into account through genuine participatory processes in natural resource management and environmental problem solving (Agarwal, 2001; Zografos and Howarth, 2010).

The environment is often a site of conflict between competing values and interests represented by different classes and groups, such as conservation of nature, livelihood, sacredness, money, or aesthetics (Healy et al., 2013: 103). In order to solve such valuation conflicts, economics proposes to reduce all values into a single unit of measure, namely money. This monetary valuation can be used for cost-benefit analysis (CBA), an approach used to calculate benefits and costs of a decision (be it a policy or a project), so as to estimate the strengths and weaknesses of alternatives. This approach, rooted in utilitarianism, assumes the existence of value commensurability, meaning that there is a common measure of the different consequences of an action based on a cardinal scale of measurement. In simple terms, all values can be translated into money (e.g. a monetary compensation for damages in a court of law in a civil suit).

However, values are often incommensurable (e.g. How much for your god? How much for someone's life?). This simply means that they cannot be measured in the same units. Therefore, as alternative to conventional economics, Martinez Alier et al. (1998) proposed weak comparability of values as a foundation of ecological economics. Weak commensurability refers to a common measure based on an ordinal scale of measurement, and is derived from weak comparability where irreducible value conflict is unavoidable but compatible with rational choice employing practical judgement. Instead of cost-benefit analysis (CBA), multicriteria evaluation offers the methodological and mathematical tools to operationalize the concept of incommensurability at both macro and micro levels of analysis (Munda, 1995, 2008). This approach of EE highlights the existence of a conflict between competing values and interests. Therefore, it recognizes the existence of multiple, and incommensurable, languages of valuation (Martinez Alier, 2002). In fact, in environmental conflicts, there is often not only a discrepancy but also incommensurability in valuation (Martinez Alier, 2003).

Apart from PE, also for EE, social change is characterized by conflict rather than harmony, so the existence of power and privilege is at the centre of interest (Røpke, 2005). Ultimately, as Martinez-Alier (2002) has argued, the fundamental question is who has the power to simplify complexity? Or else, who has the power to impose the economic language of valuation? In decision-making processes, economics becomes a tool of power in the hands of those who know how to wield it. Against the economic logic, the languages of valuation used by vulnerable groups go unheeded. This will also be the case of the EDCs that we discuss in this book.

In the following section, we introduce waste studies discussing: (1) waste definition and legislation, (2) waste generation, (3) waste management, and (4) recycling. We conclude by theorizing waste recyclers that we compare to decomposers in natural ecosystems, stressing why and how both ecological economics and political ecology should pay more attention to these important actors.

2.3 Waste Studies

Waste is a quintessentially ecological economic issue (Bisson and Proops, 2002). It deals with the thermodynamics of production processes, hence the generation of waste is rooted in the very laws of nature. However, waste is also a social construct, and what we understand to be waste has evolved with human societies. From the viewpoint of political ecology, waste is 'socio-nature', both medium and outcome of social struggles and the complex reorderings of nature-society relations (Swyngedouw, 2004: 25). What Perrault (2012: 5) argues for water, could be said for waste: 'the ways that water flow, quality, and quantity, as well as access and rights to water, both reflect and reproduce relations of social power'.

This book focuses on waste management. First, today there is a growing call for scholars to expand their inquiry from resource extraction, through production processes and consumption, to the disposal of waste (Bridge, 2011; Martinez Alier et al., 2010).

Second, waste is a growing problem for the pollutants released into the ecosystems, for the need of new disposal space, for the resulting social problems related to localization of the facilities and for the loss in terms of resources and energy. These issues are being amplified by economic development, demographic change, technological developments, and socio-environmental conflicts related to specific social contexts often resulting from locally undesirable land uses (LULUs).

Third, waste management involves a wide range of actors, from informal waste pickers to multinational corporations, and present simultaneously different levels of industrialization at different places in the world. Integrated sustainable waste management involves much more than perfectly matched technical options of waste treatment. Waste management should be addressed more also as a social and political process, and not only as a technical matter (Bisson and Proops, 2002; Winiwarter, 2002).

Fourth, capital looks at waste management as a new emergent global market, where a rentier position can be acquired and profits realized. Waste management is a multi-billion dollar industry that is increasingly attracting the attention of large-scale institutional investors (e.g. Bank of America Merrill Lynch, 2013). Indeed, capitalists consider waste management as one among several economic spaces to be occupied for the expansion of the scale and scope of capital accumulation (Harvey, 2003). This leads to the emergence of waste-based commodity frontiers. As we will see, the complexity of waste management represents nowadays an opportunity for profit making, else a very tempting market for the over-accumulated capital looking for new profitable business to seize hold of (Harvey, 2003). Our hypothesis is that that the appropriation of a 'common bad' such as waste is one of several strategies for expanding the scale and scope of capital accumulation as Prudham (2007) explains for the case of biotechnology.

Last, this book can be seen as a contribution to Critical Discard Studies,[10] an emerging interdisciplinary sub-field that takes waste and wasting, broadly defined, as its topic of study. Its tasks rely on interrogating how waste comes to be, and offers critical alternatives to popular and normative notions of waste.

Hereafter we present different definitions and categories of waste, and how this is reflected in the Indian legislation.

2.3.1 Defining Waste and Its Legislation

In ecological economics, waste is the output of social metabolism in all its forms: liquid, solid, and gas. Hereafter, when referring to waste, we will mean just solid waste. Broadly, solid waste can be classified into two major categories depending on the way it is generated: (1) those generated as undesired by-products in the production process such as mining or industrial waste, and (2) those originally produced as goods but turned to waste with the passage of time, such as old paper or discarded consumer durables (Nakamura, 1999). The first category is generated in the places of extraction, production, and transportation. The second is the result of consumption, the place of final use, and therefore tends to be distributed over a wide geographical area. Simplifying, we propose to call the first production waste and the second consumption waste. In relation to waste management there is a paradox: while production waste is much more important in terms of weight, volume, and toxicity, it is also the least well known and safely managed. This is exemplified by the lack of comprehensive data sets and a proper legislation that would ensure proper treatment, resulting in serious social and environmental consequences.

In this book, an example for each one of these categories is explored, with a focus on recycling. For the first one, we discuss a case of infrastructure waste, namely the management of ocean going ships at the end of their useful life. For the second one, we investigate the struggles over municipal solid waste management in Delhi, the capital of India. In both cases the management of waste is carried out in India, but it involves different geographical scales: shipbreaking occurs on a global scale,

---

[10] See: https://discardstudies.com (Accessed on 16 October 2022).

involving international trade and multinational corporations, while the second takes place at the urban scale.

Both in the academic literature and in the different legislations, there are many definitions of waste. They normally depend upon different concepts such as collection (e.g. municipal), source (e.g. domestic activity, commercial, industry or mining) and type (e.g. paper, plastic, and glass; or hazardous and non-hazardous). If classified by the source, as we proposed above, the legislation normally uses a more detailed classification, like in the United States: (1) residential, (2) commercial, (3) institutional, (4) construction and demolition, (5) municipal services, (6) treatment plant sites, (7) industrial, and (8) agricultural (Tchobanoglous and Kreith, 2002). Municipal Solid Waste would include residential, commercial, institutional, and industrial (but only non-processes waste); this is what we called above consumption waste. Other types of waste are often treated differently, such as hazardous (special or not) waste or biomedical waste.

The most well-known form of solid waste is municipal waste, informally called trash or garbage and technically municipal solid waste (hereafter MSW). The concerned Indian legislation is the Municipal Solid Wastes (Management and Handling) Rules, 1999. The law clarifies that 'municipal solid waste includes commercial and residential wastes generated in a municipal or notified areas in either solid or semi-solid form excluding industrial hazardous wastes but including treated bio-medical wastes'. This law has been updated in 2016, and now mentions the integration of recyclers from the informal sector to the formal sector by the state government. The implementation of this is another matter, as we shall see.[11]

In India, waste is regulated in general by the Central government with The Environmental Protection Act, 1986 (with general principles, like the Polluter Pays Principle), but then specific legislations are concerned with different types of waste, namely:

—*Bio-medical Waste (Management and Handling) Rules, 1998*: it aims to ensure that bio-medical wastes are safely disposed of, defined as

[11] Swati Singh Sambyal, 'Government notifies new solid waste management rules'. Down to Earth, 5 April 2016. Available at: https://www.downtoearth.org.in/news/waste/solid-waste-management-rules-2016-53443 (Accessed on 16 October 2022).

any waste or by-product generated during treatment, immuniza-
tion and treatment of human beings or animals or in medical research activities.

— *The Hazardous Wastes (Management, Handling and Transboundary
   Movement) Rules, 2008*: it defines hazardous waste as any waste
   which by virtue of its physical or other characteristics (described
   as chemical, toxic, inflammable, reactive, explosive, etc.) cause or
   can cause danger to health or environment, either standalone or
   in combination with other substances. It is also concerned with
   the trans-boundary shipment of hazardous waste regulated by the
   Basel convention, of which India is a signatory.

— *The Batteries (Management and Handling) Rules, 2001*: it is meant
   to set up a mechanism in place to deal with the disposal of lead acid
   batteries.

— *The E-waste (Management and Handling) Rules, 2011*: it is meant to
   put in place a system which manages e-waste in an environment-
   friendly way by regulating the issue of recycling and disposal of e-
   waste (including the imported e-waste, mostly illegally).

— *The Plastic Waste (Management and Handling) Rules, 2011*: it is a
   regulatory framework set up to control the manufacture, usage and
   recycling of plastic waste.

— *Construction   and   Demolition   Waste   Management   Rules,
   2016*: it grants the responsibility of every waste generator to recover, recycle and reuse the waste generated through construction
   and demolition.

Demonstrating what we argued above, in India there is no specific legislation that comprehensively deals with 'production waste', for example
non-hazardous industrial waste. This is then reflected also in the national
statistics.

In India,[12] the Ministry of Environment and Forests estimates that in
2016 the country generated 62 mn tonnes of waste, out of which 5.6 mn
tonnes was plastic waste, 0.17 mn tonnes was biomedical waste, 7.90 mn

---

[12] 'Solid Waste Management Rules Revised After 16 Years; Rules Now Extend to Urban and
Industrial Areas': Javadekar. By Ministry of Environment and Forests. Available at: http://pib.
nic.in/newsite/PrintRelease.aspx? relid = 138591 (Accessed on 15 March 2017).

tonnes was hazardous waste generation and 15,000 tonnes was e-waste. Out of 62, only 43 mn tonnes was collected, 11.9 mn was treated and 31 mn was dumped in landfill sites, which means that only about 75–80% of the municipal waste was collected and only 22–28% of this waste was processed and treated in 2016. Waste generation is expected to increase from 62 mn tonnes to about 165 mn tonnes in 2030.

Hereafter we present the background for consumption waste, namely Solid Waste Management, which has been the main focus of both research and legislation. I focus on MSW generation and management.

2.3.2 Waste Generation

Waste generation encompasses those activities in which materials are identified as no longer being of value and are either thrown away or gathered together for disposal.[13] This is an identification step and it varies with each individual. Waste generation is, at present, an activity that is not very controllable. In fact, waste generation is steadily increasing, especially in low-income countries where it is approaching the levels of high-income countries. The World Bank (2012) has estimated that in 2002 the global average generation was about 0.64 kg of MSW per person per day (pppd), while in 2012 it had increased at 1.2 kg pppd. This is expected to increase to 1.42 pppd by 2025. Urban population is also on the rise, so that if in 2012 there were 3 bn urban residents (leading to 1.3 bn tonnes per year), they are expected to be about 4.3 bn by 2025 (2.2 bn tonnes per day). Every two hours humans generate enough waste to fill the world's largest containership, 12 ships every day and 4,380 every year.

Obviously, global averages are broad estimates, rates vary considerably by region, country, city, and even within cities. For example, urban residents produce about twice as much waste as their rural counterparts. Overall, the higher the income level and rate of urbanization, the

---

[13] If not specified, data presented in the following two sections comes from the 2012 World Bank report 'What a waste'. These data should be considered with a degree of caution due to global inconsistencies in definitions, data collection methodologies, and completeness. Thus, their reliability is limited and comparison across income levels and regions is difficult. Many countries do not even collect waste data at the national level. However, they are useful to provide a general picture and show certain trends.

Table 2.1 Waste generation projections for 2025 by region

Region	Total urban population	Per capita (kg/capita/day)	Total (Tonnes/day)
Africa	260	0.65	169
East Asia & Pacific	777	0.95	738.15
Eastern & Central Asia	227	1.1	249.7
Latin America & the Caribbean	399	1.1	438.9
Middle East & North Africa	162	1.1	178.2
OECD	729	2.2	1603.8
South Asia	426	0.45	191.7
Total	2980	1.2	3569.45

Source: World Bank, 2012.

Table 2.2 Average Municipal Solid Waste (MSW) generation rates by income

Income level	Average MSW generation (kg/capita/day)
Low-Income	0.6–1.0
Middle-Income	0.8–1.5
High-Income	1.1–4.5

Source: World Bank, 2012.

greater the amount of solid waste produced. In fact, OECD (Organisation for Economic Co-operation and Development) countries produce almost half of the world's waste (with an average of 2.2 kg/capita/day), while Africa and South Asia produce the least waste, with respectively an average of 0.65 and 0.45 kg/capita/day (see Table 2.1). The range from the lower to the upper boundary varies more as inequality is higher, so for example, in Latin America it goes from 0.11 to 5.5 kg/capita/day, in India from 0.2 to 0.6. Generally speaking, the richer you are, the more waste you generate (see Table 2.2). So that one could argue that waste generation varies as a function of affluence and, to a lesser extent, population. The same World Bank report (2012: 3) explicitly admits that 'In most cities, the quickest way to reduce waste volumes is to reduce economic activity—not generally an attractive option'. This resonates clearly with the debates on degrowth (D'Alisa et al., 2015).

A recent comment in *Nature* argues that 'Waste production must peak this century' (Hoornweg et al., 2013). However, the authors show that—if current trends continue—'peak waste' will not happen this century. OECD countries could peak by 2050 and Asia-Pacific countries by 2075, but would be fast-growing in other regions. Using 'business-as-usual' projections, they predict that, by 2100, solid-waste generation rates will exceed 11 mn tonnes per day—more than three times today's rate.

The figures given here for MSW are significant for the problems related to its management, and expected to increase. However, this is just a small percentage of the overall waste produced. For example, for the United States, as a percentage of industrial waste, MSW is 3%.[14] In the EU, municipal waste corresponds to only approximately 10% of the total amount of the overall waste generated, in terms of weight (EEA, 2000). Worldwide, there are very few comprehensive statistics about industrial waste. This is also because regulations often do not require industries to report on their non-hazardous waste. The GrassRoots Recycling Network (2000) has reported that 'Few studies have documented how much manufacturing, mining, and energy related wasting could actually be eliminated for every ton of municipally generated discards reduced or recovered'.[15]

This mismatch is confirmed by assessments of the world economy metabolism. Hass et al. (2015) estimated the material flows, waste production, and recycling in the European Union and the world in 2005. The processed materials account for 64 Gt per year, including energy, biomass, and materials. The total output was about 41 Gt per year (28 for energy, 4 for waste rock and 13 for end of life), of which 13Gt per year were recyclable and only 4 Gt per year actually got recycled, meaning just 6% of the total. The study distinguishes between domestic processed output (DPO) and end of life (EOL). DPO comprises all wastes and emissions (including CO_2) that leave the socio-economic system (SES). EOL accounts for the materials that are used within one year, mainly

---

[14] The United States produces 250 mn tonnes of municipal solid waste every year, but 7.6 bn tonnes of non-hazardous industrial waste per year.

[15] https://zerowasteusa.org/

consumables. The largest part of this fraction is potentially available for recycling after use. Typically, these are consumer goods, such as packaging, newspapers, batteries, plastic bags, and so on. In other words, this is what corresponds, more or less, to municipal solid waste. In contrast to these consumables, by far the largest amount of materials is used to build up and maintain long-life stocks of buildings, infrastructures, and other long-life goods, which remain in the socioeconomic system as in-use stocks for more than a year. Once these materials leave the SES, they are accounted as DPO. The global average per person of DPO was 6.3 tonnes per year, meaning about 17 kg per day. For EOL it was 2 tonnes per year, meaning 5.5 kg per day. In order to compare these results with the data provided above, since DPO also includes emissions from energy production, we should account only for waste rock and EOL, which is about 7 kg pppd. This is about 11 times the global average of waste generation estimated by the World Bank (2012) for 2002 (0.64 kg pppd), or 6 times the values of 2012 (1.2 kg pppd). This is the difference between consumption and production waste.

Filling this gap would require a life cycle assessment (LCA) analysis for every product or service. This would allow to account for the ecological rucksack, meaning the total quantity (in kg) of materials removed from nature to create a product or service, minus the actual weight of the product. It considers the entire production process, from the cradle to the point when the product is ready for use. The rucksack factor (MI) is the total amount of natural materials used (kg) to make 1 kg of the resource, raw or starting (e.g. wood, iron).

Five different rucksacks have been delineated by the Wuppertal Institute to describe the overall natural resource intensity of products. These correspond to the five environmental spheres of water, air, soil, renewable biomass, and non-renewable (abiotic) materials (Schmidt-Bleek, 1999). On average, industrial products carry non-renewable rucksacks that are about 30 times their own weight. Only about 5% of non-renewable natural material disturbed in the ecosphere typically ends up in a technically useful form. This is consistent with saying that MSW is only about 3% of the overall waste generated. In the case of a Personal Computer, the ecological (abiotic) rucksack weighs at least 200 kg per kg of product. For base materials (such as iron, plastic or copper), MI values allow the comparison of technical starting materials regarding their resource intensities and thus allow the computation of the rucksack of products, so long as the material compositions of these products are known. MI values (rucksack factors) for non-renewable resources of base materials are, for example, round wood = 1.2, glass = 2, plastics = 2–7, steel = 7, paper = 15, aluminium = 85, copper = 500, platinum = 500,000 (Schmidt-Bleek, 1999). These are just broad estimation, since the figures can vary significantly based on the methodology used.

The existence of the ecological rucksack raises issues of responsibility allocation, for instance if it should be the responsibility of the producer and/ or the consumer. For example, for a computer sold in Europe, who should be held responsible for its management once it becomes waste, and the end of its useful life? Plus, who should be held responsible for the waste generated during its production? The principle of extended producer responsibility (EPR) tackles the first question. It is a strategy designed to promote the integration of environmental costs associated with goods throughout their life cycles into the market price of the products. EPR may take the form of a reuse, buy-back, or recycling program. The rationale beyond EPR has to do with financial incentives to encourage manufacturers to design environmentally friendly products by holding producers responsible for the costs of managing their products at end of life. This is based on the idea that producers (usually brand owners) have the greatest control over product design and marketing, and that therefore they have the greatest ability and responsibility to reduce toxicity and waste. Instead, the second question remains often untackled, but is of great relevance given we live in a globalized world with high levels of international trade. The same holds true for other forms of waste, like greenhouse gases (GHG). For example, who should be held responsible for GHG emitted in China to manufacture products sold in the international market?

In the next section we present the most important aspects of any waste management systems.

2.3.3 Functional Elements of a Solid Waste Management System

Solid waste management is a fundamental service provided to residents by the city government, and serves as a prerequisite for other municipal action. Here we briefly review the different functional elements of a solid waste management system.

— *Composition.* Waste is broadly classified into organic and inorganic. For planning purposes, the categories used are often organic, paper, plastic, metals, and others (e.g. textile, rubber, or ash). The lower the income of countries, the higher the proportion of organic waste, ranging between 30% and 80%. Waste composition depends upon many factors including economic development, cultural norms, geographical location, energy sources, and climate conditions.

— *Waste handling and separation, storage, and processing at the source.* This involves the activities associated with managing wastes until it is collected. On-site storage is of primary importance because of public health concerns and aesthetic considerations. The fact that waste is separated into categories at source influences also how it can then be managed (e.g. if paper is mixed, or not, with organic matter influences whether it can be recycled, or not).

— *Collection (including transport and transportation).* The average waste collection rates are directly related to income levels. Low-income countries have low collection rates, around 40%, while high-income countries have higher collection rates averaging 98%. The difference between the waste generated, and the waste collected and managed is sometimes called 'ghost waste' (Armiero and D'Alisa, 2012). This phenomenon is of particular importance in case of toxic waste since it is a dangerous practice intentionally carried out by businesses to save the costs of proper management.

— *Separation, processing, and transformation of solid waste.* This stage depends on whether waste has been separated at source or not. These operations normally occur at materials recovery facilities, transfer stations, combustion facilities, and/or disposal sites. Transformation processes are used to reduce the volume and weight of waste requiring disposal and to recover conversion products and energy (e.g. composting or incineration).

— *Disposal.* Landfilling or land spreading is the ultimate fate of all solid wastes, despite of their source or type. A modern sanitary landfill differs from a dump, since it is a method of disposing of solid wastes on land or within the earth's mantle without creating public health hazards or nuisances. Landfilling is the most common method of MSW disposal in all countries, generally over 50% (see Table 2.3). The exception is high-income countries where recycling (22%), composting (11%), and incineration (21%) account for more than 50%, and landfilling about 42%. In low-income countries, if we sum up open dumps and landfills, then this accounts for up to 80% of waste disposal. However, in low- and middle-income countries there is an important flaw recognized by the World Bank (2012: 22): 'compostable and recyclable material is removed before the waste reaches the disposal site and is not included in waste disposal statistics'. Chapter 5 of this book attempts to fill this gap, and discusses how the informal recycling sector could be taken into account.

— *The economic cost of waste management.* Solid waste management costs are expected to increase from today's annual $205.4 bn to about $375.5 bn in 2025. This is equivalent to China's military expenditure ($215 bn, and half of the US one, $596 bn). Waste management costs represent a large share of a municipality's budget: 10% in high-income countries, 50% to 80% in middle-income, and 80% to 90% in low-income countries. Most of this budget goes in to collection, and the proportion allocated toward disposal increases from low- to high-income countries. There are important social and environmental

Table 2.3 Total Municipal Solid Waste (MSW) disposed of worldwide, million tonnes per year

Types of waste disposal	Million tonnes/year	Percentage
Landfill	340	47
Recycled	130	18
Incineration	120	17
Dump	70	10
Compost	60	8
Other	40	8
Total MSW disposed of worldwide	720	100

Source: World Bank, 2012.

costs related to MSW management that are not accounted for, and that—as we will show—are shifted to vulnerable groups.

—*Integrated Solid Waste Management.* The accepted hierarchy for waste disposal options, from the most to the least preferred option, is Reduce, Reuse, Recycle, Recover (digestion and composting), Incinerate (with energy recovery), Landfill and Controlled Dump. This is considered to be the policy aim and is based on four principles: (1) *equity* for all citizens to have access to waste management systems for public health reasons; (2) *effectiveness* of the waste management system to safely remove waste; (3) *efficiency* to maximize benefits, minimize costs, and optimize the use of resources; and (4) *sustainability* from a technical, social, cultural, economic, financial, institutional, and political perspective (van de Klundert and Asnschutz, 2001).

UN-Habitat (2009) has identified three key system elements in ISWM:

(1) Public health: Waste not properly managed can be a breeding ground for insects, vermin and scavenging animals; thus can pass on air and water-borne diseases.

(2) Environmental protection: contamination of groundwater and surface water by leachate as well as air pollution from burning waste. Moreover, MSW is reported to account for about 5% of total greenhouse gas emissions (1,460 mtCo2e).

(3) Resource management: MSW can represent a considerable potential resource. The global market for recyclables is significant (400 mn tonnes of scrap metal and 175 mn tonnes for paper and cardboard per year). Recycling in low- and middle-income countries is taken care of by the informal sector, with relatively high recycling rates, for example estimated to be about 20% in China (Hoornweg et al., 2005). Secondary markets present a high volatility of the prices. The relative value of secondary materials is expected to increase as the costs of virgin materials and their environmental impact increases.

In the next section we discuss in more detail the issue of recycling.

2.3.4 Recycling

Recycling is the process of converting waste materials into new materials and objects. Mainstream economists argue that, if the cost of waste management options reflected their true environmental and social costs, then market forces could achieve the optimal mix of waste management options in efficiency terms. However, this is not the case, because prices are not correct (and it is arguable whether they could be). In the current situation, waste reduction, reuse, recycling, and recovery are too low, while incineration and landfilling are too high.

The benefits of recycling are many: conservation of resources, savings in landfill space and emissions associated with landfill and incineration, energy saving in manufacturing, and transport of waste. Recycling has significant public support, but there many barriers to it, first of all the financial cost. Capital cost for recycling in the United States varies from $10,000 to $40,000 per tonne of capacity per day (Tchobanoglous and Kreith, 2002: 1.16–1.18), while operation and maintenance costs vary from $20 to $60 per tonne. Materials for recycling need to be collected, sorted, and transported to often distant processing units. Recycling can also cause problems if it is not done in an environmentally responsible manner. The economics of recycling depends upon many factors, including the prices of other waste management options and primary materials, as well as the markets for secondary materials (meaning recycled materials), characterized by high volatility. Fostering recycling requires proper public policies,[16] stable markets, and public education.

There are three main methods that can be used to recover recyclable materials from MSW (Tchobanoglous and Kreith, 2002):

1. Collection of source-separated recyclable materials by either the generator or the collector, with and without subsequent processing.

---

[16] Policy choices that can impact market demand include: commodity-specific procurement standards, entity-specific procurement plans, equipment tax credits, tax credits for users of secondary materials, mandated use of secondary materials for certain government-controlled activities (such as landfill cover or mine reclamation projects), use of market development mechanisms in enforcement settlements, recycled content requirements for certain commodities, manufacturer take-back systems, virgin material fees, and labelling requirements.

2. Commingled recyclables collection with processing at centralized materials recovery facilities (MRFs).
3. Mixed MSW collection with processing for recovery of the recyclable materials from the waste stream at mixed-waste processing or front-end processing facilities.

However, these are methods common in high-income countries, while in low and middle (but also to a certain extent in high) income countries there is an informal recycling sector, the focus of this book. In the next section, we argue that waste recyclers—in terms of their function in social metabolism—could be compared to decomposers in natural ecosystems. This can help us to better understand why they are important, as well as to contextualize them within the realm of both EE and PE.

2.3.5 Understanding Informal Waste Recyclers from the Perspective of Ecological Economics and Political Ecology

In this section we intend to propose a theoretical framework for the recycling sector. We do this by extending the metaphor used in ecological economics to compare the metabolism of natural ecosystems to the ones of human societies with industrial processes, by comparing waste recyclers to decomposers. We argue that, as it has happened in biology, EE and PE have not paid enough attention to these actors. The role played out in our societies by waste recyclers (or else, the decomposers) is not necessarily good per se, and not for the recyclers if done under apprehensive conditions. However, (1) from the viewpoint of EE, recyclers do play an important role in social metabolism, in particular for waste; and (2) from the viewpoint of PE, they are involved in ecological distribution conflicts.

2.3.5.1 Ecosystems
In natural ecosystems, the energy to drive processes of change comes almost exclusively from the sun. The transformation of solar radiation into chemical or mechanical energy, in order to sustain a structured non-equilibrium state of plants and animals, requires at least one

material cycle. In nature the cycle of synthesis and respiration involves not just one, but usually five different cycles of chemical elements and compounds, namely water, carbon, nitrogen, phosphorous, and sulphur (Ricklefs and Miller, 2000).

Numerous species of plants, animals, and microbes move matter in cycles. According to their role within ecosystems they may be classified as producers, consumers, and decomposers (Folke, 1999). Producers are those organisms which use sunlight as the only source of energy. In the process of photosynthesis they build up complex and energy-rich molecules from simple constituents taken from soil or the air. Green plants are the most important producers in most terrestrial ecosystems. Animals that feed on green plants or other animals are called consumers. They make their living on the chemical energy and nutrients stored in other organisms. The so-called decomposers, mainly bacteria and fungi, break up the 'wastes' and the dead material from producers and consumers. They bring the nutrients back into the material cycle. Like consumers, they rely on the chemical energy provided by producers as their source of energy. To be more precise, and simplifying, we could distinguish between two categories of decomposers: physical and chemical. The first, called scavengers, are animals that eat organic matter from dead plants or animals (e.g. insects or worms). By eating, they break them into small pieces. Subsequently chemical decomposers (e.g. bacteria or fungi) intervene by breaking down the materials into its chemical composites that become nutrients for the producers.

As almost all matter involved in processes of transformation in natural ecosystems stays in closed cycles, the dominant form of waste is waste heat. The latter is radiated into space.

2.3.5.2 Human societies
In natural ecosystems, the waste of a process constitutes the input of another process. This is a model that is certainly not reproduced by the industrial companies despite the efforts of industrial ecology (which tries to emulate ecosystems by closing the loops of industrial processes). The most commonly used example is the eco-industrial park Kalundbork in Denmark, an industrial symbiosis network in which companies in the region collaborate to use each other's by-products and otherwise share resources. Societies' economies do not close the loop, and therefore are

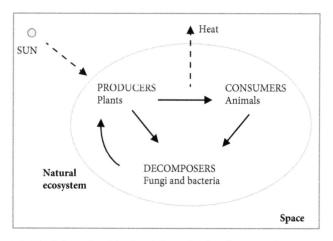

Figure 2.2 The life cycle of the food chain (or food): A circular process.

not circular. This has also been called the metabolic rift, or more recently the circularity gap. Energy cannot be recycled, and materials only up to a certain extent.

Nature is based on cyclic operation, therefore potentially infinite (at least as far as there is sunlight (see Figure 2.2). Instead, industrial societies are based on linear processes, therefore unsustainable by definition (see Figure 2.3). Ecosystems, in order to close the loop of life cycles (via the trophic chain) require organisms, called decomposers (such as fungi, bacteria or worms), which degrade both the dead organisms (plants and animals) and the organic waste.

Historically underestimated to other biological organisms higher in the food chain, decomposers play a fundamental role in any ecosystem. If they did not exist, the plants would not get essential nutrients and dead matter would accumulate (such as plastic in a landfill).

It is therefore possible to continue the parallelism between ecosystems and industrial processes, or human societies. In fact, society's recyclers play a similar role to nature's recyclers, or else the decomposers. Unlike ecosystems, in industrial processes the waste of one industry doesn't always become a resource for another one, so that it should be discarded at the same time that new materials introduced. Energy from fossil fuels and some materials cannot be recovered (e.g. polystyrene) or, although physically possible, it is economically unviable; other materials can be

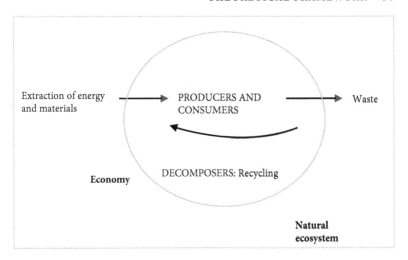

Figure 2.3 The relationship between the economy and the ecosystem: A linear process.

recycled only for a limited number of times (e.g. paper), and others potentially indefinitely (e.g. aluminium), assuming they don't get lost. In case it is possible to recycle materials, the decision whether to do it or not, depends on many factors including the energy and economic costs. We can imagine a public policy that shifts taxation from labour income to resources (so-called green tax reform), and that therefore both fosters the creation of jobs, and the preservation of materials. Otherwise, recycling tends to be expensive (compared to newly extracted materials) or carried out by those who are extremely poor, because it tends to be a sector with high labour intensity, for example, because the segregation can be mechanized only up to a certain point. Therefore, one could call decomposers those workers in society dealing with recycling. The recycling industry plays the function of chemical decomposers, while those workers involved with the collection, segregation, and processing of materials are the physical decomposers.

In this book, we present two cases of (physical) decomposers of waste of human society in India, the first involved in the dismantling of ships for recycling the steel, and the second with the recycling of municipal solid waste. In the next section we discuss the main theoretical contribution of this book that emerges out of the analysis of these two case studies. We frame our contribution within debates in political economy regarding capital accumulation showing how my case studies suggest the need to introduce the concept of *Accumulation by contamination*, along with the one of Accumulation by dispossession (Harvey, 2003).

2.4 Theoretical Contribution: Capital Accumulation by Contamination

'*Accumulate, accumulate!*
That is Moses and the prophets!'

Karl Marx (Capital I, ch. 24, sect. 3)

In this section we draw mainly from Marxist theory and critical geography, but with an explicit link both with political ecology and ecological economics.[17] We propose a detailed exploration of key political economy concepts, that allows us to introduce the new concept of accumulation by contamination and explains how it differs from the one of accumulation by dispossession. This will be of help to clarify what are the driving forces which influence the way metabolism changes. This discussion relates in particular to our second research question: How do capitalist dynamics and power relations shape unevenly waste metabolisms? These reflections were formulated after we conducted our research and are meant to constitute a central part of our theoretical contribution.

[17] The ideas discussed in this section have been developed together with Giacomo D'Alisa, that should be considered a co-author. Early thoughts have been published in this short article: Demaria, F., D'Alisa, G. (2013) 'Dispossession and contamination. Strategies for capital accumulation in the waste market'. Special Issue: Garbage and Wastes; *Lo Squaderno* 29: 37–39. The term 'accumulation by contamination' was first proposed by Joan Martinez-Alier in a seminar at the University of Manchester in 2010 on the financialization of the environment. With Giacomo, we had the chance to discuss our ideas at length with David Harvey in the Syros summer school of 2013 organized by the ENTITLE project, and we are grateful for his support. There are many other people with which we have discussed these ideas in the last ten years. They are too many to mention them all, but special thanks to Giorgos Kallis, Massimo De Angelis, Susan Paulson, Erik Swyngedouw, Maria Kaika, Diego Andreucci, Marco Armiero, Stefania Barca, Emanuele Leonardi, Julien Francois Gerber, Christos Zografos, Seth Schindler, Dianne Rocheleau, Silvia Federici, Lourdes Beneria, Ariel Salleh and all members of the European network of political ecology (ENTITLE), and political ecology network (POLLEN).

The multidimensional crises that our societies are facing show the instability and the crisis tendencies of capitalism. This offers the opportunity to revitalize the Marxist theory of over-accumulation, meaning that economic crises are due to a lack of profitable investment opportunities for capital. Potential ways out are found in the search for lower costs of input (i.e. land, raw materials or labour) and widening of markets (i.e. trade with non-capitalist formations). Capitalist development appears in need of something 'outside of itself' and for this reason continuously opens up 'territories' (Harvey, 2003), for example colonies, or new realms of accumulation such as ecosystem services. We will argue that there is an additional strategy that needs more attention, which could be called 'lower costs of output' via cost-shifting, namely contamination.

Marxists have highlighted the importance of capital accumulation as the driving force of capitalist societies. Ecological economists have highlighted the systematic tendencies of enterprises to cost-shift the environmental damages generated by the running of their business. We intend to attempt a synthesis looking at the role and importance of cost-shifting for capital accumulation, or else 'how capital is made to circulate through biophysical nature' (Prudham, 2007: 407). For this, we need to clarify what we mean by Capitalism, capital accumulation (CA), primitive accumulation (PA) and accumulation by dispossession (AbD). This will allow us to propose and properly define accumulation by contamination (AbC). This concept will hopefully help to shed some light upon the driving forces behind the cost-shifting taking place in both case studies presented: shipbreaking in Alang and waste management in Delhi.

2.4.1 Accumulate, Accumulate!

Capitalism is understood here as a social production relation where labourers have no control over the means of production. So, among the different approaches to capitalism, we follow the 'classical' one, meaning that it exists when 'direct producers are separated from the means of production and proletarianized, while the means of production are held by capitalists as private property' (Hall, 2012: 1191). The separation is often referred to as dispossession or expropriation, while the proletarianization means that wage labourers (previously producers) have nothing to sell but their labour power. The state provides the legal infrastructure, enforcing the institutions, like private property and wage labour, without which capital social relations cannot exist.

Capital accumulation is the maintenance and production of the (capitalist) social relations. It refers to the generation of wealth in the form of capital, where capitalists produce commodities for the purpose of exchange, and therefore for the self-expansion of capital. For Marx accumulation is the essence of capital. It is the process in which the separation between wage labourers and their means of production is continuously reproduced. In this sense, capital accumulation emerges from expanded reproduction, when surplus value is reinvested into the production process and the scale of production increases (i.e. production and trade). The essence of capital is that it must be accumulated. Marx put it with a religious metaphor: 'Accumulate, accumulate! That is Moses and the prophets!' (Capital I, ch. 24, sect. 3). Because of competition, the mere preservation of capital is impossible unless it is, in addition, expanded. Capital accumulation is thus an economic process through which capitalists realize the value of the production and exchange. Thus, accumulation is first and foremost a relationship between the production and capitalization of surplus value, meaning the appropriation of what is produced by the workers but not paid back as wages.

However, accumulation is also a relationship of reproduction. The accumulation process is never simply an economic process but also involves the general development of social relations (i.e. institutions like private property and wage labour) and changing roles for the state. For Marx, the process would never be a smooth, harmonious or simple expansion; at times it would be interrupted by crises and recessions. For instance, over-accumulation crises are the result of the accumulation process which generate exceeding capital capacity that does not find profitable opportunities if new dispossession processes do not take place (Harvey, 2003). For this reason, accumulation does not only take place via 'expanded reproduction' (i.e. production and trade), but also via 'primitive accumulation' (i.e. expropriation).

In relation to the origins of the surplus that made the first process of capitalist accumulation possible (how capitalism historically established itself), Marx proposed the concept of '*primitive accumulation*' (Capital

I, pt. VII; hereafter PA). Primitive accumulation is, for Marx, 'the historical process of divorcing the producer from the means of production', transforming 'the social means of subsistence and of production into capital' and 'the immediate producers into wage labourers' (1967: 714, cited by Glassman, 2006). The classical example would be the enclosure of land that expels the resident population of farmers rendering them a landless proletariat. This changes the social relations of production and releases both means of production (land) and surplus labour for capital accumulation. It's therefore a process of privatization and proletarianization, which involves changes in property relations (Glassman, 2006). In this case, the transformations in human-environment relations are its by-product. Examples of primitive accumulation for Marx include, apart from enclosures, colonialism, slave trade, modern taxation, usury, and the national debt.

In Marx's theory, primitive accumulation of capital by enclosures and colonial robbery would be substituted in due course by the exploitation of labour as the capital/labour ratio in the economy increased, and new technologies enhanced labour productivity together with new methods of disciplining wage labour. Therefore, the processes of capital accumulation would progressively overcome in importance primitive accumulation.

However, there is a long-lasting debate among Marxists on whether primitive accumulation is a historical process (in this sense Marx called it primitive or original) or a continuous process (De Angelis, 2001). In the first case, primitive accumulation is a clear-cut historical process that gave birth to the preconditions of a capitalist mode of production (what De Angelis, 2001 calls 'Historical Primitive Accumulation'). In the second case, primitive accumulation is an ongoing process whereby the extra-economic prerequisite to capitalist production is an inherent and continuous element of modern societies ('Inherent-continuous Primitive Accumulation'). De Angelis (2001) has made a synthesis of this debate, that we subscribe to, and put the emphasis on the fact that accumulation is the separation between workers and means of production. So, primitive accumulation involves both the ex-novo creation of this separation and its continuous reproduction in response to challenges (Hall, 2012: 1192). In order to differentiate the primitive or original (and therefore historical) character of primitive accumulation, the Marxist geographer David

Harvey (2003) has famously proposed the term of '*Accumulation by Dispossession*' (hereafter AbD).

The understanding of primitive accumulation is first determined by which approach to capitalism one embraces (Hall, 2012). Having clarified our position in this sense, we report here some further clarifications on the concept of PA by Levien (2012), which are directly relevant to our main argument because they will allow us to highlight the shortcomings we intend to overcome.

First, scholars debate whether primitive accumulation is defined above all by its function for capitalism or the means specific to it. In the first case, PA is defined by its result, notably the 'freeing up' of (natural) resources and labourers. Therefore, the preconditions of capital are created by 'the two transformations, whereby the social means of subsistence and production are turned into capital, and the immediate producers are turned into wage-labourers' (Marx, 1957: 875). In the second case, PA is defined by its means, meaning the extra-economic force in contrast to 'the silent compulsion of economic relations' that characterized accumulation in fully developed capitalism (Marx 1957: 899). Capital originates in violent dispossession, a history 'written in letters of blood and fire'. Marx further sustains that 'It is a notorious fact that conquest, enslavement, robbery, murder, in short, *force*, played the greatest part' (1957: 874; emphasis added). This clarifies that force is necessary to generate the two major transformations mentioned above which are the prerequisites of capitalist social relations (i.e. separation and proletarianization). However, Levien (2012) argues that 'for many, primitive accumulation came to be defined by its results—first and foremost proletarianization—rather than its extra-economic means'. If we accept his position, then the second explanation regards the issue of how much emphasis is placed on each of the two transformations: (1) the forces seeking to turn assets (such as land and natural resources) into capital, and (2) the creation of a class of wage labourers separated from the means of production. The focus depends on whether one is looking into historical or contemporary processes.

Leaving aside the debate upon the historical account of how the preconditions of capitalism came into being, we want to focus on the contemporary processes. Since the 2000s, there has been a renewed interest on primitive accumulation within Marxist debates. Without doubt, the formulation of 'accumulation by dispossession' (hereafter AbD) by David

Harvey (Harvey 2003), in line with De Angelis (2001), has been the most popular in reviving the research agenda on these issues. Although similar to PA, AbD broke with the historicism of production's modes. AbD places emphasis on the first of the two transformations: the dispossession of assets. Levien (2012: 938) recognizes that 'The significance of Harvey's reconstruction of primitive accumulation as AbD lies, above all, in its attempt to explain the contemporary upsurge in political struggles centred on the dispossession of land and various other resources rather than the exploitation of labour'.

The use of dialectics by Harvey makes it difficult to identify in his work a clear-cut definition (see Levien, 2012). The main argument relies upon the fact that AbD has increased in importance to expanded reproduction under neoliberalism. The examples given include land grabs, privatizations of collective social assets, biopiracy and the various predatory machinations of financial capital, including the partial recapture of wage-labourers' income (e.g. lottery). Harvey offers also four general forms: privatization and commodification of previously non-commodified assets, financialization, the management and manipulation of crises, and state redistributions of wealth from the poor to the rich (2005: 160–165). The concept of AbD can be mobilized to explain a number of ecological distribution conflicts, for example the development of shrimp farming understood as a modern case of enclosure movement (Veuthey and Gerber, 2012).

Glassman (2006) provides a means-specific definition for AbD (and PA) as the 'deployment of extra-economic coercion in the process of accumulation' (Levien, 2012: 939), which is rejected by Harvey as it would not cover all examples, because—for instance—the credit system and financial power are economic. Harvey himself argues that 'What accumulation by dispossession does is release a set of assets (including labour power) at very low (and in some instances zero) cost. Over-accumulated capital can seize hold of such assets and immediately turn them to profitable use' (Harvey, 2003: 149). Instead, Levien (2012: 940) proposes an alternative one: 'AbD is the use of extra-economic means of coercion to expropriate means of production, subsistence or common social wealth for capital accumulation. It is not simply an economic process of over-accumulated capital seizing hold of under-commodified assets, but fundamentally a political process in which states—or other coercion wielding entities—use extra-economic force to help capitalists overcome barriers to accumulation.'

In our opinion, AbD could be defined as the inherent necessity of the capital system to separate, through extra-economic means, the labourers from the means of production in order to relaunch the capitalist social relations of production and to find new profitable opportunities for the over-accumulated capital. AbD implies 'means to expand the scale and scope of capital accumulation via so-called "extra-economic" means' (Prudham, 2007: 411). These means include dynamics that—in principle—have nothing to do with the market itself ('the economic' in its strict sense), such as conquest, enslavement, robbery, violence, legal changes, and ideological-discursive changes.

Despite these clarifications, what concerns us here is the argument made by Brenner (2006: 101) that Harvey gives an overly expansive definition of AbD, notably that 'the huge redistributions of income and wealth away from workers that are indeed sometimes entailed by the operations of financial markets are, for the most part, no less straightforward results of the capitalist game than is exploitation through the purchase of labour-power'. For what concerns us here, the conceptualizations of AbD, as well as the ones of PA, miss to account for important dynamics of capital accumulation different from expanded reproduction and dispossession. In general, we refer to cost-shifting, but with a special focus on contamination. Let us first put in evidence how contamination has not been sufficiently accounted for, and second how this gap could be filled.

The debate on PA and AbD focus exclusively on the means of production (and subsistence) but leave aside what could be called the 'means of existence', meaning those means that are necessary for the physiological reproduction of both human and non-human life, although not directly (but of course often indirectly) necessary for production. Examples could be the air we breathe, the food we eat or the water we drink, but also ecosystem services (i.e. a certain climate) or, following the feminists, care work (Beneria et al., 2015). The means of existence have to do, first and foremost, with the physiological needs where a set of metabolic requirements have to be met in order to ensure the survival of beings. We will focus upon them because they are the *condicio sine qua non* for life, as acknowledged from the hierarchy of Maslow (1943) to the fundamental human needs of Max-Neef (1991). Max-Neef (1991) calls 'subsistence', what here we propose to call 'means of existence', but these differ from what Marxists tend to call 'means of subsistence'. They in fact refer mainly to 'subsistence production', and more specifically to 'subsistence agriculture', a non-capitalist mode of production defined as 'A form of organizing food production such that a group (household, village, society) secures food sufficient for its own reproduction over time' (Gregory et al., 2009: 731). Orthodox Marxists therefore maintain the focus upon 'production', while here we want to put emphasis upon 'reproduction', along the lines of what feminist scholars have done since the 1970s (for example, see Federici, 2004). Marxists have certainly discussed issues around the 'reproduction of labour power', and more in general the 'social reproduction', a term that encompasses 'the daily and long-term reproduction of the means of production, the labour power to make them work and the social relations that hold them in place. [...] At its most rudimentary, social reproduction is contingent upon the biological reproduction of the labour force—both day to day and generationally—through the production, acquisition, distribution and/or preparation of the *means of existence*, including food, shelter, clothing and health care' (Gregory et al., 2009: 696–697; emphasis added). However, we consider that (1) insufficient emphasis has been given to the importance of the means of existence and (2) that it has not been related to debates about PA and ABD.

In particular, we intend to explore how contamination, via cost-shifting, negatively affects the means of existence and contributes to capital accumulation.

Perreault (2012: 1051) argues that, in reference to water, there are different forms of dispossession, apart from privatization and marketization, 'including *contamination*, which remove it from the public sphere and effectively enclose it' (emphasis added). This is in line with the calls to account for (1) 'contingent role of nature in shaping pathways of accumulation and dispossession' (Sneddon, 2007) and (2) for 'the ways dispossession shapes patterns of, and opportunities for, social reproduction' (Roberts, 2008). However, the analysis is limited to the dispossession of livelihood and fails to consider the effects of contamination for humans, as well as non-human being, which is not directly related to the means of subsistence and production. Perreault (2012) rightly concludes that 'mining is subsidized by the lands, livelihoods, and bodies of the indigenous campesino peoples who bear its environmental costs'. But what about the subsidies to miners with compromised health or loss of bio-diversity in the locality?

In this book, we not only propose to examine 'how the materiality of specific forms of nature shapes processes of dispossession' (Perreault, 2012: 1052), but also how it shapes processes of contamination. Beyond dispossession, and its consequent separation of labourers from their means of production, we argue contamination endangers existence means of both human and non-human beings.

2.4.2 Our Contribution: Capital Accumulation by Contamination, or Else Cost-Shifting Successes

We argue that, apart from dispossession, there is an additional strategy of capital accumulation that needs more attention, which could be called 'lower costs of output' via cost-shifting, namely contamination.[18] Kapp (1950), a proto ecological economist, had already discussed cost-shifting as extra-economics means. Social costs affect means of existence, as well as means of subsistence and production. As previously argued, the phenomenon of cost-shifting, meant as the socialization of costs, is described as a systematic ability to displace the costs to others, one that is pervasive and external to the economic process (in this sense extra-economic), the reason for which cannot be simply considered an 'externality' (as if it was accidental or a particular case, and therefore possible to internalize). The idea that contamination makes the others pay for the costs is very much part of the ecological economics epistemology (Berger, 2008). Therefore, for Kapp, economic change generally occurs for the benefit of some groups and at the expense of other existing or future groups (Hornborg, 2009). Once cost-shifting is interpreted as a successful practice of business entities, it is easy to understand the logic that underpins it. We argue it is the logic of capital accumulation by cost-shifting. There are different

---

[18] We are aware that the words pollution and contamination have slightly different meanings, although they are often use as synonyms and etymologically they are equivalent (meaning 'to defile'). Following the Oxford dictionary, we prefer 'contamination' as it expresses 'the action or state of making or being made impure by polluting or poisoning', while pollution is defined as 'the presence in or introduction into the environment of a substance which has harmful or poisonous effects'. In brief, we interpret contamination as the act, while pollution is the state.

types of cost-shifting including, for example, the bail out of banks where private debt is socialized or the fact that reproductive work unequally falls upon women, but we intend to focus on contamination. In fact, we want to demonstrate that contamination is an important strategy in the modern processes of accumulation. Cost-shifting encounters social resistance that resists the socialization of costs by enterprises, in the form of ecological distribution conflicts.

We examine a complementary strategy of capital forces with the aim to relaunch the capitalistic relation and find new profitable opportunities for the over-accumulated capital. We propose to call it *accumulation by contamination* (here after AbC). We define it as the process by which the capital system socializes costs, through successful costs-shifting, which degrades the means of existence and bodies of human beings (as well as of other species) in order to find new possibilities for capital valorization. Examples of AbC are waste dumping, air pollution, alteration of biogeochemical cycles, and epidemic health problems.

If AbD is defined as freeing up assets like a resource (therefore by its function), as we proposed, then AbC is a different category. Instead, if AbD is defined by extra-economic means (Harvey, 2003; Glassman, 2006) and is different from expanded reproduction, then AbC is a subcategory of AbD. In our understanding, following the focus of De Angelis (2001) on separation, AbC is a different category since it has to do with lowering the costs of output, else with shifting-costs with extra-economic means. As Kapp (1963) argued, social costs are a form of non-market interdependencies; they do not appear on accounting books, although they are a normal part of the business practice.

Cost-shifting (or socialization of costs), and consequent capital accumulation happens in two ways:

1. *Direct profits due to subsidies.* For example, subsidies to the incinerator (a subsidized and concentrated right to contaminate, i.e. carbon credits).

2. *Indirect profits due to saved costs (indirect subsidies).* For example, toxic waste dumping leading to health problems or productivity loss of other economic activities such as farming or fishing; remediation costs. These social costs are often so high, that if they were

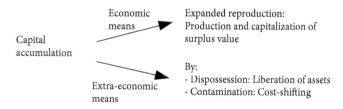

Figure 2.4 The circuits of capital accumulation.

accounted for, they would in fact inhibit the activity in itself (e.g. see the calls to leave the oil in the ground).

In conclusion, we have identified two main circuits of capital accumulation (see Figure 2.4): (1) expanded reproduction, through economic means, which means the production and capitalization of surplus value (i.e. the appropriation of what is produced by the workers, but not paid back as wages); and (2) capital accumulation by extra-economic means, via both dispossession (i.e. the liberation of assets, or separation) and contamination (i.e. cost-shifting, or socialization of costs).

As we will explore in the next chapters, AbC plays a central role in both case studies presented. In the case of shipbreaking, the conflict emerges out of cost-shifting alone, and therefore AbC; while in the case of Delhi, there is a shifting of costs to middle-class residents but also dispossession of the recyclers' means of production. Capitalism has a lot to do with two simultaneous, but distinct, processes: the privatization of assets and the socialization of costs.

3

Shipbreaking in Alang

A Conflict Against Capital Accumulation by Contamination

3.1 Introduction: The Metabolism of a Global Infrastructure, Namely Shipping

In August 2009, a fire broke out aboard the European containership *MSC Jessica*[1] killing six workers on the Indian shipbreaking beaches of Alang.[2] This kind of tragedy is rather common. The fire erupted as they were dismantling the cargoship's engine room. It took place as the ship had neither been decontaminated by the original owner nor made safe by the local enterprise. The Geneva-based Mediterranean Shipping Company (MSC), the world's second-largest shipping line in terms of container vessel capacity, had profitably used the ship since its construction in 1980. MSC denied all responsibilities as, officially, the owner of the vessel was a Panamanian company and the vessel was registered in Panama while under bare-boat charter to MSC; after the vessel left MSC's service it was sold to a Saint Vincent company.[3] In other words, MSC, along with most shipping companies, normally uses flags of convenience, cash buyers, and shell companies to bypass the international regulations. This chapter

---

[1] An earlier version of this chapter has been first published as an article in the journal *Ecological Economics* in 2010, as part of a Special Section on 'Ecological Distribution Conflicts' edited by Joan Martinez Alier, Giorgos Kallis, Sandra Veuthey, Mariana Walter, and Leah Temper. Demaria, F. (2010). Shipbreaking at Alang-Sosiya (India): An ecological distribution conflict. *Ecological Economics* 70(2): 250–260. http://www.indianexpress.com/news/six-die-in-fire-at-alang-ship-breaking-yard/498063/ (Accessed in January 2012).

[2] An earlier version of this chapter has been first published as an article in the journal *Ecological Economics* in 2010, as part of a Special Section on 'Ecological Distribution Conflicts' edited by Joan Martinez Alier, Giorgos Kallis, Sandra Veuthey, Mariana Walter, and Leah Temper. Demaria, F. (2010). Shipbreaking at Alang-Sosiya (India): An ecological distribution distribution conflict. *Ecological Economics* 70(2): 250–260.

[3] Mediterranean Shipping Company (MSC) response regarding allegations of a fire causing six deaths on *MSC Jessica* shipbreaking operation. 17 October 2012. Available at http://www.business-humanrights.org

The Political Ecology of Informal Waste Recyclers in India. Federico Demaria, Oxford University Press.
© Federico Demaria 2023. DOI: 10.1093/oso/9780192869050.003.0003

investigates, through the lens of an ecological distribution conflict related to shipbreaking in Alang-Sosiya (India), how to understand the linkages among nature, economy, and society.

Rich societies use large amounts of resources. Conflicts of resource extraction and waste disposal, such as the conflict over the excessive production of carbon dioxide, arise as a consequence of this. Rich societies generate large quantities of other kinds of waste, encountering opposition to local waste treatment and disposal sites, such as incinerators and landfills (Pellow, 2007) and rising management costs (Pearson, 1987). This is the background of a rapidly changing and lucrative trade, global in nature, in which waste flows towards developing countries or poorer areas of developed countries (McKee, 1996). Under a world-system perspective, the core, through unequal power relations, manages to export entropy to distant sinks in the periphery (Scott Frey, 1998; Hornborg et al., 2007). These flows, legal or not (with organized criminal groups as important players), consist of urban and industrial waste, hazardous and non-hazardous waste, and waste intended for reuse, recycling, and final disposal (Clapp, 1994; D'Alisa et al., 2012).

In the 1970s and 1980s scandals of toxic waste dumping in the South led to attempts to stem these flows, such as the Basel Convention on the Control of Transboundary Movements of Hazardous Wastes and their Disposal of 1989. Yet, India, among others, has been increasingly used as a dumping ground for toxic industrial waste (like asbestos and mercury) from developed countries (Singh, 2001).

The issue of shipbreaking is examined here as an example of toxic waste trade (Alter, 1997). Shipbreaking is the process of dismantling an obsolete vessel's structure for scrapping or disposal. Conducted at pier or dry dock, or directly on the beach as in Alang-Sosiya, it includes a wide range of activities, from removing all machineries and equipment to cutting down the ship infrastructure. It is the destiny of ocean-going ships like oil tankers, bulk carriers, general cargo, containerships, and passenger ships, among others. Depending on their interests, stakeholders will call it breaking, recycling, dismantling, or scrapping (Stuer-Lauridsen et al., 2004). It is a challenging process, owing to the many problems of safety, health, and environmental protection (OSHA, 2001).

The industry provides steel at cheap prices and employment, which contribute to economic growth. On the other hand there are concerns about the health and safety of workers, and the impact on the environment. These are the premises of the debate on whether shipbreaking in India falls under a WIMBY (Welcome Into My Backyard) logic or is a case of (environmental) injustice (Singh, 2001) and application of Lawrence Summers' Principle (Martínez-Alier, 2002). This chapter discusses the controversy under a framework of ecological economics and political ecology.

Changing social metabolism (meaning the flow of energy and material in the economy) (Fischer-Kowalski, 1998; Foster, 1999), driven by economic and population growth, generates growing quantities of waste. Georgescu-Roegen proposed a paradox highlighting that 'technical evolution leads to an increase in the rate at which society "wastes resources" ... the economic process actually is more efficient than automatic shuffling in producing higher entropy, i.e. waste' (Georgescu-Roegen, 1971: 34). In other words, the more developed a society, the higher its rate of generation of wastes per capita (Giampietro and Mayumi, 2009). It is generally accepted that under a fair allocation of responsibility, developed countries should deal with their own waste. Principles such as 'the polluter pays' and 'producer liability' appear to be legally settled. However, cases in which countries from the North 'externalize the costs' of toxic waste disposal outside their own national borders (notably to the South) are not rare. The pollution haven hypothesis (Antweiler, 2001) refers to the idea that lower trade barriers will shift pollution to those countries with less stringent environmental regulations, which are normally also poorer. According to the Lawrence Summers Principle, Southern countries have an environmental 'comparative advantage' regarding waste treatment (Pearson, 1987). In an internal memo leaked to the press,[4] Lawrence Summers, then chief economist at the World Bank in 1991, wrote: 'I think the economic logic behind dumping a load of toxic waste in the lowest-wage country is impeccable and we should face up to that.' Pollution should be sent to places where there are no people, or where the people are poor, since 'the measurements of the costs of health impairing pollution depend on the foregone earnings from increased morbidity and mortality. From this point of view a given amount of health impairing pollution should be done in the country with the lowest cost, which will

[4] 'Let them eat pollution.' *The Economist*, 8 February 1992.

be the country with the lowest wages.' The cost of internalizing the externalities would be the lowest.

The question is whether decisions on matters of life and death should be taken only on economic grounds. Poor people that meet the 'Lawrence Summers' criteria often complain, as several studies from political ecology document (Martínez-Alier, 2002). Such ecological distribution conflicts express underlying valuation conflicts, actors deploying different languages to affirm their right to use a safe environment (Martinez Alier, 2009).

This chapter investigates shipbreaking in India from the vantage point of political ecology, paying attention to the unequal distribution of benefits and burdens (already in the present generation) in a context of growing global social metabolism that leads to greater generation of waste, and with an analytical focus on the ways actors express alternative claims in the political arena and the valuation conflicts that hence emerge.

Section 3.2 describes the methods and the study region. Then Section 3.3 introduces the shipbreaking industry, describing the process through which a ship becomes waste for the ship owner, enters the scrapping market through a cash buyer, and is finally dismantled by a shipbreaker. Section 3.4 presents different options for the management of the ship's toxic waste and analyses the socio-environmental impacts resulting from current practices. The conflict in the *Blue Lady* case at the Supreme Court of India is analysed in Section 3.5 with particular attention to the valuation languages used by the different social groups. Finally, conclusions are drawn in Section 3.6.

3.2 Methods and Study Region

Data from interviews, official documents, direct and participant observation have been combined using the case study research methodology (Yin, 2003). Fieldwork was carried out from April to July 2009. The access of researchers to the industry site is strictly regulated and workers' freedom of expression is limited. Semi-structured or in-depth interviews with 64 respondents were conducted with local villagers (10), farmers (8), fishers (9), shipbreaking entrepreneurs (4), workers (11), political and administrative authorities (6), legal experts (4), academics (5), and activists (7). Interviewees were selected to represent a broad spectrum of interests and knowledge regarding shipbreaking, using both random and snowball sampling methods. Moreover, focus groups have been led with farmers, fishers, and workers. Interviews were conducted in English or with the help of local translators in Hindi and Gujarati. National and international documentation was researched with special focus on the *Blue Lady* case at the Indian Supreme Court during 2006 and 2007 (Civil Writ Petition No. 657 of 1995). Official documents were examined under the guidance of the lawyer Sanjay Parikh and the petitioner Gopal Krishna. Media coverage on shipbreaking has been extensively examined on the Internet and at the Centre for Education and Documentation in Mumbai.

The case study is located in the Gulf of Cambay, Bhavnagar District of Gujarat State in the north-west of India (see Figure 3.1). Alang and Sosiya are the two local villages that give the name to the Alang-Sosiya Ship

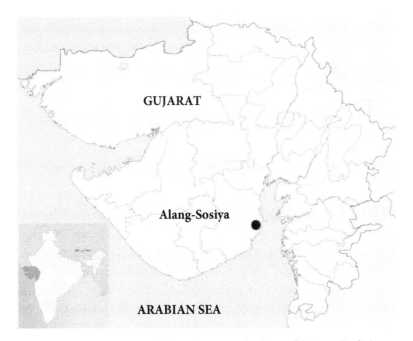

Figure 3.1 Location map of Alang-Sosiya in the State of Gujarat (India).
Source: Author's own.

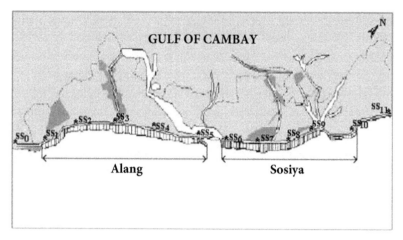

Figure 3.2 Map showing shipbreaking plots at Alang and Sosiya.
Source: Author's own.

Breaking Yard (ASSBY) (see Figure 3.2). The District, originally based
on farming and fishing, is under rapid industrialization and urbanization
which resulted in the degradation of the environment and decline in bio-
diversity. Gujarat State, historically a main centre of trade and commerce,
has one of the fastest-growing economies in India.

3.3 The Shipbreaking Industry

3.3.1 The Shipping Industry

The shipping industry constitutes a key infrastructure for the world's social
metabolism as more than 80% of international trade in goods (both raw
materials and manufactured goods) by volume is carried by sea.[5] Material
flows resulting from international trade (direct import and export flows
in terms of their weight) are part of physical accounting methods, such
as material flow analysis (MFA) (EUROSTAT, 2001; Vallejo, 2010), used
to quantify 'social metabolism' processes (Fischer-Kowalski, 1998). In

[5] If not diversely specified, data for this section comes from Review of Maritime Transport
(UNCTAD, 2011). All presented data refers to vessels of 100 gross tonnes (GT) and above.

2010 developed countries accounted for 34% of goods loaded and 43% of goods unloaded in tonnes, while developing countries accounted for 60% and 56% respectively (post-communist European transition economies account for the rest). Some regions are characterized by a physical import surplus while others face a physical trade deficit (Giljum and Eisenmenger, 2004).

Since the 1990s 'international seaborne trade' (goods loaded) increased faster than world gross domestic product, highlighting the effects of changing production processes, consumption patterns, and the deepening of economic integration (globalization). In 2010 this trade reached 8.4 bn tonnes, from 2.5 bn tonnes in 1970. Figure 3.3 shows the historical evolution per type of cargo for selected years. Data from 2009 reflects the economic crisis.

As a direct consequence, the number and capacity of ships has significantly increased. In 1960, the world ocean-going fleet comprised 15,000 ships (84 mn of deadweight tonnage; DWT a measure of how much

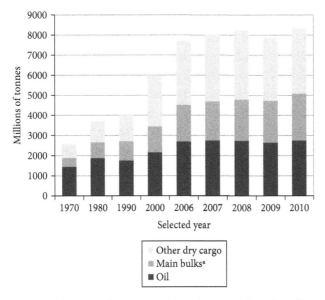

Figure 3.3 Development of international seaborne trade, selected years (millions of tonnes loaded).

Note: ª Iron ore, grain, coal, bauxite/alumina, and phosphate.

Source: UNCTAD, Review of Maritime Transport, various issues.

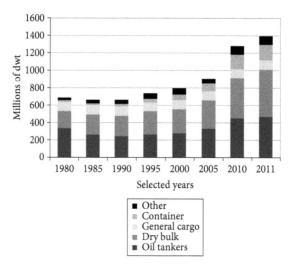

Figure 3.4 World fleet by principal types of vessel, selected years.

Note: Vessels of 100 GT and above.

Source: UNCTAD (United Nations Conference on Trade and Development), 2011.

weight a ship is carrying or can safely carry), while in 2011 it had reached 103,392 (1,396 mn of DWT). Figure 3.4 shows the composition of the world fleet by principal types of vessel, selected years.

In 2007, developed countries controlled about 65.9% of the world DWT, developing countries 31.2%, and economies in transition the remaining 2.9%. In 2011 the four top ship owning economies (Greece, Japan, Germany, and China) together controlled 50% of the world fleet. Fleet ownership, however, does not always reflect ship registration. Foreign-flagged ships accounted in 2011 for 68.1% of the world total, most of them registered in the so-called states of convenience (or open registers). The top five registries (Panama, Liberia, Marshall Islands, China Hong Kong, and Greece) together accounted for 52.6% of the world's DWT. Figure 3.5 shows ship entries at Alang-Sosiya Shipbreaking Yard (India) in 2004–2005 by ship owner's country: 82.5% of them used a flag of convenience.

Flags of convenience, together with fiscal havens, shell companies, and cash buyers, allow under-invoicing (resulting in evasion of import tax and money laundering) and facilitate ship owner's access to the shipbreaking

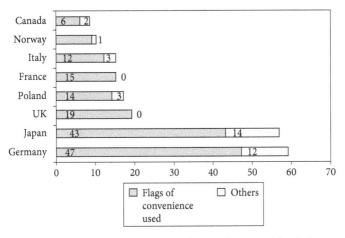

Figure 3.5 Ship entries at Alang-Sosiya Shipbreaking Yard (India), 2004–2005.
Source: GMB (Gujarat Maritime Board; www.gmbports.org).

market. This increase in the size of the world fleet does not immediately lead to a general increase in the supply of ships for scrap (see Figure 3.6).

Ship owners evaluate the expected future earning potential and the expected cost of keeping the ship in operation against the revenue obtained when the vessel is sold for scrap. This mainly depends on the price of steel. Potential earnings are more important in the decision than the scrapping price. The 2008–2009 economic crisis resulted in a boom of shipbreaking because of excess shipping capacity (see Figure 3.7 and Figure 3.8), with ship owners associations planning to eliminate 25% of the world fleet. In fact, according to the data elaborated by the French NGO Robin de Bois, if in 2006 demolitions were equivalent to only 0.6% of the existing fleet (293 vessels), the economic crisis reversed the situation (288 vessels in 2007; 456 in 2008; 1,006 in 2009[6]; 956 in 2010[7]; and 1,020 in

[6] In 2009 of 1,006 vessels (8.2 mn tonnes), 435 were demolished in India (43%), 214 in Bangladesh (21%), 173 in China (17%), 87 in Pakistan (9%), 42 in Turkey (4%). Robin de Bois, Information Bulletins on Ship Demolition: #17, September 2009; #18, January 2010. www.robin desbois.org.
[7] In 2010 of 956 vessels (6.5 mn tonnes), 422 were demolished in India (44%), 135 in Turkey (14%), 125 in China (13%), 90 in Pakistan (9%), 79 in Bangladesh (8%), 5 in Europe (1%), 100 in other countries (10%). Robin de Bois, Information Bulletins on Ship Demolition: #19 to 22, January 2011. www.robindesbois.org.

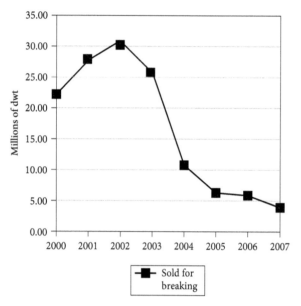

Figure 3.6 Tonnage reported sold for breaking at the world level, 2000–2007 (millions of DWT).

Source: UNCTAD (United Nations Conference on Trade and Development), 2007.

2011[8]). The excess supply is reflected since 2009 in the spectacular fall in the Baltic Dry Index that measures the rates charged for chartering dry bulk cargoes. In 2011 strong steel prices and the recovery of maritime business increased costs for ship procurement but at the same time significantly increased the margins in the ship scrapping business.[9] In general ship owning companies look to sell their ships for demolition at the best price.

The 2011 UNCTAD report rightly argues that 'the competitiveness of a country's scrapping industry is mostly influenced by labour costs and the regulatory environment. All major ship scrapping countries are developing countries' (p. 151). In other words, ships go for scrapping wherever

[8] In 2011 of 1,020 vessels (8.2 mn tonnes), 458 were demolished in India (45%), 154 in Bangladesh (14%), 142 in China (14%), 108 in Pakistan (7%), 19 in Turkey (2%). Robin de Bois, Information Bulletins on Ship Demolition: #23 to 26 February 2012. www.robindesbois.org.

[9] Article by Xu Hui, Executive Manager, China Ship Fund. Available at http://www.chinadaily.com.cn/bizchina/2010-04/08/content_9703387.htm (Accessed in January 2012).

Figure 3.7 The Alang-Sosiya Shipbreaking Yard during low tide (April 2009).
Source: Federico Demaria.

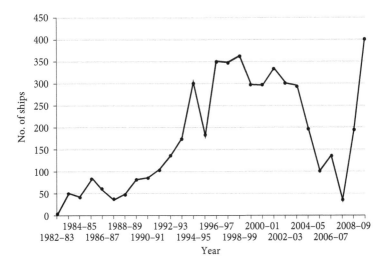

Figure 3.8 Number of ships broken per year at ASSBY.
Source: GMB (Gujarat Maritime Board; www.gmbports.org).

Table 3.1 Numbers and tonnage of ships dismantled (2011)

2011	N° of vessels	%	Tonnes of metal	%
India	458	45	35,00,000	43
Bangladesh	145	14	16,00,000	19
China	142	14	10,00,000	17
Pakistan	108	11	10,00,000	13
Turkey	72	7	2,06,000	3
USA	19	2	1,31,000	1
Europe	5	1	–	–
Others	55	6	–	–

Source: Robin de Bois, Information Bulletins on Ship Demolition: 23 to 26 February 2012.

it is easier to externalize social and environmental costs, which means cost-shifting.

Companies look to sell their ships for demolition at the best price. South Asian yards are the main destinations. For processing capacity ASSBY in India (see Figure 3.7) and Chittagong in Bangladesh are the world's biggest yards (see Table 3.1); Chinese yards are catching up to them.

Again, according to Robin de Bois (see Table 3.2), in 2011 India continues to be the undisputed leading country not only per number of units, but also for tonnage (45% of the total 8.2 mn tonnes) followed by Bangladesh (14%), China (14%), Pakistan (11%), and Turkey (7%).[10]

Data on ships sent for scrapping are not easily accessible.[11] The 2011 report by UNCTAD presents statistics (see Table 3.2) based on data from the information company IHS Fairplay (Maritime Intelligence and Publications). Data differ significantly in terms of tonnage but the country ranking remains the same, where the four largest ship scrapping

[10] Robin de Bois, Information Bulletins on Ship Demolition: #23 to 26 February 2012. www.robindesbois.org.
[11] Database from the French NGO Robin de bois is public and presents a lot of details for each ship sent for scrapping. Instead IHS Fairplay data might be more exhaustive, but is less transparent and detailed (therefore difficult to assess), and only accessible by paying an expensive fee. For the purpose of this analysis the two are complementary and do not contradict each other.

Table 3.2 Top 10 ship-scrapping nations, 2010

Country	Scrapped amount, dwt	Number of ships scrapped	Rank	Scrapped ships, percentage of total volume				
				Bulk carries	Dry cargo/ passenger	Offshore	Tankers	Others
India	9, 287,775.00	451	1	9.7	32.8	5.3	46.2	5.9
Bangladesh	6,839,207.00	110	2	15.1	5.5	5.7	71.1	2.5
China	5,769,227.00	189	3	46.6	36.3	2.5	12.2	2.4
Pakistan	5,100,606.00	111	4	8.1	2.9	6.2	80.6	2.2
Turkey	1,082,446.00	226	5	24.3	48.7	0.2	14.1	12.8
United States	217,980.00	15	6	0.0	19.9	0.0	80.1	0.0
Romania	16,064.00	4	7	0.0	100.0	0.0	0.0	0.0
Denmark	15,802.00	25	8	0.0	53.4	22.7	0.0	23.9
Japan	13,684.00	1	9	0.0	100.0	0.0	0.0	0.0
Belgium	8,807.00	12	10	0.0	100.0	0.0	0.0	0.0

Source: Compiled by the UNCTAD secretariat on the basis of data from IHS Fairplay.

countries covered 98.1% of the activity in terms of recycled DWT in 2010. This data series allows us to see on which types of ships the different countries specialize: India on tankers, dry cargo and passenger ships; Bangladesh and Pakistan on tankers; China on bulk carriers.

In Bangladesh, since 2010 the industry has only been working periodically due to an intensification of the controversy around safety and environmental concerns. The Supreme Court had suspended the authorization of beaching following an umpteenth fatal accident in 2009 and a new action by the NGO Bangladesh lawyers Association (BELA[12]) which demanded compliance with environmental and social standards (UNCTAD, 2011). Attempts by shipyards to circumvent the Court's decision had been successful, but the activity was then again suspended due to new fatal accidents (at least 12 workers died in 2011). All site activity was stopped pending an investigation report and dismantling authorizations for new ships were suspended. Later, the industry restarted operations. In any case this is probably not the end of shipbreaking in Bangladesh.[13]

China has overtaken Pakistan and reached the levels of Bangladesh. It keeps growing rapidly thanks to modernization of its industry, lower taxes, and the complete lack of democratic control over accountability for social and environmental impacts. New large facilities have been built near Shanghai in association with major shipping and other companies (including the Peninsular & Orient Steam Navigation Company and British Petroleum) which have guaranteed a steady supply of ships for breaking. In exchange the Chinese firms have promised good environmental controls and safe working conditions for the workers. In fact ship owners are under public scrutiny in their countries for being the source of alleged misery in shipbreaking countries (Wayne Hess et al., 2001). Then, one could wonder why ship owners are doing it in the least transparent country (China) which keeps labour trade unions and environmental NGOs under strict control, as well as denying access to researchers.

---

[12] http://www.belabangla.org/
[13] http://www.recyclinginternational.com/recycling-news/5930/ferrous-metals/bangladesh/recovery-bangladesh-shipbreaking-tonnages

Shipbreaking yards in Europe and the United States receive very few ships, as the prices they can offer are close to zero, and tend to receive state-owned ships, like the ones from the navy.

3.3.2 History of an Industry

Shipbreaking first developed in the United States, UK, and Japan during the Second World War because there were many ships damaged by war, and an urgent demand for steel. In the 1960s it moved to less industrialized European countries such as Spain, Italy, and Turkey. In the 1970s it left Europe and established itself in Asia, first in Taiwan and South Korea, and then during the 1980s, in China, Bangladesh, India, Pakistan, Philippines, and Vietnam. South Asian countries have benefitted from favourable natural characteristics (high tidal ranges, gentle sloping, and rocky bottom beaches) which allow the vessels to be beached, turning a highly mechanized industry into a labour-intensive one.

3.3.3 From the Ship Owner to the Shipbreaker Through Cash Buyers

Ship owners sell their ships through brokers operating in London, Dubai, Singapore, and Hamburg. All ships are sold per tonne (LDT[14]) at a price ranging from $100 to $400, depending on the ship type and on the market. In the last 10 years 'cash buyers' have emerged as important intermediaries officially to assure fulfilment of the contract. They differ from traditional ship brokers because they acquire ship ownership, becoming themselves ship owners (although only for a limited period pending its sale or during the handing over of the ship to a recycling facility). Original (last operational) ship owners get lower prices, but this system allows them to bypass liabilities and regulations (Hillyer, 2012).

---

[14] LDT (Light Displacement Tonnage) is the mass of the ship excluding cargo, fuel, ballast water, stores, passengers, and crew.

3.3.4 ASSBY: Alang-Sosiya Ship Breaking Yard

The first ship, called *Kota Tenjong*, was beached in Alang on 13 February 1983. ASSBY, which occupies 10 km of coastline, became in the 1990s the world's largest shipbreaking yard. In 2007 India accounted for 41% of the world's recycling capacity, 90% of it taking place in ASSBY (see Figure 3.8, and Table 3.3).

3.3.5 Shipbreaking Process

Once a ship arrives in the Gulf of Cambay it is inspected and checked by the competent authorities which issue (occasionally with corruption) the relevant certificates. The ship is then beached by its own propulsion power at high tide and during low tide is laid down stable on its flat bottom. At this point cutters and their helpers, using simple LPG gas and oxygen torches, can start taking apart the vessel structure. All operations take place directly on the beach in a relatively small and congested area called a plot (see Figure 3.9). Machinery and heavy equipment (engines, compressors, generators, boilers), together with other dismantled components (navigation equipment, life-saving equipment, furniture, electrical cables, utensils, etc.) are sold to traders for reuse. These operations do not require investment in infrastructure or technology, as they are labour intensive and moving cranes and motorized winches are re-used from the same ships. Depending on their size and type, scrapped ships have an unloaded weight of between 5,000 and 40,000 tonnes, with an average composition as shown in Table 3.4. It requires from 3 to 6 months for an average ship (15,000 tonnes) to be dismantled with a variable number of workers involved at different stages (from 150 to 300). The industry requires relatively low fixed capital (plot lease, machinery, and equipment) and high working capital. The cost of the vessel itself corresponds to more than 50% of the total cost. Interests on investment, duties (customs, excise, value added tax, etc.) and port charges represent the second important item. Labour and energy (torch oxygen and fuel) each constitute between 3% and 6% of the total expenditure (Upadhyay, 2002; Dubey, 2005). Environmental, safety, and health insurance costs do not appear in the accounting.

Table 3.3 Number and LDT (Light Displacement
Tonnage) of ships broken at ASSBY

Year	No. of ships	IDT
1982–1983	5	24.716
1983–1984	51	259.387
1984–1985	42	228.237
1985–1986	84	516.602
1986–1987	61	359.139
1987–1988	3	244.776
1988–1989	48	253.991
1989–1990	82	451.243
1990–1991	86	577.124
1991–1992	104	563.568
1992–1993	137	942.601
1993–1994	175	1.256.077
1994–1995	301	2.173.249
1995–1996	183	1.252.809
1996–1997	348	2.635.830
1997–1998	347	2.452.019
1998–1999	361	3.037.882
1999–2000	296	2.752.14
2000–2001	295	1.943.825
2001–2002	333	2.752.414
2002–2003	300	2.424.522
2003–2004	294	1.986.121
2004–2005	196	938.975
2005–2006	101	480.405
2006–2007	136	760.800
2007–2008	36	643.437
2008–2009	193	–
2009–2010 (estimated)	400	–
Total	5033	31.877.972

Note: (Light Displacement Tonnage) is the mass of the ship
excluding cargo, fuel, ballast water, stores, passengers and crew.

GMB (Gujarat Maritime Board; www.gmbports.org).

Figure 3.9 A shipbreaking plot in Alang (April 2009).
Source: Federico Demaria.

Table 3.4 Average components (both in weight and value) obtained by a demolished ship

	Weight (%)	Value (%)
Re-rollable ferrous scrap and iron plates	75–85	65
Re-conditioned machinery	10–15	25
Re-melting scrap	3	2
Non-ferrous scrap	1	7
Furnace oil and oils	2	0.50
Wooden and furniture	2	0.50
Burning, cutting losses, and waste	5–10	0
	100	100

Sources: Interviews with shipbreakers; Upadhyay, 2002.

3.4 Hazardous Waste and Socio-Environmental Impacts

3.4.1 Hazardous Waste Generation and Management

Ships contain (in-built and on-board) hazardous and non-hazardous substances, significant both in quantity and toxicity, which cannot (or should not) be totally reused or recycled. The waste output of the process represents between 0.5% and 10% of the ship's total weight (see Table 3.4). Composition is diverse, mainly constituted by scrap wood, plastic, paper, rubber, glass wool, thermocol, sponge, PVC pipes, oil, metals, heavy metals, paints, cement, asbestos, and radioactive waste. Independent and reliable statistics on quantity and composition are not available, while estimates are difficult because there are many different types of ships, which vary considerably in their structure (Reddy et al., 2005a,b).

The controversy over shipbreaking mainly concerns the disposal of hazardous waste. There are three methods of disposal:

(1) Decontamination prior to export
   Decontamination is the process of removing hazardous materials contained in the ship structure (partially or totally), normally without endangering seaworthiness. This must be done by ship owners. It is a costly operation that requires expertise and technology. A totally decontaminated ship would not fall under the Basel Convention.

(2) Environmental sound management on site
   Hazardous materials are safely removed and then properly disposed once the ship has been beached. This is the option recommended by the International Convention for the Safe and Environmentally Sound Recycling of Ships adopted in May 2009 by the IMO (International Maritime Organization).

(3) Dumping
   Hazardous materials are freely released into the environment. ASSBY, since the beginning, has used the third method (High Powered Committee, 2003; Reddy et al., 2003, 2005a,b). Waste, hazardous or not, has generally been directly released into the sea from the ship or the plot, burnt on the plot, or dumped during the night in surrounding villages (see Figure 3.10). Some has been transported

Figure 3.10 A dumping site close to the shipbreaking yard of Alang-Sosiya (April 2009).
Source: Federico Demaria.

and dumped in areas (like the surroundings of the city of Surat in the Golden Corridor) where other industries undertake similar actions so that it is impossible to identify the source and enforce any liability.

3.4.2 Pollutants Discharged

Scrapping activity discharges a number of liquid, gaseous, and solid pollutants which are hazardous for the environment and human beings (Islam and Hossain, 1986; Zhijie, 1988; Hossain and Islam, 2006, Neşer et al., 2012). Most common are oil, bacteria, asbestos, heavy metals,[15] and persistent organic pollutants.[16]

---

[15] Mercury (Hg), Lead (Pb), Arsenic (As), Chromium (Cr), Copper (Cu), Manganese (Mn), Zinc (Zn), and Nickel (Ni).
[16] Polychlorinated Biphenyl Compounds (PCBs), Dioxins, Polyvinyl Chloride (PVC), Polycyclic Aromatic Hydrocarbons (PAHs) and Organotins (Monobutyltin—MBT, Dibutyltin—DBT, Tributyltin—TBT, etc.).

3.4.3 Socio-Environmental Impacts

3.4.3.1 Environmental impacts

In ASSBY waste materials accumulate over the soil and then ramify incrementally to seawaters in a stepwise manner through tidal and subtidal zones, deep sea and their respective sediments. This has led to a deterioration of physico-chemical properties of seawater and intertidal sediments. COD (chemical oxygen demand) and BOD (biological oxygen demand), used as indicators of water quality (organic degradation and tension in the system), are present at high levels. Shipbreaking activity has substantially affected the ecosystem at Alang–Sosiya (Gujarat Ecology Commission, 1997; Tewari et al., 2001; Reddy et al., 2003; Reddy et al., 2004a,b, 2005a,b). System stress has led to a decline in biotic structure: a decrease in biomass, abundance, and species diversity has been measured. Pollutants mix with suspended solid and migrate long distances, carried by high currents (Bhatt, 2004). They have been found, to a lesser extent, together with floating objects and oil, all along the 100 km of coastline on the East and West side of Alang (Pathak, 1997; Mehta, 1997). The exact spatial dispersion of contaminants remains unknown as all selected control sites (10, 30, or 50 km away from Alang) have always been affected by pollution (Dholakia, 1997). The intertidal zone around ASSBY has practically no vegetation. Mangroves disappeared many years ago, soon after the industry began. The sea off ASSBY has very poor biological production potential with very low phytoplankton pigment concentration, low zooplankton standing stock, very poor macrobenthic standing stock, and low numerical abundance of fish eggs and larvae (Soni, 1997; Majumdar, 1997). Exotic species might have been carried in with ballast water, which represents a serious biological risk. The population and diversity of fish have decreased and species tolerant to petroleum hydrocarbons seem to have adapted better to the environmental stress (Mandal, 2004). The absence of sanitation facilities for the workers has led to the presence of pathogenic and non-pathogenic bacteria (faecal and nonfaecal coliforms, salmonella, clostridium, staphylococcus) in the water of the ASSBY area (surface and underground), rendering it unsafe for human consumption, while marine coastal water has become harmful for fish population and unsuitable for recreation (Desai and Vyas, 1997; Trivedi, 1997; MECON, 1997).

There is a lack of studies into the potential impacts on local terrestrial ecosystems. GPCB (Gujarat Pollution Control Board), a local government agency, claims to keep a complete monitoring, but it has not made data available. For a comprehensive environmental impact assessment one should go beyond local impacts and analyse the complete material recycling chain (ancillary industries). The furnace emissions of rerolling mills are rendered toxic by the presence of volatile organic matter of marine paints and anti-fouling paints (such as lead, arsenic, and pesticides) which has resulted in acid rain during the monsoon season (Bhatt, 2004).

The 1997 Report by the Gujarat Ecology Commission, 'Ecological Restoration and Planning for Alang-Sosiya' (GEC, 1997), remains the most comprehensive study to date. None of its suggestions have been followed, so that the assessment maintains its validity as confirmed by more recent studies of the Central Salt & Marine Chemicals Research Institute (Tewari et al., 2001; Reddy et al., 2003, 2004a,b, 2005a,b; Mandal, 2004).

3.4.3.2 Impacts on workers

Workers in ASSBY, mainly seasonal migrants from the poorer states of India (Orissa, Bihar, Uttar Pradesh, Jharkhand), live and work in pitiable conditions (International Federation for Human Rights, 2002; International Metalworkers' Federation, 2006). They migrate as a survival strategy because with their previous jobs (at $1 per day) and small farms they are unable to maintain their families. Their number varies from 5,000 to 50,000. They work under contractors, on a daily basis and with no contract or rights. They work 12 hours per day, six days per week. During the field work in Spring 2009, their daily salaries ranged from a minimum of 150 Rs. (US$3) for helpers and loaders to a maximum of 375 Rs. (US$7) for experienced cutters.

They live, without their families, in shared shanties, locally called Kholi, close to the yard with no running water, electricity, or sanitation (see Figure 3.11). They are continuously exposed to pollutants, from the air they breathe, the water they drink, and the fish they eat (Deshpande et al., 2012). Notably their jobs present a number of hazards. Frequent accidents find their causes in fire and explosion, falling objects, trapping or compression, snapping of cables, falls from heights, and lack of personal protective equipment, housekeeping standards, and safety signs

Figure 3.11 Shipbreaking yard in Alang-Sosiya: A cutter at work (left) and workers' shanties (right).
Source: Federico Demaria.

(International Labour Organization, 2004). In case of injury or death, they are rarely compensated (Rousmaniere and Raj, 2007). Local fishers report that severely injured workers are sometimes dumped at sea and left to drown. The Final Report of the Technical Experts Committee (TEC), presented in 2006 to the Indian Supreme Court, offers an insight of the hazards faced by these workers. With regard to accidents, the Final Report notes that 'the average annual incidence of fatal accidents in the shipbreaking industry is 2.0 per 1000 workers while the all-India incidence of fatal accidents during the same period in the mining industry, which is considered to be the most accident-prone industry, is 0.34 per 1000 workers'. This is based on official data from 1995 to 2005 (roughly 40 traumatic work fatalities per year). It would be methodologically more accurate to correlate the number of fatal accidents to the number of dismantled ships, as workers do when they say 'one ship, one death'. Others say, 'one per day'. With regard to pollutants, the Final Report cites the 'Medical Examination of the Asbestos Handlers' by a team from the National Institute of Occupational Health (NIOH) which concludes: 'The X ray examination by NIOH showed linear shadows on chest X rays of 15 (16%) of 94 workers occupationally exposed to asbestos. These are consistent with asbestosis ... ' There are no medical records on the short- and long-term effects of the workers' exposure to contaminants.

3.4.3.3 Impacts on fishing communities
The South Saurashtra coastal area has always been well known for fisheries of Bombay Ducks (Harpodon neherius), Hilsa, Prawns, and other

species. Fish catch in the gulf of Khambat is found to be rich on the western side over 100 km away. Data for fish catch for 1991 and 1995 are indicative. Table 3.5 shows the fish landing situation at Gogha, Bhavnagar Lockgate, and Katpar. Gogha and Bhavnagar Lockgate are on the East side of ASSBY about 50 km away. Katpar is on the West side of ASSBY again 50 km away. From the data available for the commercially important fishes, a definite fall can be observed in the fish catch, besides the disappearance of certain species.

In the same area there are about 2,500 fishers living in small communities on the beach and in villages (from East to West: Gogha, Mithi Virdi, Sosiya, Alang, Talaja, Sartampar, Gopnath—Gadhula, Mahuva—Katpar). Fishing activity constitutes the main source of livelihood for about 10,000 people. Apart from Gogha where the majority is Muslim, they all belong to the Koli community. Kolis belongs to the scheduled

Table 3.5   Fish landing in kg for some species at different centres near ASSBY; Dholakia, 1997

Name of fish	Ghogha		Katpar		Bhavnagar Lockgate	
	1991	1995	1991	1995	1991	1995
Bombay Duck	102,069	93,862	116,865	46,129	74,762	32,596
Hilsa	7020	Nil	31,762	15,860	–	–
Culpid	1860	Nil	22,905	23,390	–	–
Mullet	44,308	24,809	112,695	12,776	–	5689
Catfish	21,715	–	13,950	2250	Nil	–
Colmi (shrimp)	175,250	909,151	30,015	48,072	20,240	62,004
Medium prawn	704,179	408,121	108,534	18,690	78,180	27,831
Jumbo prawn	214,314	80,400	30,225	Nil	–	–
Lobster	87,141	21,199	1500	2769	3162	110,639
Colia	–	–	3348	–	–	–
Dhoma	–	–	11,487	3565	–	–
Other fish	420,538	186,427	106,951	27,854	34,056	–

tribes (ST), that (together with the scheduled castes, SC) are unprivileged population groups explicitly recognized by the Constitution of India.

Fishers report that, since shipbreaking began, the quantity, variety, and size of fish has decreased, the flavour has changed, and a number of species have disappeared. Others like mudskippers (an amphibious fish with a special air breathing system) have better adapted, but are normally less commercially valuable (apart from being contaminated).

Fishers report not to have noticed any damage to their own health due to pollution (see Figure 3.12). However a number of pollutants can bioaccumulate and enter the food chain. Heavy metals bioconcentrated in the fish have been found to be many times higher than the maximum prescribed (Mehta, 1997). These highly toxic fish are not suitable for human consumption. However they are locally caught, consumed (mainly by fishers and shipbreaking workers) and go in dried or fresh form all over India and abroad. Fish can swim long distances and be caught elsewhere. High levels of butyltin, a POP, have been found in fish for consumption in the entire Asian–Pacific region. Shipbreaking, along with sewage disposal and anti-fouling paints, is considered the main source of this (Kannan et al., 1995).

There is no simple solution for fishers. They cannot easily fish elsewhere for a better quality of catch: the area of pollution is very wide, and fishers are not readily mobile. They are also constrained by legal restrictions on where they may fish. In consequence, the quality of life of all the community has worsened significantly. The most vulnerable have

Figure 3.12 Fishing community next to the shipbreaking yard in Alang-Sosiya: A fisher explaining to me that contaminated water provokes itching.
Source: Federico Demaria.

to work as unskilled labourers while others have emigrated in search of better opportunities. This picture is very similar to the one of Chittagong (Bangladesh), the world's second-largest shipbreaking yard: 'As the commercially important species are replaced by low priced species and scarcity of fish, many coastal fishers are leaving their hereditary profession and moving around every day as environmental refugees in a state of under employment and poverty to unemployment and grim poverty' (Hossain and Islam, 2006).

3.4.3.4 Impacts on villagers

The 10 villages in a radius of 12 km (Alang, Sosiya, Manar, Sathara, Kathwa, Bharapara, Mathavada, Takhatgadh, Jasapara, Madva) have experienced great economic and social changes because of shipbreaking (UNESCO, 2001). Previously working mainly in agriculture, after the arrival of ASSBY they could find new employment and business opportunities (often in accordance to their caste) in transportation, trade, and retail (Chaudhari, 1999). Some of the environmental impacts are of concern for the villagers. Those living close to the operation yards are affected by noise pollution. More generally people complain to Sarpanches (heads of villages) and local authorities about the dumping of waste from the dismantled boats as there are hundreds of dumping sites in all the surroundings. Preferred sites are waste lands, traditionally used for grazing, but also farming fields; people report that oxen and cattle have died because of eating waste. Villagers report respiratory and skin problems particularly when the waste is set on fire. Most of the villages along the coastline in this region suffer from water scarcity and salinity. The industry has worsened the problem, inducing overexploitation of water reserves (through population growth and workers' immigration) leading to a decrease in groundwater level. Apart from the deterioration of agriculture and animal husbandry, villagers report kidney diseases that are related to both salinity and pollutants. A number of wells are so polluted that they have been abandoned. Modern and traditional forms of agriculture co-exist—for respectively large and small farms—growing mangos, chikos, coconuts, and onions. Since the industry has settled, land and labour prices have increased locally. On the other hand quantity and size of crops have decreased, and the flavour has changed.

3.4.4 Emergence of a Conflict: From Material Origins to Cultural Discourses

If this was the end of the story, it would simply confirm the Lawrence Summers Principle. Instead the next section shows the emergence of a conflict where disputes about values are vocalized. The conflict has material origins that are then shaped by cultural discourses. As discussed in social movement theory, diagnosing a problem (such as shipbreaking) turns out to be a very contentious process, where the different actors try to affirm and impose their interpretative frame to the detriment of representations proposed by the others (Snow et al., 1986). The construction of reality is inextricably linked to asymmetries of power (Della Porta and Diani, 2006).

3.5 Looking Closer at the Ecological Distribution Conflict: The *Blue Lady* Case at the Supreme Court (2006–2007)

3.5.1 Three Spatial Scales for the Conflict: International, National, and Local

In the late 1990s, the Alang and Sosiya landscape attracted worldwide interest in terms of its aesthetics as an industrial and social inferno. Although environmental and labour groups started structuring their complaints, its socio-environmental aspects are still neglected. The conflict has developed at three different scales (international, national, and local) with environmentalists playing a major role, accompanied by trade unions and human rights groups, together with industrial lobbies, the Gujarat and Indian governments, and as so often in India, the judiciary.

At the international level, environmental NGOs, including Greenpeace and BAN (Basel Action Network), carried out campaigns to raise public awareness in developed countries and lobby for the implementation of regulations (notably the Basel Convention). In 2005 the 'Platform on Shipbreaking' (www.shipbreakingplatform.org) was created as an International Network of environmental, human, and labour rights organizations to challenge the global shipping industry.

In India, environmental NGOs (like Toxic Links, Corporate Accountability Desk, Human Rights Law Network) and independent activists (like the researcher Gopal Krishna, the activist Madhumitta Dutta, the lawyers Bushan Oza and Colin Gonsalves) engage in judicial activism and fight to this day on the Civil Written Petition on Hazardous Waste Management first filed in 1995 to the Supreme Court by the 'Research Foundation for Science, Technology and Natural Resources policy'.

At the local level the conflict has remained latent. Seasonal workers are vulnerable because of their precarious social and economic condition and so can be easily kept under pressure and dominated. A local trade union (Alang Sosiya Ship Recycling and General Workers' Association), with limited power, exists, accepted since 2005 by shipbreakers to negotiate wages. Workers report the use of violence (by the local police) against sporadic attempts of strikes over disputes about salary, safety, working, and living conditions.

Villagers have expressed oral complaints to authorities, normally through the heads of villages. Some attempts of frame bridging (Snow et al., 1986) are being undertaken by national activists between villagers (environmental issues) and workers (working and living conditions). The alliance could potentially be strong, especially in case a common organizational base can be built. Shipbreakers actively oppose the process with threats and a 'divide and rule' strategy.

Media coverage of the human and environmental conditions at ASSBY obliged competent Indian authorities and international organizations (UNEP, ILO, and IMO) to react. Both attempted to assess the main issues at stake, tackling them with detailed policy-making initiatives (mostly technical guidelines) and more effective implementation (Basel Convention, 2002; International Maritime Organization, 2003; International Labour Organization, 2004). The proposed practices (i.e. technology to improve labour safety and environmental protection) are similar to the ones used in developed countries. The industry left those shores to avoid the rules. Technically correct, but politically naive, none of them has been enforced. Instead, in order to understand the situation, the case of the *Blue Lady* at the Supreme Court of India is presented hereafter. This is not the most famous one (this would be the *Clemenceau* in 2006) but it illustrates the issues at stake, the decision-making process, and the valuation languages deployed at different scales by different actors of the conflicts over this type of waste disposal.

3.5.2 History of the *Blue Lady* Last Voyage

SS France was built in 1960 by the French Line and was at that time the longest passenger ship ever built. It had a mass of 45,000 tonnes, was 316 m long and 34 m wide, and had 16 floors and 1,400 rooms.

In 1979 it was sold to Norwegian Cruise Line (the mother company Star Cruise Ltd—SCL), renamed *SS Norway* and transformed into the world's most glamorous cruiseship. Seriously damaged in 2003 by a boiler explosion in Miami, it was towed to Germany where repairs were planned. A feasibility study, in 2004, estimated that to decontaminate part of the in-built asbestos would cost €17 mn. In 2005 the ship left Germany, its official destination being Singapore, for reuse. The ship owner's intentions were to discard the ship, and therefore the *SS Norway* became 'waste' under the EU Waste Shipment Regulations. Moreover, since it contained hazardous substances, it could have been considered hazardous waste for the purpose of the Basel Convention. Under Article 9 and Basel Ban Amendment, the export of ships from OECD (Organisation for Economic Co-operation and Development) countries to non-OECD countries, should be conceived as illegal traffic (Moen, 2008). The ship arrived in Malaysia and was planned to be scrapped in Bangladesh.

However, due to protest by BELA (Bangladesh environmental lawyers association) the sale was declared invalid. In 2006 *SS Norway* left Dubai, the authorities being informed that it was going for repairs, although in reality it was sailing towards Alang to be dismantled.

In June 2006 the mother company Star Cruise (Malaysia) sold it through Norwegian Cruise Line (Bermuda) to the Liberian (shell) company Bridgeed Shipping for, officially, $10 (as indicated in the Bill of sale for Bahamian ships). Bridgeed sold it, after one month, to the Indian shipbreaking company Hariyana Steel Demolition Pvt Ltd. The ownership was then transferred again to another shipbreaking company, Priya Blue Industries Pvt Ltd. The ship, finally renamed *Blue Lady*, apart from the common practice of under-invoicing, had a real price of about $15 mn.

On May 2006, the ship was initially prevented from entering Indian waters by an application of the activist Gopal Krishna to the Supreme Court of India. On humanitarian grounds, because of the monsoon, the ship was allowed, on June 2006, to anchor at Pipavav port near Alang. It was finally beached (without permission) on 3 August 2006 and allowed to be dismantled by the Final Court Order of 11 September 2007.

3.5.3 The Case in the Supreme Court: Arguments and Languages of Valuation

The analysis of a judicial case, such as the *Blue Lady* one, offers an insight into the framing conflict, meaning the struggle over reality construction. Different actors participated in the 'politics of signification' (Hall, 1982). There were environmentalists, villagers, shipbreakers, and the Indian authorities. Actors involved are signifying agents engaged in the production of alternative and contentious meanings (Benford and Snow, 2000). They undertook two core framing tasks: diagnostic and prognostic. The first concerns the definition of what the problem is and who is responsible; the second regards the proposed solutions. In particular, this section analyses the different attitudes expressed by these actors to the three methods of waste management, and the different valuation languages they used to frame the issue.

3.5.3.1 Environmentalists

Indian environmentalists, in alliance with international organizations, challenged shipbreaking according to languages of justice, economics, and legality. Using a justice discourse and invoking the Basel Convention, they described it as an 'illegal export of toxic waste' from rich to poor countries, highlighting impacts on the environment, and the health and livelihood of workers and local communities. *Blue Lady* was a case of 'toxic imperialism', Gopal Krishna argued. The practice is perceived as environmental injustice or environmental racism on a global scale (Lipman, 1998) and a human rights violation. Orthodox economic language (such as 'internalizing externalities' or 'polluter pays principle') was also strategically adopted by Greenpeace, BAN, and the Shipbreaking Platform. While they are conscious of the pitfalls of economic values, the polluter pays principle offered a suitable language to link questions of economics with questions of justice. Finally, the last language used was one of compliance with the rule of law. Indian activists often claimed that existing legislation had been violated. Gopal Krishna, in his application, called for respect for the 2003 Supreme Court Order including prior informed consent, inventory of hazardous waste mandatory for ship owner, decontamination by the ship owner prior to export, proper removal and waste management (with special attention to asbestos) and transparent pollution monitoring by GPCB. He pointed out that the *Blue Lady* carried 1,250 tonnes of asbestos, the import of which is banned under the Basel Convention and Indian Hazardous Waste (management and handling) Rules, 2003. Lastly, he claimed that ILO standards on occupational and environmental health hazards had not been respected.

3.5.3.2 Shipbreakers

The position of shipbreaking companies has always been articulated by Mr Nagarsheth, historical president of the Iron Steel Scrap and Shipbreakers Association of India (ISCSAI). The argument was basically made on economic values, though also environmental values were employed.

In their Application on February 2006 (IA 25) they highlighted ASSBY's contributions to the economy claiming that more than 100,000 people were in direct and indirect employment, up to 2.5 mn tonnes of good-quality and cheap steel (approximately 5% of the domestic demand) had been returned to market, and that 20 bn of Rs. (US$400 mn) had been raised by the authorities in the form of customs duties, income, and sales taxes. Mr Nagarsheth presented shipbreaking as an environmentally-friendly activity because, by recycling the materials, it saves non-renewable resources (such as iron ore and the energy needed to produce primary steel). In contrast to other methods of manufacture, especially steel manufacturing, it does not produce solid waste. This position is apparently supported by the International Maritime Organization (IMO) which has declared shipbreaking a green industry.

Mr Nagarsheth claimed that occupational hazard is the issue, and not the environmental impacts as publicized by media and activists. The recognized hazard could be met by resorting to new technologies. In fact Mr Nagarsheth declared to be committed to proper waste management without causing any harm or damage to human life or to the environment. Finally he refused to see ships as hazardous waste, so that national and international legislation for the transport of hazardous waste would not apply. What is interesting here is that while business interests employ the same languages (economic, environmental, distributive) as the environmental groups, they frame very different and at very different scales the issues, to come to very different evaluative conclusions.

3.5.3.3 Indian authorities
The ministry of Environment and Forestry (MOEF) together with three other ministries (steel, shipping, and labour) are in charge of the policy-making on shipbreaking; GMB (Gujarat Maritime Board) and GPCB (Gujarat Pollution Control Board) deal with the local implementation of rules and regulations. Their valuation premises and positions were very close to those of ship owners and shipbreakers, emphasizing public benefits in terms of economic and environmental values at the national scale. According to the authorities, ships are not waste, hazardous substances are managed in an environmentally sound manner and worker safety is under control. Since there was never any pollution, no remediation is necessary. The Menon Committee (HPC), constituted by the Supreme Court in 1997, presented a Report (background to the 2003 Court Order) that represents the sole governmental admission of severe pollution and inhuman conditions of the workers.

In the *Blue Lady* case, MOEF was in charge of the technical experts committee (TEC) on management of hazardous wastes that the Supreme Court had established on March 2006, to investigate environmental protection, worker safety, and health. Committee ship inspections, such as the routine ones by GPCB, are visual, because in ASBBY there are no proper laboratory testing facilities. Gopal Krishna proved the conclusions of these inspections to be wrong. The Committee had declared that 'presence of radioactive materials in a passenger ship like the "Blue Lady" is quite unlikely'. In fact, it contained 5,500 fire detection points containing 1,100 radioactive elements in the form of Americium-241.

3.5.3.4 Villagers
On March 2007, Mr Bhagavatsinh Halubha Gohil, Sarpanch of Sosiya (head of the village), filed an application on behalf of 12 sarpanches

and 30,000 people who live within a distance of 1 to 25 km from the shipbreaking yard. The applicants were opposing the dismantling of the ship because of the damage it would do to the health of workers and villagers and the environment (the soil, sea food, water, air, flora, and fauna) on which the livelihood of the people depend (the majority of the population consists of farmers and fishers).

They acknowledged that the 'scrapping of the ship was vigorously opposed by environmental groups in India, as the Indian breakers did not have the facility or technology to safely dispose of the estimated 1000 tonnes of asbestos'. Three main reasons prompted them to take legal action. First, they presented a study that they had commissioned to a consultancy about the potential health dangers due to cancerogenic effects of the airborne dispersion of the asbestos fibres contained in the ship. Second, they mentioned how open dumping of waste into the sea had affected fishers, forcing them out into the sea beyond 5 or 6 km because of the oil that spreads over the water, ruining fishing. Third, they explained how in the past 15 to 20 years farmers had been noticing that the yield of their crops was diminishing. Even though its cause had not been easy to pinpoint, they had come to the conclusion that this was related to air, water, and soil contamination brought on by the work at ASBBY. The villagers requested their inclusion in the Civil Writ Petition No. 657 of 1995[17] (a public interest petition on the question of hazardous waste import), that the *Blue Lady* not be allowed to be dismantled at ASSBY and asked for social and environmental justice. Notably, in an interview for the Indian magazine *Frontline*, Mr Gohil, promoter of the petition and Sarpanch of Sosiya, clarified their intentions declaring: 'we don't want to stop shipbreaking because that would mean loss of jobs for hundreds of people. All we are asking is that it should be done in a responsible manner and our lives and earnings are not affected.'[18]

Witnesses report that a Judge snubbed the petition and the validity of the knowledge of the local people commenting, 'What do these people know about asbestos?'.

---

[17] Available at https://www.elaw.org/content/india-research-foundation-v-union-india-others-wp-6571995-20031014-hazardous-wastes.

[18] 'Shipload of trouble', Lyla Bavadam, *Frontline*, 16 November 2007.

3.5.4 The Final Court Order on *Blue Lady*

The final Court Order was passed on 11 September 2007. The villagers' petition was never taken into consideration. The Court considered whether permission should be granted for dismantling of the ship *Blue Lady* at Alang, Gujarat. The Court mentioned that the vessel *Blue Lady* would give employment to 700 workmen, provide the country with 41,000 tonnes of steel and reduce pressure on mining activity elsewhere. So that, in the framework of sustainable development (recognizing recycling as a key element), the precautionary and polluter pays principles (said to be accepted and settled in Indian Law) should be considered together with the concept of balance (between economic development and environment) under the principle of proportionality (declared to be important in an emergent economy). These considerations, together with the technical and scientific suggestions by the TEC, supported the conclusion that:

> It cannot be disputed that no development is possible without some adverse effect on the ecology and the environment, and the projects of public utility cannot be abandoned and it is necessary to adjust the interest of the people as well as the necessity to maintain the environment. A balance has to be struck between the two interests. Where the commercial venture or enterprise would bring in results which are far more useful for the people, difficulty of a small number of people has to be bypassed. The comparative hardships have to be balanced and the convenience and benefit to a larger section of the people has to get primacy over comparatively lesser hardship.

The intention, as declared by the Court, was to balance the priorities of development (generation of revenue, employment, and public interest) on one hand and environmental protection on the other. Under a general admission that activity needed to be strictly and properly regulated, the breaking of the *Blue Lady* was allowed. No quantification of costs and benefits was asked for by the Supreme Court, and neither was a multi-criteria evaluation carried out.

3.6 Conclusions: Capital Accumulation by Contamination at Alang

Economic development, through economic growth and globalization, has considerably increased the magnitude of the global social metabolism. The shipping industry represents the key infrastructure through which material flows travel around the world. The increase in physical trade flows leads to a proportional increase in the shipping capacity (the number and size of ships), which leads—sooner or later—to an increase in the supply of ships for scrap.

This chapter investigated shipbreaking in India's greatest yard, ASSBY, contextualizing it within the world's social metabolism and analysing the social, economic, and institutional logics at play. At the Supreme Court of India, competing value frameworks, languages of valuation, and truth claims came to clash. Environmental and civil activists as well as business interests and public authorities framed the issue as one of economic, environmental, and equity values. The former emphasized the injustice of an unequal distribution of costs and benefits and the disproportionate environmental and social damages at the local scale, considering local livelihood and ecosystem losses as incommensurable with benefits at other scales. The latter instead valued monetary and environmental benefits at the national scale, assuming them commensurable with local losses, and finding a positive balance. Facts apart, different languages of valuation clashed and the Supreme Court decided in the favour of the language of the powerful, interpreting sustainable development as a positive economic benefit at the national scale. 'Development' turned out to be the dominant ideology with a substantive power to signify. The Supreme Court's decision is based on a (controversial) utilitarian reasoning rather than on (Kantian) rights and, instead of recognizing value pluralism, the so-called principle of balance is based on a trade-off between development and environment that does not recognize the incommensurability among the expressed values. It rests upon the idea that economic benefits can compensate for environmental degradation. It would be interesting to know how would the Court undertake a cost-benefit analysis and how much would it count a worker's life, how much the loss of livelihood and how much the irreversible damage done to local ecosystems.

The above are not just rhetorical questions. They show the irreducible difficulty in the call made by economists to internalize externalities. Furthermore, our analysis shows that there are important reasons why externalities are not internalized. The dumping of toxic waste, rather than a market failure, can be seen as a cost-shifting success (Kapp, 1950), this being made possible by social asymmetries in the distribution of political and economic power, property rights, and income (Martinez Alier and O'Connor, 1999). Racism should also be accounted as a driving social force for environmental inequality (Pellow, 2007), both at international and national levels. In the Indian context, caste plays an important role. This means that in environmental conflicts, losers tend to be of lower caste than winners. Shipbreaking can also be seen as an ecologically unequal exchange because of the 'externalization' of environmentally damaging disposal activities to the periphery of the world-system as a consequence of exchange relations with more industrialized countries (Hornborg, 1998). This is based upon the usurpation of waste assimilation properties of ecological systems in a manner that enlarges the domestic carrying capacity of the industrialized countries to the detriment of peripheral societies (Rice, 2009).

Last, shipbreaking can also be interpreted as a case of 'accumulation by contamination'. Marxist theory of over-accumulation argues that the economic crisis is due to a lack for capital of profitable investments opportunities. Dispossession is one strategy, among others, to overcome such crisis (Harvey, 2003). Accumulation by dispossession is the inherent necessity of the capital system to separate, through extra-economic means (such as a change in law or violence), the labourers from the means of production to perpetuate the capitalistic relation (e.g. bio-prospecting, patent rights, privatization of public utilities). Our analysis suggests the existence of a second strategy: accumulation by contamination. This is the process by which the capital system endangers, through cost-shifting, the means of existence (and subsistence) of human beings to perpetuate the capitalistic relation (e.g. marine pollution, alteration of biogeochemical cycles). In the case of dispossession, something that was pre-existing outside the capitalist system is brought inside, that is, privatization of the public assets or commons (Harvey, 2003). Normally a specific social group is dispossessed by another one to obtain profit (e.g. farmers are dispossessed of their land by land grabbers). In the case of contamination,

SHIPBREAKING IN ALANG   103

an appropriation of de facto property rights takes place resulting in the shifting of costs and risks, that is, exploiting the sinks over their sustainable assimilative capacity (e.g. climate change or shipbreaking). The consequences most likely fall upon the most vulnerable social groups (e.g. small-scale farmers or fishers in the South, like those in Alang), but the society as a whole can be affected.

Things could be done in a different (better) way and it is technically feasible to have a proper if more expensive dismantling operation (as in Europe). There are in fact many guidelines (Basel Convention, 2002; International Maritime Organization, 2003; International Labour Organization, 2004; European Commission, 2007) which are simply not implemented. Ship owners could pay a deposit (or guarantee) throughout the ship life to be spent for proper dismantling, established as a requirement for allowing entrance at any harbour. This could allow investments to take the activity off the beach because dry docks operations potentially offer better labour and environmental standards. But all this would increase their costs, which is precisely the reason why they send boats to unregulated shipyards like those of ASSBY in the first place. This is why the calls for a green shipbreaking have actually failed (Neşer et al., 2008; Khan et al., 2012). Using the terminology proposed by Martinez Alier, ASSBY is therefore an example of the waste-based commodity frontier of the world's social metabolism, where those who maintain the power (ship owners, shipbreakers, and authorities) manage to perpetuate a system of 'accumulation by contamination', exercising de facto property rights. Just as in the case with climate change, the crucial question is not only who is to pay and who is to be paid, but who is the owner of the sinks?

We have attempted to highlight the complexity of the linkages among nature, economy, and society, showing how ecological economics and political ecology can contribute to its understanding. Whether improvements in ASSBY or other wasteyards of the global economy will ever become true, are then a question of social and political struggle and the ability of those who currently lose out to affirm their own rights. From this perspective, greater and effective opposition encountered by ship owners and shipbreakers regarding their shifting of environmental costs would result in improved sustainability, potentially both locally and globally: locally for the pollutants that would not be discharged into the environment; globally because an increment in the operations' costs for the shipping industry might slow down the social metabolism (by increasing the costs of trade) and its multiple impacts. People who struggle for environmental justice potentially contribute to the environmental sustainability of the economy (Martínez-Alier, 2002). They do so by challenging not only accumulation by contamination, as in the case of shipbreaking, but also accumulation by dispossession, as we will show in the next chapter.

4

Delhi's Waste Conflict

An Unlikely Alliance Against Capital Accumulation by Dispossession and Contamination

4.1 Introduction: A Political Ecology of Urban Metabolism

Residents of south Delhi's Okhla area were delighted to see what they thought was the season's first snowfall. But they were enraged after realizing that it was toxic ash from a large waste-to-energy plant.

Rediff News
27 December 2012

The above quote is from an online news article about a waste-to-energy incinerator in Delhi, India. It highlights the importance of materiality—in this case toxic ash—in the lives of the people residing in the neighbourhood adjacent to the incinerator.[1] Indeed, the euphoria elicited when residents thought they were witnessing the season's first snowfall quickly gave way to visceral rage as the neighbourhood was engulfed in hazardous particulate matter. The story of Delhi's first waste-to-energy plant could be narrated as a case of neoliberalism par excellence—a series of non-transparent deals led to the transfer of land

---

[1] This chapter was published in the journal *Antipode* in 2015, with the geographer from Manchester University Seth Schindler as a co-author. An earlier version, shorter and more policy-oriented, was published in the *Economic and Political Weekly* in 2012 with the title 'Delhi Waste Conflict', with Seth Schindler and Shashi Bhushan, general secretary of the Delhi-based informal recyclers union AIKMM.
   Demaria, F., Schindler, S. (2015). Contesting urban metabolism: Struggles over waste-to-energy in Delhi, India. *Antipode* 48(2): 293–313. Schindler, S., Demaria, F., Bhushan, S. (2012). Delhi Waste Conflict. *Economic and Political Weekly* XLVII: 42, pp. 18–21.

The Political Ecology of Informal Waste Recyclers in India. Federico Demaria, Oxford University Press.
© Federico Demaria 2023. DOI: 10.1093/oso/9780192869050.003.0004

and the right to build the incinerator from a parastatal institution to a large corporation owned by a sitting Parliamentarian. However, this narrative would omit the emotional and physical toll that the incinerator has taken on nearby residents, who launched a protracted campaign to have the plant closed. This movement is focused on materiality, as the constant exposure to particulate matter has become a defining feature of the everyday lives of nearby residents and has produced a collective anxiety. In addition to middle-class residents, waste-to-energy technology has faced opposition from workers in the informal waste management sector and NGOs that lobby on their behalf. 'Waste pickers' collect, segregate, and sell waste to recyclers, and to them the incinerator represents a bitter economic injustice because it threatens to dispossess them of a resource, that is, waste (Wilson et al., 2006). An incipient alliance has emerged between middle-class residents and waste pickers in opposition to the incinerator and it emerges in spite of the fact that they are motivated by 'conflicting rationalities' (Watson, 2003). To the former this struggle is material in essence as they seek to reduce their exposure to waste on the grounds that it poses a health risk, while the latter are engaged in a political economic contestation whose aim is to defend a source of livelihood. This unlikely alliance could be explained by the fact that middle-class residents resist accumulation by contamination, while waste pickers resist accumulation by dispossession.

This chapter speaks to ongoing scholarly debates surrounding the need to expand the scope of urban political ecology (UPE) on the one hand (Heynen, 2014), while situating it within local contexts on the other hand (Lawhon et al., 2014). To this end we draw on industrial ecology and ecological economics (see Newell and Cousins, 2014), for which materiality lacks agency but must be accounted for and can be quantified; in this particular case we focus on the composition, volume, and density of Delhi's waste. This approach demonstrates that neither political economy nor materiality can be considered in context as they are always already co-constituted. It is distinguishable from classical urban political ecology's (UPE) use of the metabolism metaphor as a heuristic device employed to better understand and critique capitalism, as well as 'second wave UPE' wherein post-humanist approaches focus on the distribution of agency across complex assemblages composed of human and non-human act-ants (see Heynen, 2014).

The politics surrounding metabolic flows give rise to antagonisms and alliances that are not necessarily re-enactments of twentieth-century struggles; instead of epic contestations between capital and organized la-bour, or demands for recognition and rights that characterize so-called new social movements, metabolic conflicts erupt and alliances are formed and fragment as people struggle to define their 'place' in, and relation to, dynamic situated urban political ecologies. Metabolic contestations in cities in the Global South—and waste conflicts in particular—involve struggles over value and livelihood *as well as* health and wellbeing. While it is clear that political opportunities are fostered or foreclosed according to the resources that serve as metabolic inputs and the ways in which they are processed (e.g. coal vs oil) (Mitchell, 2011), we show that the same is true of outputs (e.g. interring waste in landfills vs incineration).

This chapter is divided into four sections. In Section 4.2 we introduce our conceptualization of urban metabolism, which is influenced by in-dustrial ecology and ecological economics. In Section 4.3 we describe Delhi's solid waste management (SWM) system, explain how it has been transformed in recent years, and show how this has provoked opposition which coalesced into an unlikely alliance. In Section 4.4 we conclude by exploring the implications of unlikely alliances for environmental pol-itics in general.

4.2 Materiality and the Making of Urban Metabolisms

The conceptualization of cities as metabolisms has a long history (Geddes, 1885; Mumford, 1938; Wolman, 1965; Martinez Alier, 1987; Decker et al., 2000; Giampietro et al., 2012; see Newell and Cousins, 2014 for an overview) and over the course of the past decades there has been a 'virtual explosion' (Fischer-Kowalski, 1998: 62) of research on urban me-tabolisms. Ecological economists and industrial ecologists have been at the forefront of this revival, and to these scholars urban metabolisms are 'exchange processes whereby cities transform raw materials, energy, and water into the built environment, human biomass, and waste' (Castan Broto et al., 2012: 851). The aim of many of these researchers is to quantify material inputs and outputs, and capture the biophysical processes that result as resources are assembled and transformed, and waste is produced (Kennedy et al., 2007; Daniels and Moore, 2001; Fischer-Kowalski et al., 2011). This approach has been influential in policy surrounding environmental sustainability which is increasingly geared towards the quantification of material flows and biophysical processes (While et al., 2010). For example, the United Nations Environmental Program's recently published report entitled *City-Level Decoupling: Urban Resource Flows and the Governance of Infrastructure Transitions* (2013: 2) 'makes the case for examining cities from a material flow perspective, presenting the city as a living organism with a dynamic and continuous flow of inputs and outputs as its "metabolism", while also placing the city within the broader system of flows that make it possible for it to function'.

Urban metabolisms can remain stable over long periods of time, but they are inherently subject to change according to resource availability, technological innovation, and political contingency. Joan Martinez Alier (2002) has demonstrated that the chance of social and political conflict is heightened when metabolic flows are suddenly increased, interrupted, or redirected. While most scholarship focused on the quantification of material flows within a given metabolic system has largely failed to explicitly show how power relations condition the (re-)configuration of metabolisms (for exceptions see Martinez Alier et al., 2010; Anguelovski and Martinez Alier, 2014), urban political ecologists have put these contestations front and centre. For these scholars urban infrastructure is a manifestation of power relations within and between cities, as it facilitates the throughput of metabolic flows, their transformation and unequal distribution (Kaika and Swyngedouw, 2000; Kaika, 2006; Keil and Graham, 1998; Swyngedouw and Heynen, 2003; Swyngedouw, 1996). Accordingly, UPE demonstrates that metabolic processes cannot be understood in isolation from governance regimes that determine the social relations of production, division of labour, and distribution of resources (Swyngedouw and Heynen, 2003; Heynen et al., 2006). In much of this scholarship there is an a priori assumption that metabolic flows are determined by political economic processes, so in contrast to quantitative analyses of urban metabolisms UPE tends to employ the metabolism metaphor as a heuristic device through which capitalism can be understood and critiqued. For example, Matthew Gandy (2002: 8) criticizes earlier scholarship on metabolism whose 'metabolic conceptions of urban form tend to neglect the flow of capital ... [which] represents the most powerful circulatory dynamic in the production of modern cities'.

Urban political ecology is witnessing a number of robust debates, and Heynen (2014) traces the emergence of 'second wave UPE' which draws on post-humanism to critically analyse the role of things. Much of this scholarship employs the Deleuzoguattarian concept of 'assemblage' to describe the rhizomatic coming together of humans and non-humans, and/or it examines the ways in which actants mediate durable actor-networks (see Farias and Bender, 2010; McFarlane, 2011a; 2011b; Harris, 2013; Bennett, 2010; Holifield, 2009; Lancione, 2013; Meehan, 2014; Shaw and Meehan, 2013; Ranganathan, 2015). Much of this scholarship is not geared towards understanding or critiquing capitalism, but rather it seeks to develop a deeper understanding of everyday life and cities (see Heynen, 2014; Derickson, 2014). In this vein Lawhon et al. (2014) argue that UPE risks universalizing particular Northern ecologies because of its unwavering focus on the power of capital. They suggest that scholarship on African urbanism can inform the development of a *situated* urban political ecology, by beginning with local context, identities, and everyday practice, and then using non-Northern epistemologies to explain actually existing ecologies. Rather than generating a critique of capitalism whose remedy is systemic change, they argue that this situated UPE can lead to 'radical incrementalism' (Pieterse, 2008). This approach has already paid dividends by situating actually existing metabolic flows, the production of landscape and urban space in the context of local contingencies, ecologies, and politics (Lawhon, 2013b; Ernston, 2012; Silver, 2014). Importantly, for these authors African urbanism is not meant to replace Marxian-inspired UPE as an alternative universal epistemological framework, but by situating UPE they hope to expand the 'range of urban experiences to inform theory on how urban environments are shaped, politicized and contested' (Lawhon et al., 2014: 489).

We are sympathetic to the argument that UPE should be broadened theoretically and situated empirically, and we argue that this can be achieved by developing a deeper understanding of the contested nature of urban metabolisms. Colin McFarlane (2013: 500) argues that peering at a city through a 'metabolic lens' offers the potential to multiply 'the potential sites of intervention, from water pipes, drains and power stations to laws, policies and officials, widening the objects of analysis and the epistemology of social change'. However, this potential remains largely unfulfilled in much UPE scholarship because of the way in which capital is portrayed as the primary determinant of urban metabolisms. By embracing an understanding of metabolism influenced by industrial ecology and ecological economics whose focus is actual material flows, we seek to develop a situated understanding of waste in Delhi at the core of which is a complex relationship between its materiality (e.g. volume, composition, density, and its biophysical transformation) and political economy (e.g. ownership, access, and value struggles). In this urban metabolism non-human entities lack agency but must be accounted for in a literal sense because a change in their character or quantity, or the way in which they are acted upon, can profoundly impact political economic processes. We do not simply seek to 'empower' materiality as a determinant of political economy, rather we demonstrate that materiality and political economy are dialectically related and co-constitute urban metabolisms. While a change in one or the other may disrupt a stable metabolic configuration in particular instances, there is no moment when either serves as context or structure. Ultimately, the coevolution of materiality and political economy transforms urban metabolisms and as a result political opportunities are fostered and foreclosed.

4.3 Delhi's Urban Metabolism

Waste management in Southern metropolises is a multi-billion dollar industry that is increasingly attracting the attention of large-scale institutional investors (Bank of America Merrill Lynch, 2013). This is due to the fact that the volume of generated waste, its metabolic density and proportion of recyclable materials (and thus calorific value) has increased in many cities (Martinez Alier et al., 2014), and as a result there are new opportunities for capital accumulation through incineration (World Bank, 1999). In most cases municipal officials are left with little choice but to process/dispose of waste within cities given an increasing metabolic density of waste, difficulties establishing new landfills within cities, and high costs transporting waste to landfills in outlying areas (D'Alisa et al., 2012).[2] Incineration appears an attractive option because it 'eliminates' waste while it also produces energy.

Indian cities exhibit these trends, and they are also being transformed through complex economic, political, social, and ecological processes that are contested in a range of spaces and ways by numerous actors (Shatkin, 2014). Powerful local actors typically embrace and work towards grandiose visions of urban transformation, the pursuit of which significantly impacts cities and urban residents as slums are demolished and cityscapes are remade (Benjamin, 2008; Dupont, 2010; Ghertner, 2011; Goldman, 2011; Schindler, 2014a). Nevertheless, visions of 'world class' cities remain perpetually postponed because they are contested by a bewildering array of actors who employ a range of techniques in places that vary from courts and corporate boardrooms (see Bhan, 2009; Searle, 2014) to everyday politics that unfold on the street (see Chatterjee, 2011; Doshi, 2013; Datta, 2013; Schindler, 2014b).

Recent scholarship demonstrates that urban ecologies in India are embedded in these broader processes of transformation and contestation, and serve as a field upon which the middle-class and the poor are engaged in political and material struggle. Negi (2010) has narrated an 'environmental turn' in Indian politics in which courts have ruled in favour of public interest litigation (PIL) initiated by middle-class residents, which forces municipal authorities to demolish slums and close so-called hazardous industries in the name of environmentalism. While Mawdsley (2004: 81) cautions against essentializing a single environmentalism of the middle class, she notes that 'the middle classes exert a disproportionate influence in shaping the terms of public debate on environmental issues'. Meanwhile, the poor have resisted displacement and metabolic reconfiguration that threaten their livelihoods. A recent edited volume by Rademacher and Sivaramakrishnan (2013: 30) presents 'the emergence of a set of conflicts that involve not merely the material conditions of

---

[2] D'Alisa et al. (2012) define metabolic density of waste as the product of the pace of waste disposed per capita and area (kg/d)/km². This indicator is calculated with the Multi-Scale Integrated Analysis of Societal and Ecosystem Metabolism (MuSIASEM).

urban life—security, green spaces, municipal services, unimpeded mobility through the city—but also the very people, mostly slum dwellers, who might undermine these conditions'.

The political positions taken by these groups are not immutable, and the transformation of urban India's dynamic metabolism can foster unlikely alliances between them. We draw on a combined 16 months of experience collaborating with organizations working in Delhi's waste management sector—one an NGO and the other a waste workers' trade union—in 2011–2012. During this time we interacted with key stakeholders involved in everyday struggles over waste management, and we augmented these experiences with semi-structured interviews during follow-up visits in 2013 and 2014.

4.3.1 Solid Waste Management in Delhi

The metabolization of waste in Delhi—that is, the production, throughput, and processing of waste—is best understood as a single production network comprised of two interlinked value chains, one formal and the other informal (see Figure 4.1). The generators of waste—for example, households and firms—are legally obliged to deposit their waste at a transfer station where it becomes the property of the municipal government. These transfer stations are typically approximately 15 square metres and are located throughout the city in both residential and commercial areas. From the transfer station onwards the collection, removal, and disposal of waste is the responsibility of municipal authorities.

The formal waste management system has historically been overburdened and it is complemented by a large informal value chain that channels waste into the formal and informal recycling sectors. The relationship between the formal and informal value chains is mediated by approximately 150,000–200,000 waste pickers (Chaturvedi and Gidwani, 2011: 131) who gather recyclable waste at various leakage points along the formal value chain (see green arrows in Figure 4.1; and Figure 4.2). They segregate it and then sell it to small-scale junk dealers (see Figure 4.3), who, in turn, sell it to wholesalers (see Gill, 2010; Agarwal et al., 2005; Hayami et al., 2006; Gidwani and Reddy, 2011). These wholesalers ultimately sell recyclable waste in bulk to formal and informal recycling

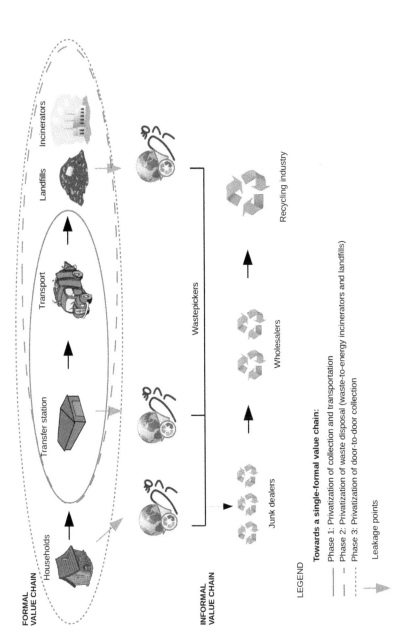

FORMAL VALUE CHAIN

Households   Transfer station   Transport   Landfills   Incinerators

INFORMAL VALUE CHAIN

Junk dealers   Wholesalers   Wastepickers   Recycling industry

LEGEND

Towards a single-formal value chain:

——— Phase 1: Privatization of collection and transportation

– – – Phase 2: Privatization of waste disposal (waste-to-energy incinerators and landfills)

········· Phase 3: Privatization of door-to-door collection

➤ Leakage points

Figure 4.1 Flow diagram of waste management in Delhi and the three stages of the policy shift.
Source: Federico Demaria.

Figure 4.2 Waste pickers (father and son) collecting waste door-to-door in Delhi.
Picture: Federico Demaria.

firms. This system has had a mixed record; as of 2005 approximately 15% of Delhi's waste was recycled (Agarwal et al., 2005) while approximately 20–30% remained uncollected and was illegally dumped or burned in the open (Talyan et al., 2008). What is indisputable, however, is that the informal waste sector provided livelihoods of last resort to thousands of people (Gill, 2010). Most waste pickers collect approximately 50 kg of recyclable material per day, mostly plastic and paper (60% and 30% of their income, respectively), but also metals, hair, and organic materials, and they earn roughly 8,000 Rupees per month (about US$125) (AIKMM, 2015; Figure 4.3).

Solid waste management in Delhi is undergoing a prolonged and thorough reconfiguration as successive phases of privatization of the formal waste management system have served to strengthen connections within the formal value chain at the expense of linkages with the informal value chain. These institutional reforms have been accompanied by the introduction of new techniques of waste processing which rework the material

Figure 4.3 Waste pickers segregating waste in Delhi.
Picture: Federico Demaria.

Table 4.1 Physical composition of (as wt. %) of Municipal Solid Waste in Delhi

Year	Organic	Recyclable	Inert	Total
1982	57.7	8.3	34	100
1995	38.3	12.9	48.8	100
2002	36.6	17.2	46.2	100

Source: Talyan et al., 2008.

flows of waste and determine who is exposed to environmental hazards. These political economic and technological changes are driven by the dramatic material increase in the volume and density of waste, and a change in its composition. The roots of these material changes date back to the mid-1980s when only 8.3% of Delhi's waste was recyclable. By 2002 the proportion of recyclable waste had increased to 17.2% (see Table 4.1), and this compositional shift is even more striking when one considers

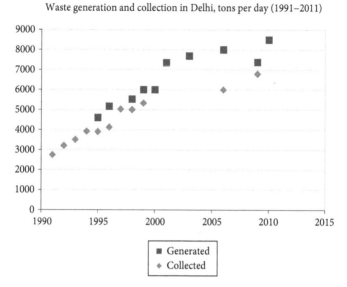

Figure 4.4 Generation and collection of municipal solid waste in Delhi (1991–2011).
Source: CPCB 2006; MCD 2012.

that there was an unprecedented trebling of the amount of waste generated from 1990 to 2010 (see Figure 4.4).

Delhi's landfills struggled to absorb the material increase of waste, and municipal authorities were urgently tasked with locating new sites for sanitary landfills in order to avoid a public health crisis. Middle-class residents filed numerous lawsuits that demanded authorities develop more effective SWM systems, the result of which was the creation of a number of expert committees at multiple levels of government (Gidwani, 2013). Numerous policy options could have responded to the increased volume of waste in Delhi. One would have been to promote segregation of waste at the point of generation, improve collection rates, and invest in sanitary landfills. This could have been complemented by institutionalizing the linkages between the formal and informal value chains with the objective of fostering recycling (see Schindler et al., 2012; WIEGO, 2013). Instead, authorities embraced techno-managerial solutions which entailed transforming the production network of waste management into a single formal value chain under the control of private sector enterprises.

The privatization of waste management in Delhi has unfolded in three phases (see Figure 4.1), the first of which began in 2005 when municipal authorities started to contract private firms for the collection and transportation of waste from transfer stations to landfills (Chaturvedi and Gidwani, 2011). Authorities opted for a second phase of privatization in which waste-to-energy plants—that is, the incineration of waste rather than its burial—became the cornerstone of Delhi's waste management system. Currently two waste-to-energy plants are operational in Okhla and Ghazipur (south and east Delhi, respectively), and a third is under construction in the north of the city in Narela Bawana.

The third phase of privatization has just begun and it is geared towards developing a single value chain under control of private-sector enterprises, and this policy is driven by a material exigency because waste-to-energy plants can only produce energy from high-calorific waste. In Delhi, the calorific value of formally collected waste at disposal sites (i.e. after recyclable waste is removed by waste pickers) is approximately 1000 kcal/kg (NEERI, 2005), while combustion incinerators require waste with a minimum calorific value of 1500 kcal/kg. Thus, Delhi's incinerators require the elimination of leakage points whereby high-calorific recyclable waste is transferred to the informal value chain by waste pickers. In order to obtain waste with a high enough calorific value, privatization vertically integrates SWM—from collection to disposal—under the direction of a small number of large-scale enterprises. One example is a 2009 contract between the Municipal Corporation of Delhi and a subsidiary of Ramky (Delhi MSW Solutions Limited), one of India's largest waste management firms, which grants the firm exclusive rights to collect and process waste in four zones in Delhi (Civil Lines, Rohini, Vasant Kunj, and Dwarka Pappankalan).

The progressive privatization of SWM in Delhi was a response to—and made possible by—the increase in volume and metabolic density of waste, as well as a change in its composition. Privatization is not only an institutional change, but it is also a comprehensive reconfiguration of the city's metabolism as the throughput of waste is redirected and new methods to process waste are introduced. This has been contested by Delhi's middle-class and waste pickers, albeit for very different reasons.

4.3.2   Conflict I—Waste Pickers

Waste pickers began to organize politically in the 1990s. They originally sought recognition from the state and their demands centred on access to services such as healthcare and schools. Beginning in the mid-2000s struggles increasingly revolved around access to waste because the reconfiguration of Delhi's waste metabolism progressively eliminated leakage points from the formal value chain. The first struggles over access to waste erupted at transfer stations because after their privatization firms often forcibly removed waste pickers or forced them to pay a fee to continue their operations (see Chaturvedi and Gidwani, 2011). One waste picker explained (personal communication, 2014):

> At first when the company came, they said that we should carry on working. But then, one by one, they started to go to the garbage bins [to collect waste]. They stated they had written permission from the municipal authority and they took control of them. Those who did not vacate them were beaten up and thrown out; the others were told that they could stay if they paid a certain sum of money.

The urgency of struggles over access to waste intensified with the announcement that waste-to-energy would become the cornerstone of SWM in Delhi. The following two comments are representative of how waste pickers typically understood the conflict as a struggle for their livelihood (personal communication, 2014):

> Since we don't have any other work we are forced to do this filthy work. We are forced to pick up this waste. Still the government is trying to force us out. They want to produce electricity by burning our livelihood.
> The work of the waste-to-energy plant is to burn things. They know that [inert and organic] waste never burns. They are trying to burn things [recyclable material] from which we earn our living. Therefore, we are opposing the waste plants.

Finally, in some areas of Delhi where the door-to-door collection of waste has been privatized, waste pickers have lost access to the last remaining leakage point. A female waste picker whose livelihood came from door-to-door collection explained (personal communication, 2014):

> Since 2012 the company has started to send a four-wheeler small truck to collect waste at the doorstep. Since then my revenue has already gone down about 30% [or] 40% and it's decreasing everyday. Then, sometimes the company employee offers to us the waste they collected under a payment of 100 Rupees or more per truck, but I can't afford it. Where should I go to get support?

A number of trade unions have been formed to demand access to waste, such as All India Kabadi Mazdoor Mahasangh (AIKMM), Safai Sena, Delhi Kabadi Mazdoor Sangh, and Green Flag. They have primarily (1) lobbied municipal authorities to grant waste pickers access to waste in publicly owned facilities and (2) organized networks of waste pickers in order to secure flows of waste. For example, Safai Sena (meaning 'Army of Cleaners') is 'a registered group of waste pickers, doorstep waste collectors, itinerant and other small buyers, small junk dealers, and other types of recyclers' that was formed in 2009 (see http://www.safaisena.net/index.htm). It successfully outbid competitors for the exclusive rights to collect and remove waste from Delhi's three train stations in 2011. This waste then enters Safai Sena's network and it is channelled into the recycling industry. Similarly, AIKMM, formed in 2005, claims to have approximately 17,000 members in the Delhi metropolitan area (see: https://www.facebook.com/profile.php?id=100064402343565). Its director Shashi Bhushan explained (personal communication, 2013, https://academicguides.waldenu.edu/formandstyle/apa/citations/personalcommunications):

> We work with a trade union perspective. We organize waste pickers to get them their livelihood and fundamental rights as citizens. If one of us faces a problem [e.g. get harassed by the police], we call fifty or more members and run in his support. In this way we have managed to stop the demand for bribes by private companies at the transfer stations in the centre of Delhi. Nobody wants to hear our voice . . . no policy makers reply to our letters of complaint. So we organize demonstrations with

hundreds of our members in front of the public authorities' offices and sit there until they receive us. It is the only chance for us to meet and talk to them about our demands, starting from right to waste.

Both of these unions organize rallies and demonstrations (Figure 4.5), and their demands have targeted local officials and private firms. For example, AIKMM organized a demonstration outside the Delhi headquarters of the United Nations in 2011 to protest the inclusion of the Okhla and Ghazipur waste-to-energy plants in the Clean Development Mechanism's carbon credits scheme. The effectiveness of grassroots unions is limited, however, because they have scarce resources and many waste pickers earn a subsistence livelihood and cannot afford to spend much time attending political rallies. Furthermore, there is no legal basis for them to make a lawful claim regarding access to waste since its management is the responsibility of municipal authorities.

Figure 4.5 Waste pickers affiliated to the trade union AIKMM demonstrating in Delhi.
Picture: Federico Demaria.

Trade unions are complemented by a host of social and environmental justice organizations that advocate on behalf of waste pickers, such as Toxic Watch Alliance, Hazards Center, Toxics Link, Chintan, Nidan, and Global Alliance for Incinerator Alternatives (GAIA). Many of these organizations collaborated with grassroots unions to host the Global Strategic Workshop for Waste Pickers in 2012 in Pune, in which waste pickers and activists from around the world gathered and identified privatization and waste-to-energy as the two main threats to waste pickers globally. While all of these unions and organizations consistently demand that waste pickers should have access to waste, tensions emerge regarding how they relate with private-sector firms. For example, Safai Sena's website explains that a private firm was granted exclusive rights to collect waste in a Delhi suburb, and 'Safai Sena worked with them to ensure that the existing waste pickers were able to upgrade their work through becoming the doorstep collectors under the new system'. (http://www.safais ena.net/our-activities.htm). In other words, this union demanded that the firm hire its members as wage labourers. Alternatively, AIKMM has steadfastly opposed bargaining with private-sector firms for fear that this could legitimize privatization. Its website demands that privatization be halted altogether and most recently its demands have focused on door-to-door collection: 'Informal sector waste collectors should be given exclusive rights for door-to-door collection at the housing cluster and neighbourhood levels. The private sector companies should be kept out of door-to-door waste collection' (see http://aikmm.org/demands-2/).

All of the NGOs that advocate on behalf of waste pickers link their demands to both environmental sustainability and social justice, but tensions have emerged over which issue to prioritize. Some of the organizations frame their opposition to waste-to-energy plants as an environmental struggle while for others it is first and foremost an issue of social justice and their demands are focused on livelihood issues. For example, an organization called Chintan released a report that framed waste-to-energy as a livelihood issue that should 'not be accepted blindly without regard to the *socio-economic context*' [emphasis added] (Chaturvedi et al., 2012: 17). Alternatively, an NGO called Toxic Watch Alliance (http://www.toxicswatch.org/) has focused on waste-to-energy's environmental impacts, and its director Gopal Krishna (2013) explained that 'this plant will emit large quantities of hazardous emissions (such as dioxins) due to burning of MSW [Municipal Solid Waste], and will profoundly affect the health of the people living in the surrounding areas and environmental for all times to come in future'.

In summary, issues surrounding access to waste have become increasingly politicized, and a number of trade unions and NGOs have emerged to contest the reconfiguration of Delhi's waste metabolism. Since waste pickers operate informally they cannot make lawful claims to waste, and this may explain why some organizations committed to social justice frame their opposition to waste-to-energy plants in environmental terms. We could talk of an urban environmentalism of the poor, where people that fight to defend their livelihood also contribute to environmental sustainability (Martinez-Alier, 2002). This implies that, despite the motivation of waste pickers is mainly due to the will to oppose accumulation by dispossession, they also instrumentally relate to the opposition to accumulation by contamination. This provides a basis for the unlikely alliance with middle-class residents.

4.3.3 Conflict II—Middle-Class Residents

Informal dumping grounds proliferated in large Indian cities in the 1980s as government subsidies for commercial fertilizers reduced demand among farmers for organic waste, which they had hitherto used as fertilizer (Almitra Patel, personal communication, 2014, https://academi cguides.waldenu.edu/formandstyle/apa/citations/personalcommunicati ons). Economic growth in the 1980s and 1990s resulted in the widespread use of cheap plastic, and a concomitant boom in construction increased the volume of inert waste. This prompted the emergence of a middle-class mobilization demanding more effective SWM with the slogan 'clean up and flourish or pile up and perish' (Almitra Patel, personal communication, 2014).[3] Legal proceedings were initiated against municipalities for their failure to handle solid waste and to enforce anti-dumping laws. The petitioners ultimately prevailed and the Supreme Court appointed

---

[3] We use the term 'middle-class' broadly, to refer to Delhi residents who are formally employed in white-collar work. This includes people employed in hi-tech sectors but also accountants, journalists, teachers, and small business owners.

a committee that drafted India's first Municipal Solid Waste (MSW) Rules in September 2000 (PIL No.W.P. (C) 888 of 1996 Almitra H. Patel vs Union of India and Others). The lead petitioner in the case, Almitra Patel, explained that 'this regulation advocates that "wet" food wastes and "dry" recyclable wastes should not be mixed at the source (household or commercial level), so that the organic waste can be composted, while the dry waste can be left to the informal sector's ragpickers and *kabadiwalas* for recycling' (personal communication, 2014). The avenues available to India's middle-class to make lawful claims against poorly performing municipal governments have proliferated as the MSW Rules have given municipal governments more responsibility. Almitra Patel claims that the MSW Rules are 'a powerful weapon that any Indian citizen can use to demand improved performance and accountability' (http://www.almit rapatel.com/).

Most middle-class residents in Delhi either supported or failed to no-tice the initial wave of privatization of the city's SWM system. Complaints among middle-class residents only surfaced in instances where private firms failed to improve waste collection, but there was not opposition to privatization per se. Thus, for most middle-class Delhi residents waste be-comes a political issue when the failure of municipal authorities to meet legal obligations regarding its handling and management threatens to contaminate their surroundings. This explains why the reconfiguration of Delhi's waste metabolism engendered resistance among middle-class residents of neighbourhoods located near the proposed waste-to-energy plants, who were fearful that the plants would contribute to the rapid de-terioration of air quality.

The first waste-to-energy plant in Delhi was built in a populated area called Okhla and it is India's largest. The second plant is somewhat smaller and is located in an area called Ghazipur which is somewhat peripheral but nevertheless densely populated. The proponents of the Okhla waste-to-energy plant conducted an environmental impact assessment in 2006, and unsurprisingly they concluded that the plant would not have serious adverse environmental impacts. The assessment explained that although there would be continuous emissions of particulate matter and ash, the plant would only have a 'minor negative impact' on ambient air quality (p. 87).

Local residents claim that they were not informed about the project in its early stages and they formed the Okhla Anti-Incinerator Committee in 2009 to oppose the waste-to-energy plant (Figure 4.6). They sought to mobilize support through social media and they organized public actions such as street plays (see: https://www.facebook.com/pages/Okhla-Anti-Incinerator-Committee/203624043005125). Consistent with earlier middle-class mobilizations regarding environmental issues, the opposition demanded accountability from public officials and insisted that the plant posed an environmental hazard. One of the leaders of the movement explained that municipal authorities (personal communication, 2014)

> are not interested in solving the waste crisis at all, all that rhetoric on technology and development is nonsense. They have a hidden agenda, the waste crisis is just used as an excuse. These are acres of prime real estate land. They [Jindal Ecopolis] got it for a few Rupees and will sell it for several crores of Rupees in the future.

Figure 4.6 Middle-class residents, affiliated to the Okhla Anti-Incinerator Committee, protesting in front of the Okhla waste-to-energy plant under construction.

Picture: Federico Demaria.

These allegations of corruption are consistent with an ongoing anti-corruption movement in Delhi, yet even if proven true this is unlikely to halt the operations of the waste-to-energy plant. Furthermore, demands to have the plant relocated were futile because city officials could simply assert their authority to determine land-use on publicly held land. Thus, rather than lobby to have the plant relocated, the Okhla Anti-Incinerator Committee was forced to contest the waste-to-energy plant on the grounds that it was inherently unsafe. During interviews our repeated attempts to focus the discussion on the political economy of opaque land deals were rebuffed. Indeed, the political economy of corruption was narrated as a matter of course, but what motivated residents to take to the streets and demonstrate was the feeling that particulate matter produced by the plant is all-pervasive and inescapable. Thus, these residents are first and foremost focused on materiality; particulate matter has invaded their bedrooms, and implanted itself in their clothes, blankets, and even bodies. As one of their leaders explained: 'This is a question of the health of our children and elders and we cannot compromise. Most of us have been living in this area for decades and cannot relocate' (personal communication, 2013).

Residents met with the acting Minister of Environment and Forests, Jairam Ramesh, and he promised to launch an inquiry into the approval of the plant given its proximity to residential areas. The stakes were raised in the meantime when the plant began operating and promptly covered the surrounding neighbourhoods in a blanket of ash. The *Deccan Herald* (Sethi, 2012) reported that the area 'is slowly turning into a toxic gas chamber'. Residents had already launched a number of legal challenges to the plant, and a member of the Okhla Anti-Incinerator Committee explained that 'we are now planning to file a case for human rights violation at the National Human Rights Commission. We feel our fundamental rights have been violated, in particular the right to life and the right to a clean environment.' The Public Interest Litigation (PIL) that the residents filed in 2009 made its way to the Delhi High Court in 2013. The presiding justices opted to refer it to India's recently created National Green Tribunal, which was created in 2010 'for effective and expeditious disposal of cases relating to environmental protection' (http://www.greentribunal.gov.in/index.php). The case is currently pending.

4.3.4 Unlikely Alliances and the Institutionalization of Waste Politics

An incipient—and at times uneasy—alliance has been forged between waste pickers and middle-class residents in their opposition to Delhi's waste-to-energy plants. The Okhla Anti-Incineration Committee has highlighted the threat to waste pickers' livelihoods posed by the Okhla waste-to-energy plant through social media, and a more collaborative relationship has developed in the contestation over the Ghazipur waste-to-energy plant. In March 2012 a demonstration was spearheaded by resident welfare associations from neighbourhoods located near the Ghazipur plant in collaboration with AIKMM. In a letter to inform Delhi police of their intention to stage a demonstration, AIKMM General Secretary Shashi Busan explained that 'local residents are concerned about the potential injurious consequences to the health of their families due to the plant toxic emissions (i.e. carcinogenic dioxins and furans). Instead, waste pickers are concerned about the loss of their livelihood, as they fear that recyclable materials will be burnt in the incinerator.'

The resident welfare association and AIKMM subsequently formed the Ghazipur Anti-Incinerator Committee, and issued a press release (2012) with four demands:

1. Stop all on-going work on the Ghazipur incinerator immediately;
2. Dismiss all waste-to-energy incinerator project proposals;
3. Adopt participatory and decentralized waste management policies that do not disproportionately force any single community to live with the city's waste;
4. Recognize and support the informal waste recycling sector by adopting policies that include the waste pickers.

The Okhla Anti-Incinerator Committee took notice and happily announced that 'Ghazipur has picked up the baton!' There was evidence that the thinking of Okhla residents had evolved from being narrowly focused on closing the Okhla plant, to more broadly-focused environmental justice issues. One very active member of the Okhla Anti-Incinerator Committee explained this shift (personal communication, 2013):

Earlier some people used to say 'shift it, shift it' [to another location] but I said no. From both the cases [Okhla and Ghazipur waste-to-energy plants] these technologies are not good. Either we should need some good technologies or we should use some other way [to safely process waste] ... They should find some other ways to dispose of garbage.

Another active member of the Okhla Anti-Incineration Committee is a professional journalist who has publicly defended the interests of waste pickers (Makri and Devraj, 2015):

> For rag pickers, rubbish is a resource and a survival strategy. Even under unhealthy conditions, their work earns them enough to support their families. And in the absence of a municipal recycling system and segregation of waste at source, such as people's homes, they play a key part in the city's waste management.

While Okhla residents demonstrate a willingness to explore alternative metabolic configurations which can serve as the basis for augmenting waste pickers' access to waste, in general the two groups have remained at arm's length. In contrast, waste pickers and Ghazipur residents have cooperated closely by holding joint demonstrations and issuing joint statements. The primary explanation for these differences is the socio-economic status of residents in Okhla and Ghazipur, respectively. Many of the former affluent professionals are capable of engaging in formal politics and litigation. Prior to the completion of the incinerator they were able to secure a much-publicized visit from the erstwhile Minister of Environment, Jairam Ramesh, in which he promised to review the procedure whereby environmental clearance was issued to the plant (The Hindu, 2011). They were also able to gain an audience with Delhi's erstwhile Chief Minister Sheila Dikshit, and in addition to engaging public officials and leveraging media coverage, Okhla residents can afford to wage a lengthy legal battle.

Ghazipur residents tend to be from a lower socio-economic status (e.g. low-level officials, small entrepreneurs and low-level office workers) whose demands do not command the attention of public officials or the media. Thus, they are forced to take to the streets and agitate, and AIKMM has proven a valuable ally because of its ability to mobilize waste pickers. The relationship between AIKMM and Ghazipur residents has been symbiotic. The Ghazipur residents required assistance from AIKMM to register their joint demonstration with police because they lacked knowledge regarding street politics. Negotiations with police surrounding the registration of the demonstrations was handled by AIKMM, and initially it appeared as if permission would not be granted. In response AIKMM members considered escalating the situation by blocking roads, but Ghazipur residents refused to participate in direct action that was not sanctioned by authorities. Permission to hold a demonstration was finally obtained and the presence of Ghazipur residents lent it legitimacy in the eyes of authorities whose patience with waste pickers is thin because they are unable to make lawful claims to waste. Thus, there are clear reasons why waste pickers and residents aligned; the question that remains surrounds the durability of this alliance and whether it represents a newfound willingness among both groups to combine demands regarding environment and livelihoods. They envision different situated ecologies, so the limits to their cooperation will likely become apparent after the issue of waste-to-energy plants is settled by India's judiciary. For waste pickers the struggle against the reconfiguration of Delhi's SWM system is over their means of subsistence. Just as many farmers and small-scale producers of non-agricultural products in rural areas depend on ecosystems for their livelihoods (what Gadgil and Guha, 1995, call 'ecosystem people'), waste pickers' livelihoods are dependent on a metabolic configuration characterized by a high volume of accessible recyclable material. This urban metabolism emerged after India's economic reforms in the early 1990s, which, combined with a certain degree of political decentralization, empowered urban middle-classes who increasingly demand government officials enforce environmental laws and reduce pollution (i.e. so-called bourgeois environmentalism, Baviskar, 2003). While their immediate motivation is to reduce their exposure to environmental hazards, they also embrace the creation of urban nature, access to which is restricted and serves as a status symbol and evidence of membership in the middle-class. Thus, while waste pickers' main objective is to configure Delhi's metabolism in such a way that they maintain access to waste, middle-class residents envision a metabolism that produces a situated political ecology that insulates them from waste and enables a desired lifestyle. In other words, waste pickers want to revert dispossession, while residents want to be protected from contamination.

These diverse objectives have recently been incorporated into Delhi's formal politics. There was a longstanding consensus among India's rival nationwide parties, India National Congress and Bharatiya Janata Party, surrounding the privatization of waste management and incineration. After a prolonged movement the Aam Aadmi Party (AAP), an upstart party headed by a social reformer, came to power in city-wide elections in 2013.[4] Okhla residents were assured by Delhi's erstwhile Environment Minister, Saurabh Bhardwaj, that the AAP government would address their demands and recently the *India Times* reported that Chief Minister Arvind Kejriwal committed to closing the plant (Nandi, 2015). The Deputy Chief Minister subsequently inspected both Okhla and Ghazipur facilities, indicating that the joint efforts of waste pickers and residents in Ghazipur ultimately garnered an official response (TNN, 2015).

The AAP released a Manifesto on Sanitation and Waste Management, wherein the 'Mohalla Sabha[5] [neighbourhood assemblies] would be given complete authority and funds for local waste management'. If implemented this would provide a formal platform for waste pickers and residents to devise localized solutions to waste management. While it is unclear if AAP has the authority to close the Ghazipur and Okhla plants, *mohalla sabhas* could conceivably ensure that waste pickers retain access to high-calorific recyclable material, thereby channelling waste away from waste-to-energy plants. The politics of waste took a further turn in June 2015, when municipal waste workers went on strike for 12 days.[6] As waste piled up in Delhi's streets, political parties sought to lay the blame with their rivals. Thus, the politics of waste have taken centre stage in Delhi and although change will likely be incremental, it is significant

---

[4] Delhi's AAP Chief Minister resigned in order to contest national elections, and the party formed a majority government after a landslide victory in city-wide elections in 2015.

[5] Each ward is divided into 10 *mohallas*, and all residents of a mohalla are members of the *mohalla sabha*. Each *mohalla sabha* meets bi-monthly. The councilor and all local municipal officials are present and people decide how the municipal funds should be used in that *mohalla*. Source: http://mohallasabha.delhi.gov.in/faq.html#:~:text=An%20open%20meeting%20of%20the,Mohalla%2C%20and%20monitor%20their%20progress.

[6] http://www.ndtv.com/cheat-sheet/money-for-mongolia-not-for-mongolpuri-aaps-dig-at-pm-narendra-over-delhi-garbage-crisis-771037 (Accessed 18 October 2022).

that the party in power advocates institutionalizing a decentralized waste management system that includes waste pickers and residents.

4.4 Conclusions: Contesting Urban Metabolism

In this chapter we have examined the contestation of Delhi's urban metabolism. Like many Indian cities, Delhi faced a looming public health crisis in the 1990s due to the rapid increase of waste that had been expanding for decades. This metabolic configuration required a response from authorities, enabled waste pickers to earn livelihoods, and inhibited middle-class residents from practising the lifestyles to which they aspire. Conflicts erupted, however, when municipal authorities opted to embrace waste-to-energy technology. Waste pickers contest the reworking of Delhi's metabolism because it threatens the access to the waste upon which their livelihoods depend, and middle-class residents oppose waste-to-energy because of its perceived deleterious impact on air quality and the concomitant health risks. While environmental politics in urban India has hitherto been understood as the preserve of a bourgeoisie intent on imposing revanchist order and disciplining the poor, this case demonstrates that environmental politics can foster unlikely alliances among these groups. In this case, and as we will discuss in the conclusions of this book, the alliance between middle-class residents and waste pickers could be seen as an alliance against capital accumulation by both dispossession and contamination.

In order to capture the complexity of the politics surrounding waste in Delhi, it is necessary to balance critical urban theory with attention to materiality. These approaches can be complementary, so instead of an a priori allegiance to one of these theoretical traditions, they should be combined according to local circumstances. In our estimation the concept of an urban metabolism—as conceived by ecological economists and industrial ecologists—allows for the incorporation of an awareness of materiality with critical approaches concerned with power relations and political economy. Urban metabolisms are inherently produced through material and political economic processes—there is no 'original' or 'real' moment in which either materiality or political economy serves as context or structure. While one or the other may drive change in a particular time/place, they are both always already co-constituted. A sudden change in one or the other can generate feedback that affects the overall metabolism. In the case we presented, material flows of waste are subject to conflicting logics and rationalities (see Watson, 2003), yet what ultimately develops is a metabolic configuration that consolidates the throughput of waste in a single formal value chain that ends at a waste-to-energy plant and negatively impacts air quality. This has produced a situated political ecology in which the actual places where waste is collected and processed (e.g. doorsteps, transfer stations, and landfills) have become a 'commodity frontier'. Commodity frontiers have historically been located in hinterlands where the resources upon which cities depend are extracted (Moore, 2000; Martinez Alier et al., 2010), and the emergence of a commodity frontier within Delhi indicates that we can expect the conflicts surrounding waste to increasingly resemble resource conflicts. In this sense waste represents investment opportunities and its 'extraction' produces environmental hazards that jeopardize the health of local residents and inhibit the production of desirable situated political ecologies. In this context, groups whose rationalities may indeed be in conflict can occasionally find common cause in their efforts to affect the situated ecology on this commodity frontier. The city is only habitable for those who can integrate themselves within these systems in ways that allow them to earn livelihoods and also socially reproduce. As we demonstrated, there are innumerable ways in which people can connect with an urban metabolism, for a range of goals and on highly uneven terms. Given the number of actors seeking access and influence, many of whom pursue divergent goals, urban metabolisms are shaping up to be the primary focal point of sociality and contestation in Southern metropolises. The open question remains: Who—if anyone—will promote more sustainable situated political ecologies and why? The answer to this question remains elusive, but our understanding of how social, political, and economic struggles produce actually existing urban space will be limited if we do not account for the relationship between political economy and materiality. The concepts of accumulation by dispossession and contamination contribute to understand why different actors become actively involved.

5

Informal Waste Recyclers and Their Environmental Services

A Case for Recognition and Capital De-Accumulation

5.1 Introduction: The Black Box of the Informal Recycling Sector

Despite the recognition of the existence of millions of informal recyclers, there are no reliable estimates of the number of people engaged in this activity, or of its economic and environmental impact.[1] We argue for an urgent need for better understanding of the informal recycling sector, so as to improve waste management under economic, social, and environmental criteria. Calls for integrating the informal recycling sector into the formal waste management systems have mainly gone unheard. Improving our understanding of this sector is a first essential step if we intend to improve the conditions of its workers and the sustainability of the economy.

In this chapter we investigate the social relations of recycling, which means the social relationships that recyclers must enter into in order to survive, to produce, and to reproduce their means of life. In Section 5.2 we present the methods, and in Section 5.3 we discuss the informal recycling sector in Delhi by (1) assessing the currently available data set on waste management, (2) proposing a taxonomy of recyclers, and (3) making suggestions on how to estimate their number. In Section 5.4, we present a methodology to evaluate the contribution of informal recycling, and in Section 5.5 the results, namely an estimation of how much they recycle,

---

[1] This chapter is published here for the first time. I have discussed the same data and issues in a policy-oriented report for the recyclers union AIKMM in Delhi.

Demaria, F. (2015) 'Rights for waste workers as service providers: A comprehensive valuation of Delhi's informal recycling sector.' All India Kabadi Mazdoor Mahansangh (AIKMM).

The Political Ecology of Informal Waste Recyclers in India. Federico Demaria, Oxford University Press.
© Federico Demaria 2023. DOI: 10.1093/oso/9780192869050.003.0005

what type of materials, and how much they earn. In Section 5.6 we make a case for the recognition of the important contribution of informal recyclers in making social metabolism more circular (i.e. high recycling rates). In particular, we present the most common demands of recyclers groups, and introduce two complementary options for the public authorities to compensate them for their waste management and recycling services. In Section 5.7 we conclude that if we can properly evaluate the contribution of the informal recycling sector, then we can find ways to compensate them for the services they provide, instead of dispossessing them of their means of production (or better, recycling and therefore existence). These inclusive policies could significantly improve their living and working conditions.

5.2 Methods: Interviews, Focus Groups, Official Documents, Direct and Participant Observation

Data from interviews, focus groups, official documents, direct and participant observation have been combined using the case study research methodology (Yin, 2003). We draw on a combined 16 months in 2011–2015 of experience collaborating with a waste workers' trade union in Delhi: All India Kabadi Mazdoor Mahasangh (hereafter AIKMM). During this time we interacted with key stakeholders involved in waste management, and we augmented these experiences with semi-structured interviews during follow-up visits.

We collected, combined, and analysed the available set data on waste in Delhi from different secondary sources, including scientific, NGOs and public authorities, reports, and data sets. Public authorities included Municipal Corporation of Delhi, New Delhi Municipal Corporation, Delhi Pollution Control Committee, Central Pollution Control Board, Ministry of Environment and Forests and Ministry of Urban Development. Official public data and reports are often not easily available. Therefore, often they were obtained from official sources by AIKMM through the Right to Information Act.[2] This was helpful also for

---

[2] Right to Information (RTI) is an Act of the Parliament of India to provide for setting out the practical regime of right to information for citizens. Under the provisions of the Act, any citizen of India may request information from a 'public authority' which is required to reply

obtaining the methodology through which the data had been generated, of particular interest for this chapter.

However, given both the difficulty to access data and the shortcomings of the methodology to obtain them, we focused on collecting data from primary sources, namely waste pickers and junk dealers (locally called *kabaris*). Previous studies have attempted to estimate quantities and revenue generated by waste pickers but these estimates are usually derived from what the waste pickers themselves would declare. In contrast, this chapter proposes an innovative methodology that provides more accurate data and could be replicated elsewhere.

5.3 Formal Waste Management and the Informal Recycling Sector in Delhi, India

As we explained in Chapter 4, among the Global South metropolises, Delhi is at the forefront of the policy shift in solid waste management, which involves the privatization of the collection system(s) and the mass incineration of waste (Schindler et al., 2012). The fundamental antagonism is over access to waste. The assignation of property rights alters the relationship between the formal and informal sectors and in the process waste recyclers lose access to waste. Given the threat that the policy shift poses to the livelihoods of waste recyclers, this chapter argues that it should be openly discussed and debated in the public sphere, rather than mandated by municipal authorities behind closed doors. For this purpose, a better understanding of waste management in general, and the informal recycling sector in particular, is needed.

The present chapter has its starting point in the recommendations put forward in the report by the Delhi-based NGO Chintan: 'Cooling agents: An Examination of the role of the Informal Recycling Sector in Mitigating Climate Change' (Chintan, 2009: 5) that urged public authorities to:

expeditiously or within 30 days. The Act also requires every public authority to computerize its records for wide dissemination and to proactively disseminate certain categories of information so that the citizens need minimum recourse to request information formally.

—Improve data. CPCB[3] should also improve the specificity and public availability of data on the material composition of recyclables (% by weight, for each type of recyclable) in the MSW of Metros and Class I and II cities urgently.

—Undertake a formal study on recycling in India. There are few comprehensive sources of information on recycling rates and materials recycled in India. Because the informal sector accounts for most recycling, such a study might be best carried out in collaboration with local NGOs that work directly with the sector.

In this section we provide an assessment of the current available data set on waste management in Delhi, leading to a first approximate estimation of recycling rates to be then compared with the results of the new methodology we propose below. We also discuss a taxonomy of informal recyclers based on their means of transport and their area of collection, as well as how we could obtain better estimates of their absolute number.

5.3.1 The Waste Equation: Opening the Black Box

Available data sets by authorities and research centres on waste generation, composition, collection, and management in Delhi are generally uncertain and unreliable. Data on generation and composition are often collected at the landfill site (Kumar et al., 2009), therefore missing both the uncollected and the recyclable materials removed by the informal sector. This ends up regularly in an underestimation of both the generated quantity (as bridge weight at the landfill is rather only the collected waste) and the percentage of recyclable materials. In addition, the exact recycling rates, mainly achieved by the informal sector, are practically undetermined. Recyclable waste is at the core of the matter as several thousand livelihoods depend on it.

The World Bank (2012: 32) has recognized that the reliability of waste data is influenced by a number of factors, including

---

[3] Central Pollution Control Board (CPCB) of India is a statutory organization under the Ministry of Environment, Forest and Climate Change. It serves as a field formation and also provides technical services to the Ministry under the provisions of the Environment (Protection) Act, 1986.

Information collected at a non-representative moment. [...] Rarely it is disclosed at what stage the waste generation rates and composition were determined, and whether they were estimated or physically measured. The most accurate method measures the waste generated at source before any recycling, composting, burning, or open dumping takes place. However, the generation rate and composition are commonly calculated using waste quantities arriving at the final disposal site. This method of measurement does not fully represent the waste stream because the waste can be diverted prior to final disposal, especially in low and middle-income countries where the informal sector removes a large fraction of recyclables.

In order to shed light upon waste management, we propose the following waste equation:

$$
\text{Generated Waste (GW)} = \text{Formally Managed Waste (FMW)} \\
+ \text{Informally Recycled Waste (IRW)} \\
+ \text{Uncollected Waste (UW)}
$$

Composition (C): unknown

—*Composition (C)*: It is unknown since no characterization has been carried out. Compared to cities in wealthy countries, in Delhi this estimation is rendered more sophisticated given the disparities of income and socio-economic conditions. In Table 5.1 we present an estimation, done at the landfill site, that represents the recyclable

Table 5.1 Physical composition of (as waste %) of Municipal Solid Waste in Delhi

Year	Organic	Recyclable	Inert	Total
1982	57.7	8.3	34	100
1995	38.3	12.9	48.8	100
2002	36.6	17.2	46.2	100

Source: Talyan, 2008.

materials missed by the recyclers, rather than its total quantity at the source (Talyan, 2008).

—*Generated waste (GW)*: This includes waste generated by households, the commercial sector, and public cleaning. Industrial waste should not be accounted for, although in many cities it is mixed with the former categories (e.g. construction waste).

—*Formally Managed Waste (FMW)*: This is the portion of GW that is managed that is formally managed by the competent authorities (normally municipalities), be it public or privatized management. This includes waste derived to mainly the landfill and incinerators, with some minor attempts of composting or recycling. The MSM cost per tonne ranges between 1,000 and 1,500 Rupees per tonne (US$15–20).[4] The MSW management expenditure is about 20% of total municipal revenue expenditure (Hanrahan et al., 2006).

In Figure 5.1 we present an estimation of GW and FMW that underestimates GW and does not take into account IRW and UW.

—*Informally Recycled Waste (IRW)*: This is the waste recycled by the informal sector, mainly plastic, paper, glass, and metals. An estimation argues that, as of 2005, approximately 15% of Delhi's waste was recycled by the informal sector (Agarwal et al., 2005), although it might be higher than this.

—*Uncollected Waste (UW)*: This is the GW that is neither collected and managed and is often illegally dumped, and sometimes burned, inside or outside the city. A study reports that approximately 20–30% of the GW remains uncollected and was illegally dumped or burned in the open (Talyan, 2008).

In Delhi, the only exactly known quantity is FMW given by the quantity of waste that enters into the landfill, and more recently to the incinerators. This is about 9,000 tonnes per day. It should be taken into account

---

[4] In this chapter, I give prices in the Indian currency, Rupees, and then provide in parenthesis the conversion to US dollars. The conversion rate is of 65 Rupees for one US dollar (April 2017). Rupees are abbreviated as Rs.

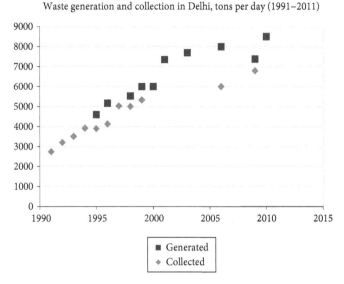

Figure 5.1 Generation and collection of municipal solid waste in Delhi (1991–2011).
Source: CPCB 2006; MCD 2012.

that irregularities in the weighting of waste occurs rather frequently, since companies get paid per tonne with an incentive to manipulate the statistics, and data are not easily made available. The exact quantities of all the other categories are unknown. From the current existing figures and the proposed waste equation, we can make the following per day estimations, as of the 2000s:

Generated Waste (GW) = Formally Managed Waste (FMW)
+ Informally Recycled Waste (IRW)
+ Uncollected Waste (UW)
100% GW = 9000 tonnes FMW + 15% IMW + 25% UW[5]
FMW = GW—(IMW + UW) = 100—(15 + 25) = 60%
15,000 t GW = 9000 t FMW + 2,250 t IMW + 3,750 t UW

---

[5] Being the known estimation between 20% and 30%, we here assume an average of 25%.

Following this estimation, if we assume that in Delhi there are about 175,000 recyclers,[6] and they collect in total 2,250 t, it means that on average they collect 13 kg of recyclable waste per day. IMW is likely underestimated. In this chapter we demonstrate that at least door-to-door recyclers collect much more. Before presenting the methodology and results of our research, in the next section we provide more details about the recyclers in Delhi, in particular showing that there are different types.

5.3.2 Who Are the Recyclers?

The informal recycling system is a sophisticated web of actors. Recyclers could be classified either by (1) their means of transport, or (2) by their area of collection:

(1) Means of transport
    —By foot: they collect waste with a bag walking around the streets, and can carry up to 50 kg (called street recyclers);
    —By cycle: they can carry up to 50/100 kg;
    —By *thela* (a tricycle with a cart): they cover a distance of a few kilometres and can carry 100/200 kg of waste.
(2) Area of collection (or leakage points; see green arrows in Figure 4.1).

Waste pickers collect recyclable waste along all the official waste management chain, from the points of generation to the disposal sites. These are the most important sites of collection:

2.1 Door-to-door collection: Here there are two main types.
    —General waste recyclers: most recyclers undertake door-to-door collection. They normally use a *thela*. Every day (one day off a week), early in the morning, they would collect waste

---

[6] Being the known estimation between 150,000 and 200,000, we here assume an average of 175,000 recyclers in Delhi.

from the households (generally from low-middle to upper class, excluding the slums) and segregate it in the neighbourhood itself. The non-recyclable (organic and other materials, like construction waste) is dumped at the transfer station. Instead, the recyclables (paper, plastic, metals, glass, rubber, etc.) are loaded on the *thela* and brought back to their communities.

—High value recyclables recyclers (*Thiawalas*): some households accumulate the most valuable recyclables materials (newspapers, glass bottles, metals, cardboard) and sell it regularly (e.g. once a month) to the recyclers. These recyclers go around neighbourhoods shouting 'kabari' (meaning waste), buy the waste and then sell it to waste dealers in the vicinity of the neighbourhood or back into their communities.

2.2 Transfer stations (also locally called dhalao or dustbins)

Normally at each transfer station there are one or more waste pickers, who further segregate the waste that is dumped there before the municipal truck comes to collect the waste and bring it to the landfill. Some of them even actually live at the transfer station.

2.3 Streets

Generally the poorest waste pickers, they walk around the city and collect whatever they can find with a preference for high-priced materials such as PET bottles, or, found rarely, glass bottles. They collect in the streets itself and in waste bins. Special occasions, like public events, or places, like the airport or markets, give them better opportunities.

2.4 Shops and offices

These places are a source of high-quality and high-priced materials (mostly paper and cardboard), often already segregated. The access to these places is often not free, in some cases there are unofficial tenders. In Delhi, the NDMC areas (the administrative, political, and financial centre of the city) represent the best example. In this case, *thela* are not allowed to enter so that the recyclable waste is collected by waste dealers' trucks, stored in the neighbourhood, and then transported to the outskirts of the city in bigger storage places.

2.5 Landfills
At both legal and illegal dumpsites, an army of waste pickers further segregates the waste that arrives there. Probably the most dangerous, unhealthy, and unpleasant workplace.

Figure 5.2 offers a summary of the different categories of recyclers. For the purpose of this study only waste pickers engaged in door-to-door collection (Figure 4.1), usually with a *thela*, were considered. This is because they are the most regular and easy to track. Plus, they offer the greatest potential for a future decentralized waste management system based on the principles of sustainability and justice.

Door-to-door recyclers in Delhi tend to be male, aged from 20 to 40 years and with no education. They might work alone, or with one or two helpers. Each covers the same neighbourhood every day, ranging from 200 to 400 houses. Their working day starts early in the morning, from 4am to 8 am, and finishes in the afternoon, with an average of about 8 working hours per day. This accounts for about half an hour for the travel to the neighbourhood, four hours for door-to-door collection and first segregation, 45 minutes for the travel back, and lasts three hours for the second segregation. The first segregation separates the recyclable materials from the non-recyclable, and the second one the recyclables by material type. They take one day off per week, and go for long holidays of between two and four weeks once a year for which they rely on a substitute. They report as their biggest fear that some private company will take away their source of livelihood.

As we discuss in the following section, although we can easily identify the different categories, it is rather difficult to estimate how many recyclers, in total and per category.

Area of collection	Means of transport		
---	Foot	Cycle	Thela (tricycle with a cart)
Households		x	x
Shops and offices	x	x	x
Transfer station	x	x	
Street	x	x	
Landfills	x		

Figure 5.2 Collection and transport of waste in Delhi's informal sector.

5.3.3 How Many Recyclers?

The total number of recyclers present in Delhi is unknown, since no official register exists. The commonly accepted estimate argues that in Delhi there are approximately 150,000–200,000 waste pickers (Chaturvedi and Gidwani, 2011: 131). At the 2011 census, the population of Delhi (officially the National Capital Territory of Delhi) was about 18.8 mn. So this figure resonates with the World Bank estimation that about 1% of the urban population is involved in the informal recycling sector.

There are different methodologies that could be used to broadly estimate their number and corroborate these broad estimations. We outline here a few possible methods:

(1) If we know GW and its composition, and we assume that 100% of the recyclable waste is collected, and we know how much each waste picker recycles on average, then we could estimate how many waste pickers. If we know also FMW and UW, then we could estimate the exact quantity of IRW.

(2) If we know the total quantity of IRW, and how much each waste picker recycles on average. IRW could be extrapolated with the data of the formal recycling industry, that however are not public. We would have to assume that all waste recycled proceeds from the informal sector, a rather reasonable assumption in Delhi.

(3) If we can estimate how many households a waste picker covers with her/his door-to-door collection, then by knowing the total population (not exactly the case in Delhi), we could estimate the number of waste pickers (however, we would be assuming that all households are the same, and this is obviously not the case).

(4) If the municipality establishes an official register. This option presents a series of obstacles, given the informality of the sector, starting from the fact that many waste pickers do not hold identification cards and are often very mobile.

The methods listed here offer an idea of the complexity of the task. A combination of different methods could be of help. However, the majority of the options can only be undertaken by public authorities given the high amount of resources needed. Therefore, the option chosen for

Date:		
Recycler name:		
Type of waste	Quantity (Kg)	Payment (Rs)
Paper		
Plastic		
Metals		
…		

Figure 5.3 Stylized model of a junk dealer record book.

our investigation has involved the selection of a sample of waste pickers in order to estimate: (1) What type and how much waste they recycle, and (2) How much they earn out of this activity. The proposed methodology does not allow for the estimation of the total number of waste pickers. However, if combined with an estimation of GW and C to be carried out by public authorities, this would start filling the gaps. For the moment, we will be able to compare our results with the ones obtained here above with the proposed waste equation, and in particular that waste pickers recycle on average 13 kg of materials per day.

5.4 Proposed Methodology: Data from the Junk Dealers' Record Books

A typical recycler would sell his/her waste to a waste dealer (locally called kabari or kabadiwala) at the end of a working day after some sorting of the day's pickings. The kabari weighs the material and takes note of both the quantity received and the payment to the waste pickers in his records books, per type of waste (Figures 5.3 and 5.4). Kabaris' record books represent a reliable and detailed source of information on the types, payments, and quantity of recyclable materials. Kabaris regularly maintain record books with details of daily and monthly transactions with each of their suppliers, the recyclers, with whom they tend to have long-term relationships (Figure 5.5). Most of the kabaris have set up their establishments in communities where recyclers live and carry out the sorting activities. Each of the communities can host a few to a 100 kabari businesses and can be considered a recovery (or recycling) hub.

Figure 5.4 An actual record book: Each column corresponds to a recycler, and on the top it indicates his/her name and the date. Below, the list of materials with weight (kg) and payment (Indian Rupees). The language is Hindi.

Figure 5.5 A junk dealer (orange t-shirt) considered in this study buying waste from a recycler, weighting it, and making notes in his record book.
Pictures: Federico Demaria.

A typical kabari's record book consists of the particulars laid out in Figures 5.3 and 5.4.

Samples were randomly collected from different recycling and informal resource recovery hubs around Delhi, in collaboration with AIKMM. Kabaris were informed about the purpose of the research and the importance of sharing their record books. The information thus gathered was transcribed to digital data sheets with the help of a local research assistant.

Record books of 11 kabaris who procured waste from 111 waste recyclers between 2011 and 2012 were analysed. All 11 kabaris and over 50 recyclers were interviewed in order to get additional insights into the

Sr. No	Waste dealer	No. of wastepickers	Neighborhood name	Area of Delhi	Time span
1	Raj Kumar	10	Madanpur Khadar	South Delhi	November 2011 – November 2012
2	Mukimji	4	Sahabad Dairy – Rohini	North Delhi	January 2012 – March 2013
3	Munvari	10	Bohapur	East Delhi	February 2011 – September 2011
4	Narender	13	Madanpur Khadar	South Delhi	January 2011 – December 2011
5	Raja	14	Seema Puri	North-East Delhi	January 2011 – October 2011
6	Rajesh Jaiswal	2	Shri Niwash Puri	South Delhi	September 2010 – September 2011
7	Sunil	12	R.K. Puram Sector 4	South-West Delhi	January 2012 – September 2012
Total	7	65			

Figure 5.6 Kabaris and waste pickers selected for the analysis; names have been changed to ensure anonymity.

system and to interpret the data sets. The real names of the participating kabaris have been withheld in order to ensure privacy. The final analysis was carried out on only 7 kabaris record books and 65 waste pickers (see Figure 5.6). This was done to ensure consistency in the data. The main criteria for this selection was that data should be available for at least six months, while the ideal target was 12 months in order to control for any potential seasonal variations.

Figure 5.6 gives a list of kabaris considered for the final analysis. The complete digital data sheet comprises 30,000 entries given by the numbers of waste pickers, the sub-types of materials sold to the kabaris, and the number of worked days (on an average 26 days per month).

The collected data provide a response to the following questions: How much do recyclers collect on average per day (total and per type)? In how many categories do the recyclers segregate the waste (paper, PET, plastic, mix, tins, etc.)? How much do they earn?

In the following section we provide the results.

5.5 Results: The Metabolism of the Informal Recycling Sector

5.5.1 Kabaris: Segregation of the Recycled Waste in Types and Sub-Types

Waste pickers collect the waste door-to-door and then segregate waste in two subsequent phases. The first phase is carried out at the neighbourhood level, right after the door-to-door collection, to eliminate the non-recyclables. These non-recyclables are disposed of in the street bins and

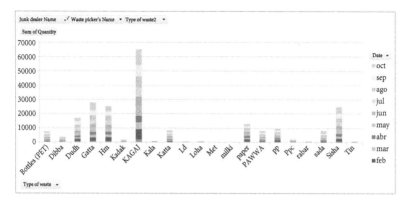

Figure 5.7 Total quantity managed by Raja (junk dealer) in 2011, by sub-type of waste (kg). For example Kagaj (paper), Gatta (cardboard), Dudh (plastic), Loha (iron), Rabar (rubber).

the recyclables are loaded into sacks and brought back to the communities for further segregation. The second segregation often takes place at the kabari shop, either by the waste-collectors themselves or by kabaris' employees. Figure 5.7 is an example of the different sub-types of materials which are sorted depending on the material type and quality (e.g. clean white paper and dirty paper). The characterization of this second segregation varies among kabaris, because of different marketing strategies, making it difficult to compare data among them. For the current analysis, it was therefore decided to limit the analysis to the type of materials— paper, plastic, metals, and glass. This also makes it comparable with international waste generation data.

5.5.2 Door-to-Door Waste Recyclers
5.5.2.1 Quantity
The average quantity of recyclable materials collected by a door-to-door waste-picker in Delhi (2011–2012) is on average 50 kg per day. Figure 5.8 and Table 5.2 show the percentage break up for each material. To this quantity reported in the kabaris' record books, one should add about 3 kg of waste food (e.g. roti and rice), which refers to food waste used as animal fodder (mainly fed to lactating cows), plus a few hundred grams for hair and metals, per day.

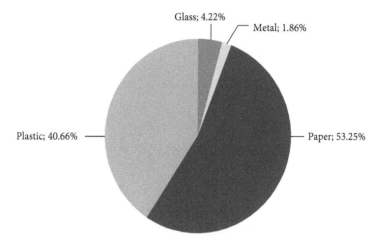

Figure 5.8 Per type percentage of the quantity of recyclable materials collected by a door-to-door waste recycler in Delhi.

Table 5.2 Average quantity of recyclable materials per type for a door-to-door waste collector in Delhi, 2011–2012

	Kg	%
Paper	27	53
Plastic	20	41
Glass	2	4
Metal	1	2
Total	50	100

5.5.2.2   Income and expenditure

The main source of income for waste pickers is from the materials they sell to the kabaris (Figure 5.9). On average, from the analysed record books between 2011 and 2012, the average monthly earnings are Rs. 6,000 (about US$100). This is the gross revenue from the daily sale of the materials. Table 5.3 shows the percentage of the revenue earned from each type of material.

The record books also point to additional sources of income that complement this revenue. This is earned by the sale of items like food waste,

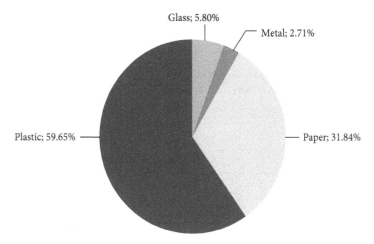

Figure 5.9 Percentages of revenue earned from various types of materials by waste pickers, on average.

Table 5.3 Average income per type for a door-to-door waste picker in Delhi, 2011–2012 (Rs., %)

	Rupees (Rs)	%
Plastic	3,579	60
Paper	1,911	31
Glass	348	6
Metal	162	3
Total	6,000	100

metals, and hair to more specialized junk dealers who offer higher rates. These items can fetch anywhere between Rs. 45 to Rs. 2500/kg: for example tin and iron, between Rs. 1 to 45/kg; hair, Rs. 2,500/kg; and food waste, Rs. 6/kg. Table 5.4 and Figure 5.10 show the average revenue per month from these complementary sources as declared by waste-collectors during the interviews. This brings the total revenue to about Rs. 8,500 per month (about US$120).

Many recyclers also reported income through monthly fees from the households they served. Some waste pickers occasionally engaged

Table 5.4 Average payments for a door-to-door waste collector in Delhi, 2011–2012

Income	Rupees (Rs)	%
Payment from Kabari	6,000	70
Metals	1,500	18
Hair	500	6
Roti	500	6
Total	8,500	100

Average income for a door-to-door waste-collector in Delhi, 2011–12

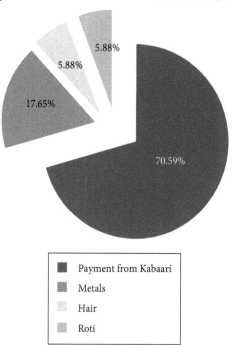

Figure 5.10 Pie chart of average payments for a door-to-door waste collector in Delhi, 2011–2012.

in other odd jobs for extra income. However, all these complementary sources of income are not regular and therefore difficult to quantify, hence they have been kept out of the general profile (Figure 5.10).

Given that the 70% of the waste pickers' income is earned from deals with the kabaris, both parties have to ensure high levels of accuracy in the book keeping. However, in order to ensure accuracy of the data on income, recyclers were also interviewed about their main expenses. The data on expenses varies significantly from family to family, depending on the size, numbers of earnings members, location, etc. The data presented here refers to a 4–5 member family where occasionally other family members earn a complementary income. About 70% of the income is allocated towards food, in other words for their mere physiological reproduction. The rest goes for expenses such as housing, health, schooling of children, clothing, phone, and transport. Such structure of the recyclers' household spending proves that their involvement in the informal recycling sector is a survival strategy. Therefore, despite door-to-door waste pickers earning an income which is about the minimum wage, it just ensures the survival of the workers and their families but is not sufficient to meet needs beyond that.

5.6 Discussion: Policy Proposals in Relation to the Waste Management and Environmental Services of Informal Recyclers

Our methodology has generated data on the informal recycling sector with a significant reliability. These data suggest the following findings.

First, the result that the average revenue is about Rs. 8,500 per month for the period between 2011 and 2012 demonstrates that the income obtained from waste picking is close to the minimum wage (which was Rs. 6,422 in 2011 and Rs. 7,254 in 2012)[7] and above the poverty line

---

[7] Current Minimum Wage. Labour Department, Delhi Government. Available at: https://lab our.delhi.gov.in/content/order-nofno14202mwviiipart-file5972-5986-dated-14102022-enha ncement-minimum-wages (Accessed 19 October 2022).

(which was Rs. 5,000 per month for a family of five in urban areas).[8] This means that the revenue is significant enough for a social group that has no other employment opportunities and therefore should not be easily dismissed. Instead, public authorities should make considerable efforts to improve both the living and working conditions of waste workers. A significant threat is posed by privatization that threatens their access to waste, while waste-to-energy incinerators compete for high-calorific recyclable materials.

Second, the result on the average quantity recycled shows the significant contribution of the sector to Delhi's waste management system which not only results in savings for the municipalities but also reduces pressure on the landfills. Door-to-door recyclers collect more than 50 kg per day of recyclable materials, that is significantly higher than the estimation we provided above based on the waste equation (13 kg). One should take into account that this category of recyclers is the one who collects the most, compared for example to those who collect in the streets or landfills. The anomaly relies upon the fact that the society receives these services completely free of cost, while for the same services private companies are remunerated handsomely by public authorities. Therefore, the need to fill this gap is urgent and should be reflected in future waste management plans. To this end, we report hereafter the key demands put forward by the organized groups of recyclers in Delhi. Then, we explore the details of two policy suggestions to compensate recyclers for the waste management and environmental services they currently provide to society as a whole free of cost. As we will show, the data provided above would be a fundamental base for such policies.

5.6.1 Policy Proposals by the Informal Recyclers

The struggles of informal recyclers could be understood in terms of capital de-accumulation, for re-appropriating the expropriated resources and against the degradation of their means of existence and bodies. Most commonly, the informal recycling sector demands the following:

---

[8] Press Note on Poverty Estimates, 2011–2012. Government of India Planning Commission July 2013. Available at: http://planningcommission.nic.in/news/pre_pov2307.pdf.

5.6.1.1 Recognition
Indian society should give recyclers the dignity, respect, and social recognition they deserve. Public authorities should grant them legal recognition.

5.6.1.2 Legalize access to waste at source
Public authorities should ensure recyclers access to waste at source, legalizing what is de facto already a reality. This could be done providing an identification card that proves recyclers' status as service providers and a waistcoat that makes them visible and easily recognizable.

5.6.1.3 Segregation at source
Public authorities should launch public awareness campaigns, in collaboration with recyclers and residents, to inform the citizens about the problems related to waste management. In particular, they should at least enforce the simple two-bin segregation system of dry and wet waste. This would significantly reduce the health hazards and time requirements currently associated with the segregation of recyclable materials. Additionally, it would also improve the quality of the segregated materials, increasing both the quantity recycled and the revenue obtained by the recyclers.

5.6.1.4 Payment for waste management and environmental services
Waste pickers should receive a payment for the services they provide to society, at least as much as the private companies receive. This would involve not only a payment on productivity base (Rupees per kg), to guarantee minimum wages but also ensure welfare benefits so as to provide a beyond-survival livelihood opportunity for recyclers. We provide more details for these here below.

5.6.1.5 A way forward: Decentralization and zero-waste strategy
In the long term, public authorities need to envision an environmentally-friendly waste management system that aims to reduce its dependence on landfills and ensures maximum recovery of resources at source—a system that relies on a participative decentralized approach in which roles and responsibilities are clearly assigned to each stakeholder. The public authorities need to take charge and all the other stakeholders should be

involved in respective activities like collection, segregation, processing, dissemination of information, and awareness building. Source segregation and door-to-door collection should be mandatory across the board and secondary segregation areas should be provided within each ward of the city to avoid transportation. Emphasis should be laid on maximizing recovery from MSW, including organic waste through compost and biogas plants.

The mobilization of recyclers has given some results. In 2016 the Ministry of Environment and Forests has revised the MSW legislation incorporating two of these claims, although the challenge rests in the implementation:[9] (1) The source segregation of waste has been mandated to channelize the waste to wealth by recovery, reuse, and recycle. Waste generators would now have to now segregate waste into three streams: Biodegradables, Dry (plastic, paper, metal, wood, etc.), and Domestic Hazardous waste before handing it over to the collector; (2) Integration of waste pickers and waste dealers, Kabadiwalas, in the formal system should be done by State Governments, and Self Help Groups, or any other group to be formed.

Hereafter we discuss possible ways to operationalize the payment to recyclers for their waste management and environmental services, based on the results obtained with this research. Whether these, or similar, policies will be implemented depends on the balance of power making it clear that these are not techno-managerial issues, but deeply political ones.

5.6.2 Waste Management Services

The public authorities have engaged different private waste management firms for the waste management services across Delhi, while they keep ignoring recyclers for similar services. For this chapter the contract between the Municipal Corporation of Delhi (hereafter MCD) and the private company Delhi MSW Solutions Limited (a subsidiary of

---

[9] Ministry of Environment and Forests (2016). 'Solid Waste Management Rules Revised after 16 Years; Rules Now Extend to Urban and Industrial Areas': Javadekar. Available at: http://pib. nic.in/newsite/PrintRelease.aspx?relid=138591 (Accessed on 20 March 2017).

Waste management services (Rs/ton)	Civil Line,...	NDMC	Waste-collectors
Door-to-door collection	Yes	No	Yes
Collection & Transportation	Yes	Yes	No
Disposal in landfill	Yes	No	No
Recycling	No	No	Yes
Total	**1440**	**800**	**0**

Figure 5.11 Distribution of waste management services, and public remuneration thereof, in Delhi.

the Hyderabad-based Ramky Group) was considered. The contract between the two parties was signed in 2008 for Door-to-Door Collection, Transportation and developing an integrated municipal solid waste processing (ISWM) facility and Sanitary Landfill to serve the following areas: Civil Lines, Rohini Vasant Kunj, and Dwaraka-Pappankala. The company receives a tipping fee (predetermined amount) per tonne based on the quantity of waste they dispose every month. The tipping fee model disincentivizes any environmentally-friendly practices such as waste prevention, recycling, or diversion. It is no surprise then that despite MSW Solutions' contractual obligation to set up a 'Waste processing facility', no recycling actually takes place despite the clear indications in this sense specified in the contract.[10] There is also a lack of transparency in the payment and decisions regarding the 'tipping fee rates'. We failed to obtain this information, despite the Right to Information applications by AIKMM.

It was unofficially ascertained that the 'tipping rate fee' for this contract is about Rs. 1,500 per tonne. For example, a previously existing contract in NDMC area, which only included Collection and Transportation from the transfer station to the landfill, was about Rs. 800 per tonne. Normally the rates are decided through a tender, ideally in two stages, first technical and then financial.

[10] North corporation raps firm tasked with waste management. 5 June 2013. Times of India. Available at: http://timesofindia.indiatimes.com/city/delhi/North-corporation-raps-firm-tasked-with-waste-management/articleshow/20434098.cms (Accessed on 19 October 2022). Households not sorting waste before disposal; contractors doing a poor job. 23 June 2015. Times of India. Available at: http://timesofindia.indiatimes.com/city/delhi/Households-not-sorting-waste-before-disposal-contractors-doing-a-poor-job/articleshow/18141049.cms (Accessed on 19 October 2022).

Figure 5.11 shows that while private companies are remunerated for their waste management services, waste collectors are not. This represents an anomaly for the following reasons:

(1) Waste pickers do not carry out 'Collection and Transportation' and 'Disposal in Landfill'; because they recycle the materials, these two steps are not required.

(2) If on average they recycle about 50 kg of materials per day, they actually collect about 300 kg at the doorstep, assuming that recyclable materials would be at most 20% of the total generated waste. The remaining 80%, about 250 kg, is left at the dustbin as residual. This means recyclers provide for free a service of door-to-door collection, right at the doorstep.

(3) Recycling is by all means, economic and environmentally, a preferable option to dispose in landfill and incineration.

Therefore, waste pickers should be at least be equally remunerated for their services as private companies. By a calculation, if MSW Solutions receive about Rs. 1.4/kg, then each waste recycler should receive, on average, about Rs. 70 per day (50 kg at 1.4 Rs./kg), more or less one US dollar. They could then be additionally compensated for the door-to-door collection (250 kg per day) with, for example, another 70 Rs. This means that each recycler should receive about 2,100 Rs. for each of these services, for a total of about 4,200 Rs. per month (about US$65). At the least, minimum wages (as per Act) should be guaranteed as they are for private company workers.

The idea of recognizing waste collectors as service providers is not new. The proposal of compensating them for their services has already been implemented in other countries. For instance, in Bogota (Colombia) waste pickers are being paid on the basis of how much they collect (US$50/tonne; about 3 Rs./kg) since December 2012.[11]

---

[11] Victory for wastepickers. 25 March 2013. EJOLT Blog. Available at: http://www.ejolt.org/2013/03/victory-for-waste-pickers/ (Accessed on 19 October 2022).

5.6.3   Environmental Services

In environmental economics, there is a growing debate on 'payment for ecosystems services' where the argument is that monetary compensation is needed in order to value nature. For instance, waste-to-energy incinerators in Delhi receive subsidies from the Clean Development Mechanism of the Kyoto Protocol because they supposedly reduce greenhouse gas emissions compared to the landfill as a baseline. Now, considering recycling holds a higher position in the hierarchy of waste management options to both incineration and landfilling, similar incentives need to be put in place. Recycling presents a number of environmental benefits, of which the most important are:

(1) A reduction in water and energy consumption;
(2) a reduction in greenhouse gas emissions;
(3) avoided impact on biodiversity;
(4) avoided pressure on landfills.

Economists at the Brazilian Institute for Applied Economics (2010) have drafted a policy document regarding the payment to recyclers for their environmental services, motivated by the fact that the average income that they receive is not adequate in relation to the service they provide to the environment. Figure 5.12 reports the monetary values estimated for these environmental benefits per type of material (values given

	Environmental benefits			Quantity recycled by waste-collectors	Payment for environmental benefits
	R$/t	Rs/t	Rs/Kg	Kg per day	Rs per day
Iron	74	1937	2	1	2
Aluminium	339	8875	9	0	1
Paper	24	628	1	27	17
Plastic	56	1466	1	20	29
Glass	11	288	0	2	1
Total				50	49

Figure 5.12 Valuation of the uncompensated environmental benefits of waste pickers' work.
Source: Ijgosse, 2012.

in Brazilian Reals and Indian Rupees). For example, in the case of greenhouse gases, the cited report calculates the compensation on the basis of the avoided emissions at the price of the carbon markets. This type of subsidy is also earned by waste-to-energy plants, so that there is no reason why the recyclers should not also be renumerated.

In conclusion, if the quantity of materials recycled is considered and multiplied with the corresponding payment rate for each material, each waste collector in Delhi should receive an average of 50 Rs. per day (i.e. 1,500 Rs. per month, about €20).

The NGO report 'Cooling agents: An Examination of the role of the Informal Recycling Sector in Mitigating Climate Change' (Chintan, 2009: 3) reports that 'the informal sector in Delhi alone accounts for estimated net GHG reductions of 962,133 tonnes of carbon dioxide equivalent (TCO2e) each year. These savings are the same as removing roughly 175,000 passenger vehicle from the roads annually, or providing electricity to about 130,000 homes for one year (US estimates)'. This refers to the avoided emissions due to recycling. However, one should also add the avoided emissions due to the fact that recyclers do not use fossil fuel for the collection and transportation of waste, since they go by either foot or cycle.

5.7 Conclusions: Why Should Informal Recyclers Be Taken into Account?

In this chapter, we have attempted to move forward our understanding of the informal recycling sector. Recyclers should be taken into account: (1) To better understand waste generation and therefore implement better management; (2) To reduce the environmental impacts of waste management; and (3) To reduce poverty and inequalities.

In the case of Delhi, we have proven, first, that door-to-door recyclers obtain a revenue close to the minimum wage from recycling which only ensures their survival. Hence, if the public authorities cannot offer an alternative occupation, a focus on public policies to improve working conditions is essential.

Second, recyclers and the informal recycling sector as a whole, collect and recycle a considerable quantity of recyclable material, subsidizing society (in terms of savings in waste-handling costs for public authorities due to a significant reduction in quantity to be managed) and reducing pressure on the environment. For instance, there is no exact quantification of the savings, but we could estimate that if waste pickers recycle about 20% of the total waste generated in Delhi (e.g. 2,000 tonnes per day out of 10,000) and that public authorities pay to private companies for the management approximately 1,500 Rupees per tonne, then the total savings are about 3 mn Rs. per day (US$45,000), and 110 crores Rs. per year (US$15 mn). For this reason, they should be recognized and even compensated as in Colombia and Brazil where recyclers receive welfare benefits or monetary compensation for their waste management and environmental services. This can be an example that monetary valuation, although a simplification, can be useful under certain conditions, as argued by Kallis et al. (2013), for instance when 'it is part of socio-political processes that bring more equality and improve the environment'.

Third, further research on the informal recycling sector and waste management sector in general is needed in order to recognize its importance and inform public policies centred around social justice and ecological sustainability. In particular, basic research is needed to understand the quantity and composition of the generated waste and the economics of the informal waste sector. This should evaluate the effectiveness of existing public policies to integrate waste recyclers, so that they can be replicated elsewhere. Last, there is a need to start doing research also on informal waste recyclers in high-income countries, a growing phenomenon that finds public authorities unprepared.

6

Conclusions

How Environments Are Shaped, Politicized, and Contested

In this chapter we conclude by showing how our case studies provide a new understanding to the three research questions mentioned in Chapter 1. In particular, we show how they present a range of experiences to inform theory on how environments are shaped, politicized, and contested. Figure 6.1 summarizes the main theoretical contributions. We have shed light on the relationship between social metabolism and conflicts, with a focus on recycling and examining from a situated political ecology perspective. First, a situated understanding of waste shows that there is a complex relationship between its materiality and political economy; they are co-constituted and produce different socio-metabolic configurations. Ultimately, the co-evolution of materiality and political economy (including social and institutional dynamics) shapes metabolisms and as a result political opportunities are fostered and foreclosed. Changes in the social metabolism are mediated by the social, economic, and institutional logics at play. They ultimately lead to socio-metabolic reconfigurations which, in turn, eventually lead to ecological distribution conflicts. People struggle to defend, or realize, desirable situated urban political ecologies. Second, we showed that analysing the political economy of these processes, be it at the global or city level, can help to clarify why the metabolism changes in the way it does, meaning its driving forces. More specifically, we argue that capital accumulation takes place at waste-based commodity frontiers through extra-economic means, namely both dispossession and contamination. Third, we attempted to investigate the social relations of recycling, which means the social relationships that recyclers must enter into in order to survive, to produce, and to reproduce their means of life. These are inherently intertwined

The Political Ecology of Informal Waste Recyclers in India. Federico Demaria, Oxford University Press.
© Federico Demaria 2023. DOI: 10.1093/oso/9780192869050.003.0006

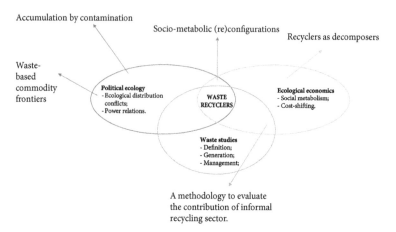

Figure 6.1 The main theoretical contributions of this book.
Source: Federico Demaria.

with the waste metabolism, be it global or urban. We suggested that re-cyclers play in human societies a similar role to the decomposers in nat-ural ecosystems. We evaluated the contribution of informal recycling in Delhi and called for a due compensation of recyclers' waste management and environmental services, instead of a dispossession from their means of production, and a shifting of social costs of enterprises and consumers to them. The struggles of recyclers constitute an attempt to re-politicize waste metabolism beyond techno-managerial solutions by fostering counter-hegemonic discourses and praxis.

Hereafter we explain more in detail what new understanding our re-sults provide to the research questions posed in Chapter 1.

(1) How and why does the metabolism of waste cause social conflicts, where, and under what conditions?

We have attempted to shed light on the relationship between social metabolism and conflicts, with a focus on recycling and looking from a situated political ecology perspective. Changes in the social metabolism lead to conflicts, but how do differences in the structure and nature of particular social metabolisms create different conflict dynamics? And when does this happen?

Obviously, different societies have distinctive metabolisms (compare, for instance, hunter-gatherer, subsistence agriculture, or industrial societies, and the many forms within these broad categories) that sometimes co-exist and surely evolve over time. Their metabolism can be characterized by both their *material dimension*, that is, the amount and composition of materials and energy they consume, as well as by their *immaterial dimension*, that is, their political economy and the institutions of society that define their sources, type of extraction, distribution, and disposal models of materials and energy across the members of a society. We proposed to use the term 'socio-metabolic configurations' to refer to both material and immaterial dimensions of society's metabolism.

We argued that any socio-metabolic re-configuration produces a new situated political ecology. Our case studies present a range of experiences to inform theory on how environments are shaped, politicized, and contested. A situated understanding of waste shows that there is a complex relationship between its materiality (e.g. volume, composition, density, and its biophysical transformation) and political economy (e.g. ownership, access, and value struggles). This represents an attempt to simultaneously mobilize the concepts of social metabolism from ecological economics and critical approaches from political ecology. Socio-metabolic configurations are inherently produced through material and political economic processes; there is no 'original' or 'real' moment in which either materiality or political economy serves as context or structure. While one or the other may drive change in a particular time/place, they are both always already co-constituted. A sudden change in one or the other can generate feedback that affects the overall metabolism. In both the cases presented, material flows of waste are subject to conflicting logics and rationalities that results in dialectical processes, where simultaneous opposing forces act. Both cases demonstrate that environmental politics can foster alliances (likely or not) among different social groups. What ultimately develops out of a conflict where different languages of valuation are deployed, is a socio-metabolic configuration.

To understand the implications for the sustainability of social metabolism, one must not only look into the quantification of metabolic flows, but also into the power relations that shape the reconfiguration of metabolism(s), that is, the political economy. Ultimately, the co-evolution of materiality and political economy (including social and institutional dynamics) transforms/shapes metabolisms and as a result political opportunities are fostered and foreclosed. Therefore, we argue that ecological distribution conflicts do not only emerge out of an increase in the social metabolism (i.e. increased extraction of materials; Martinez Alier, 2002), but out of such socio-metabolic re-configurations.[1] People struggle to defend, or realize, desirable situated urban political ecologies. Since these are often contradictory, conflicts emerge and the final outcome depends upon the balance of power to impose a certain socio-metabolic configuration.

In the case of shipbreaking in Alang and Sosiya, we showed that economic development led to an increase of the shipping capacity, which in turn leads—sooner or later—to an increase in the supply of ships for scraps. In the second half of the twentieth century, the shipbreaking industry moved from developed countries to Asia in search of lower operating costs, due to less strict labour and environmental legislation. This turned it from a highly mechanized industry into a labour-intensive one and with serious environmental impacts. Therefore, the shipbreaking industry—as a consequence of changes in the global metabolism—introduced a new socio-metabolic configuration at the local scale, that in turn is being contested. While ship owners and breakers obtained large profits, farmers and fishers resisted such re-configuration because it threatened their livelihood. They did not resist an increase in the shipping capacity per se, but how this created a new situated political ecology characterized by cost-shifting in the shipbreaking process. The materiality relates to the quantity of ships to be scrapped and their composition. The political economy has to do with how, where, and by whom ships are managed. If the political economy of shipbreaking had been different, that is, with an implemented strict international legislation that ensured a proper dismantling of the ships in dry docks, then it would have not generated such contestation.

In the case of Delhi, the rapid increase in waste generation since the 1990s led to a new socio-metabolic configuration. While on one hand this enabled waste pickers to earn livelihoods, on the other hand it required

---

[1] I acknowledge that Giacomo D'Alisa generously shared with me his ideas on this issue, in particular the fact that conflicts emerge out of the clash among different metabolisms, and not simply out of the increase of the industrial metabolism.

a response by public authorities to face a looming public health crisis. Such a response, with privatization and the introduction of incineration, consolidated the throughput of waste in a single formal value chain that constituted a new socio-metabolic configuration. For instance, the metabolization of waste in Delhi (India) has to do with the production, throughput, and processing of waste. The materiality relates to the quantity, composition, and calorific value of waste. The political economy has to do with how, where, and by whom it is managed (private, public, or informal sector; recycling, incineration, or landfill, etc.). Conflicts erupted because waste pickers saw their access to waste threatened and middle-class residents perceived deleterious impact on air quality and the concomitant health risks. The new configuration inhibited the production of desirable situated political ecologies for these two social groups and eventually leads to a social mobilization to reverse it.

The two cases investigated demonstrate that ecological distribution conflicts do not emerge merely from an increase of the social metabolism, but from socio-metabolic re-configurations. Of course the former is linked to the latter. In Alang-Sosiya it is the increase of the shipping capacity, while in Delhi it is the increase of waste generation. However, these facts per se do not lead to conflicts. They are instead mediated by the social, economic, and institutional logics at play. In fact, the conflicts are not concomitant to the increase of social metabolism, but eventually appear in a second phase—in shipbreaking, once the economic crisis materializes (and consequently the Baltic Dry Index falls); while in Delhi once public authorities implement a policy shift. Therefore, we do not seek to invalidate the theory that there is a link between the increase of social metabolism and ecological distribution conflicts, but instead we propose to introduce a nuanced approached to show that: (1) the materiality and political economy are co-constituted, and (2) contestations over the (re)configuration of urban metabolisms span these spheres as people struggle to realize situated urban political ecologies.

In the following section we explore the political economy of these processes, be it at the global or city level. This can help to clarify why the metabolism changes in the way it does, meaning its driving forces.

(2) How do capitalist dynamics and power relations shape waste metabolisms unevenly?

We proposed to understand waste metabolism looking, apart from its materiality like ecological economics does, also to the political economy. This includes different geographical scales, from the global to the urban level. Here we intend to clarify why the metabolism changes in the way it does, meaning its driving forces. We argue that capital accumulation takes place at waste-based commodity frontiers through extra-economic means, namely both dispossession and contamination. The ways that waste quality and quantity, as well as access and rights to waste, both reflect and reproduce relations of social power.

Above we argued that changes in the social metabolism mediated by the social, economic, and institutional logics at play lead to socio-metabolic reconfigurations which, in turn, eventually lead to ecological distribution conflicts. Following Martinez Alier (2002) we defined these as conflicts on the access to natural resources and services and on the burdens of pollution or other environmental impacts that arise because of unequal property rights and inequalities of power and income among humans (both international and internal to each state). Then the question remains: What drives those changes in the social metabolism, or else the socio-metabolic re-configurations?

Already in the theoretical framework we argued how insights from political economy can be of help. In particular, we put emphasis on the processes of capital accumulation. Apart from the economic processes (i.e. the production and capitalization of surplus value), there are extra-economic ones. These have to do with: (1) Dispossession, literally the liberation of assets or, said differently, the separation of workers from the means of production; and (2) Contamination, the process by which the capital system socializes costs, through successful cost-shifting, which degrades the means of existence and bodies of human beings (as well as of other species). Both are at the core of ecological distribution conflicts. For instance, the former relates to 'the access to natural resources and services', while the latter with 'the burdens of pollution or other environmental impacts'. Both aim to expand the scale and scope of capital accumulation through extra-economic means (i.e. force), therefore relying upon uneven power relations. These means include dynamics that—in principle—have nothing to do with the market itself ('the economic' in its strict sense), such as conquest, enslavement, robbery, violence, legal changes, and ideological-discursive changes. They definitively intersect with other forms of oppression, be it class, caste, gender, or race. The re-sulting environmental injustice eventually leads to conflicts where im-pacted actors attempt to resolve such unequal distribution defending desirable situated ecologies. We think it is worth recalling literally from Chapter 1 how Kapp recognized the conflictive nature of social costs remediation, and its relation with power, as the 'political history of the last 150 years can be interpreted as a revolt of large masses of people (in-cluding small business) against social costs […] an integral part of the gradual access to political power by groups formerly excluded from such power'. Where on one hand 'pressure groups and vested interests have been able to distort and abuse the legitimate struggles for a more equal distribution of social costs, to the detriment of society', on the other hand a counter-movement (in Polanyi's terms) arises with 'the emergence of an "anti-capitalist" mentality and an intense quest for greater security by large masses of people who have to bear the brunt of the social losses of rapid change'. This is exactly what we call ecological distribution conflicts, which are extensively documented by the Environmental Justice Atlas (www.ejatlas.org). These dynamics are exemplified by the presented case studies as follows.

Shipbreaking in the developing world is not just an externality but a successful case of cost-shifting, or else, capital accumulation by contam-ination. In this case, capital accumulation by contamination takes place thanks to the indirect profits due to saved costs (i.e. indirect subsidies). Ship owners and shipbreakers obtain large profits dumping the environ-mental costs on workers, local farmers, and fishers. The latter see their means of existence and bodies degraded, at the economic benefit of the former. In the Supreme Court case we analysed, environmental and civil activists emphasized the injustice of an unequal distribution of costs and benefits and the disproportionate environmental and social dam-ages at the local scale, considering local livelihood and ecosystem losses as incommensurable with benefits at other scales. Business interests and public authorities instead valued monetary and environmental benefits at the national scale, assuming them commensurable with local losses, and finding a positive balance.

Instead, the waste struggle in Delhi has to do with both dynamics. First, waste pickers protest against the dispossession of their means of livelihood (i.e. access to waste upon which their livelihoods depend), or else assets that are transformed into capital. They also struggle against cost-shifting. In fact, they complain about the health risk incurred because waste is not segregated at source by residents. Plus, they claim a compensation for their unpaid management and environmental services. Second, middle-class residents oppose waste-to-energy because of its perceived deleterious impact on air quality and the concomitant health risks. In the latter, capital accumulation by contamination not only takes place thanks to the indirect profits due to saved costs (i.e. indirect subsidies), but also with direct profits due to subsidies, for example, subsidies to the incinerator by national and international authorities (i.e. carbon credits by the Clean Development Mechanism). In fact, this could be seen as a mere rent-seeking position, because it involves seeking to increase one's share of existing wealth without creating new wealth.

In conclusion, the presented cases show how the over-accumulated capital finds new profitable opportunities (the so-called capital valorization) in two very different ways: accumulation by dispossession and accumulation by contamination. While in the former it privatizes assets, in the latter it socializes costs. These processes are rendered possible by a certain balance of power that allows extra-economic means (both material and ideological), and that conflicts seek to transform. The focus upon capital accumulation by extra-economic means should help to understand how capital is made to circulate through biophysical nature, or else how processes of capital accumulation are related to the social metabolisms. The need of capitalist development of something 'outside of itself' is strictly material. It requires continuously opening up 'territories', or else the expansion to new 'commodity frontiers' in search of 'lower costs of input' (i.e. dispossession) and 'lower costs of output' (i.e. contamination). Therefore, the circuits of capital accumulation are inherently associated with the socio-metabolic re-configurations, and consequently foster conditions of social and environmental degradation that, eventually, lead to conflict as an attempt to visualize the injustice and revert it.

This leads us to argue that the produced situated political ecologies, which means the actual places where waste is collected and processed, have become a 'commodity frontier'. Commodity frontiers have historically been located in hinterlands where the resources are extracted (Martinez Alier et al., 2010; Moore, 2000). We argue that currently there is a shift from waste-as-externality to waste-as-resource. Thus, the

production of waste-based commodity frontiers indicates that we can expect the conflicts surrounding waste to increasingly resemble resource
conflicts (see our special issue: Schindler and Demaria, 2020)[2]. In this
sense waste represents investment opportunities and its 'extraction' produces environmental hazards that jeopardize the health of local residents
as well as workers, and inhibits the production of desirable situated political ecologies.

Jason Moore's sustained intervention (2015: 2) offers an understanding
of capitalism as 'a way of organizing nature' whose cyclical expansion
is underpinned by the successive transgression of commodity frontiers which facilitates the appropriation of hitherto non-commodified
resources. He argues that capital experiences a falling rate of return as
resources become commodified, and in order to restore conditions favourable to accumulation new sources of Cheap Nature must be identified
and appropriated. This explains why capitalism cannot 'sustain itself as a
closed system' (Moore, 2000: 146) and must constantly expand in order to
'extend the domain of appropriation faster than the zone of exploitation'
(Moore, 2015: 217). Moore argues that capitalism is in terminal crisis because there are simply no more commodity frontiers whose transgression
could fuel an expansionary phase of global capitalism. We do not take
issue with the broad contours of Moore's argument, but we argue that it
ignores instances in which localized commodity frontiers are produced
and exploited. Indeed, in many instances waste has become a resource,
driven by the production of waste-based commodity frontiers. This has
been enabled by new regulations (e.g. privatization of waste management) and methods of processing (e.g. waste-to-energy incineration).
There is a need for a research agenda that focuses on the metabolic, political, economic, legal, and/or bureaucratic mechanisms underpinning the
production of these localized commodity frontiers. The same should also
focus on changing socio-technical practices surrounding waste management, the social-ecological impacts of this shift in particular places, and
the social as well as ecological resistance it has provoked.

In the following section, we move back to the commodity frontiers
of informal waste recycling presented in our case studies. We focus
upon how informal recyclers, by defending their livelihood, resist the

[2] The idea of waste-based commodity frontiers has been developed with Seth Schindler.

socio-metabolic re-configuration driven by both accumulation by dis-possession and contamination. In particular, we look at how they politicize waste metabolism to make visible the social and environmental injustice. Their quest to re-socialize the assets and privatize the costs is a call for a fairer and more ecological society.

> (3) What is the role of informal recyclers in the metabolism of waste? How and under what conditions might their work and contribution be valued and compensated? How do power relations reduce them to invisible subjects? How do they resist and attempt to transform their role in waste metabolism?

Recycling tends to be seen as an unproblematized activity, but it entails a series of complexities, from the labour conditions to environmental degradation. In this book we attempted to investigate the social relations of recycling, which means the social relationships that recyclers must enter into in order to survive, to produce, and to reproduce their means of life. These are inherently intertwined with the waste metabolism. Earlier, we suggested that recyclers play in human societies a similar role to the decomposers in natural ecosystems. We call to paying more attention to them, both in science and public policy, because (1) they play an important role in closing the material loops of waste metabolism towards a more circular economy (what has been called the circularity gap, or metabolic rift; Martinez-Alier, 2021), and therefore they are less ecologically unsustainable, but (2) they work in difficult conditions and face numerous threats (these could be understood as the social and political dimensions of the circular economy). Since waste has become a new commodity frontier, recyclers risk both the expropriation of their means of production as well as the degradation of their means of existence and bodies. Recycling has many benefits, but faces a number of barriers, such as the financial cost or its environmental impacts. We focused exclusively on the informal recycling sector, because by definition it is not monitored by any form of government. This sector is often very labour-intensive and exploitative, but recyclers are rendered invisible because they are at the bottom of the social stratification. They are seen as low-skilled and careless of their health. For instance, in the case of shipbreaking, the dismantling could be mechanized but it would require dry docks and therefore would be much more expensive (and consequently less profitable for ship owners and shipbreakers, basically impeding capital accumulation). Instead, in the case of Delhi, recyclers carry out work that could not easily be mechanized (collection at the doorstep) and then separation that could, but is not, done by the members of the households (that shift the costs to recyclers). Currently, at the base of informal recycling sector there is the extreme poverty of recyclers who often do not have alternatives to obtain a livelihood. In this sense, informal recycling is based on extreme inequalities where someone lives out of the waste of other, more well-off members of society. The reasons behind their extreme poverty go beyond the scope of this book, because it would involve the historical political economy of the means of production such as land distribution. However, it is undeniable that the economic oppression is often coupled with other forms of oppression, such as gender, caste, or race. This challenges the hypothesis that we first need to be rich in order to become environmentalists, and looks rather the contrary. In this sense, we could refer to recyclers as a case of environmentalism of the poor (urban in the case of Delhi). The environmental benefits of the recyclers' activity include conservation of resources, savings in landfill space and emissions associated with landfill and incineration, energy saving in manufacturing and transport of waste. Apart from these benefits which coincide with recycling in general, they often obtain higher recycling rates than mechanized processes while using less fossil fuels. In doing so, they improve the sustainability of waste metabolism. However, just like biology with the decomposers, both ecological economics and political ecology have not paid enough attention to the important role of recyclers. If societies want to get closer to closing the material loops, with proposals such as the circular economy, then recyclers, as well as the social relations of recycling, should be at the centre of the debate.

The International Labour Organization has referred to the role of recyclers as green jobs, if they are included in the formal waste management sector (ILO, 2013). To be more precise, recyclers are already included since de facto they are part-and-parcel of the system, but what they need is formal recognition and compensation for their services. First of all, recyclers should be recognized for their waste management services. For example, in the case of Delhi, they should be paid at least as much as the private enterprises that carry out similar activities. Second, they should be recognized for their environmental services and be compensated for this. For instance, it is anomalous that in Delhi the waste-to-energy incinerator receives subsidies by the Clean Development Mechanism for its reduction of greenhouse gases in comparison to the baseline, the landfill, while recycling doesn't receive anything, although it is clearly higher in the waste hierarchy. In Chapter 5, we proposed detailed examples of how the exact compensation might be calculated and operationalized.

Whether recyclers get recognized and compensated (or else they manage to deploy capital de-accumulation strategies), again, clearly depends upon the balance of power. Contrary to what the industry often does, it cannot afford to pay lobbyists. For instance, the Coalition for Responsible Waste Incineration or European Union for Responsible Incineration and Treatment of Special Waste (Eurits) are notoriously known as a lobby group of the incineration industry. Following Martinez Alier (2002) power can be seen here at least in two different ways: (1) the ability to impose a decision on others; and (2) to impose a language of valuation determining which is the bottom line in an ecological distribution conflict (called procedural power). Recyclers are rendered invisible and ignored, if not actively persecuted.

Recyclers have often resorted to social mobilization and attempted to redress the balance of power. In the case of urban informal recyclers, this has been increasingly done since the 1990s when threats, such as privatization and incineration, intensified. Beyond the local level, they organized nationally and regionally in networks. Then, in alliance with social and environmental groups, they have managed to organize worldwide into the Global Alliance of Wastepickers.[3] This is a networking process supported by WIEGO (Women in Informal Employment: Globalizing and Organizing), among thousands of waste picker organizations with groups from more than 28 countries covering mainly Latin America, Asia, and Africa. Its mission is 'to work for the social and economic inclusion of the waste picker population, to promote and strengthen its organizations, to help them move up the value chain and to be included and given priority in formal waste management systems'. In collaboration with WIEGO, and supported by GAIA (Global Alliance for Incinerator

---

[3] See: http://www.globalrec.org/ (Accessed on 19 October 2022).

Alternatives), recyclers participated also in several UN Climate Summits to raise awareness about their issues, with mixed results.

In the case of shipbreaking, workers have received some support from national trade unions and environmental groups, but have generally not managed to organize effectively at the local level. In fact, the mafia-like oppression carried out by shipbreakers has not been easy to overcome, and we experienced it ourselves during field work. Internationally, environmental, human, and labour rights organizations have been organized in a coalition called Shipbreaking Platform[4] since 2005. Its mission is 'to challenge the arguments from a powerful shipping industry not used to being held accountable for its substandard practices'.

More generally, recyclers struggle for participation, recognition, and a fairer distribution of resources and socio-environmental costs. Their struggles constitute an attempt to re-politicize waste metabolism beyond techno-managerial solutions by fostering counter-hegemonic discourses and praxis. Recyclers emphasize the contradictions between development, the environment, and social well-being, and envision a transformative pathway towards a more sustainable waste metabolism. Their struggles can contribute to bring more attention over waste metabolism, while simultaneously promoting social equity and ecological sustainability. Their struggles can be read in terms of capital de-accumulation, for re-appropriating the expropriated resources and against the degradation of their means of existence and bodies. Last, their struggles can contribute to make visible the invisible, and this book is humbly meant to contribute to this political process. *Hasta la victoria compañeras recicladoras!*

---

[4] See: http://www.shipbreakingplatform.org (Accessed on 19 October 2022).

References

Abbott, A., Nandeibam, S., and O'Shea, L. (2011). Explaining the variation in household recycling rates across the UK. *Ecological Economics* 70(11): 2214–2223.

Abbott, A., Nandeibam, S., and O'Shea, L. (2013). Recycling: Social norms and warmglow revisited. *Ecological Economics* 90: 10–18.

Adeola, F. O. (2002). Toxic waste. In K. Bisson and J. Proops (Eds.), *Waste in Ecological Economics* (pp. 146–177). Cheltenham: Edward Elgar.

Agarwal, B. (1992). The gender and environment debate: Lessons from India. *Feminist Studies* 18 (1): 119–158.

Agarwal, B. (2001). Participatory exclusions, community forestry, and gender: An analysis for South Asia and a conceptual framework. *World Development* 29: 1623–1648.

Agarwal, A., Singhmar A., Kulshrestha M., and Mittal, A.K. (2005). Municipal solid waste recycling and associated markets in Delhi, India. *Resources, Conservation and Recycling* 44(1): 73–90.

Agrawal, A (. 2005). *Environmentality*. Durham: Duke University Press.

AIKMM. (2015). *Rights for Waste Workers as Service Providers: A Comprehensive Valuation of Delhi's Informal Recycling Sector*. Delhi: All India Kabadi Mazdoor Mahansangh.

Alpízar, F., and Gsottbauer, E. (2015). Reputation and household recycling practices: Field experiments in Costa Rica. *Ecological Economics* 120: 366–375.

Alter, H. (1997). Industrial recycling and the basel convention. *Resource, Conservation and Recycling* 19(1): 29–53.

Anguelovski, I., and Martinez Alier, J. (2014). The 'Environmentalism of the Poor' revisited: Territory and place in disconnected global struggles. *Ecological Economics* 102: 167–176.

Antweiler, W., Copeland, B.R., and Scott Taylor, M. (2001). Is free trade good for the environment? *American Economic Review*, 91(4): 877–908.

Ari, E., and Yilmaz, V. (2016). A proposed structural model for housewives' recycling behavior: A case study from Turkey. *Ecological Economics* 129: 132–142.

Armiero, M., and D'Alisa, G. (2012). Rights of resistance: The garbage struggles for environmental justice in Campania, Italy. *Capitalism Nature Socialism* 23(4): 52–68.

Ayres, R.U. (1999). The second law, the fourth law, recycling and limits to growth. *Ecological Economics* 29(3): 473–483.

Bank of America Merrill Lynch (2013). *No Time to Waste: Global Waste Primer*. New York: Bank of America Merrill Lynch. http://www.longfinance.net/images/reports/pdf/baml_waste_2013.pdf (last accessed 13 June 2014) .

Barata, E. (2002). Municipal waste. In K. Bisson and J. Proops (Eds.), *Waste in Ecological Economics* (pp. 131–146). Cheltenham: Edward Elgar.

176   REFERENCES

Basel Convention (2002). *Technical Guidelines for the Environmentally Sound Management for Full and Partial Dismantling of Ships.* Geneva: UNEP, Basel Secretariat.

Baumgartner, S. (2002). Thermodynamics of waste generation. In K. Bisson and J. Proops (Eds.) (2002). *Waste in Ecological Economics* (pp. 119–146). Cheltenham: Edward Elgar.

Baviskar A. (2003). Between violence and desire: Space, power, and identity in the making of metropolitan Delhi. *International Social Science Journal* 55(175): 89–98.

Beneria, L., Berik, G., and Floro, M. (2015). *Gender, Development and Globalization.* London: Routledge.

Benford, R.D. and Snow, D.A. (2000). Framing processes and social movements. *Annual Review of Sociology* 26, 611–639.

Benjamin S. (2008). Occupancy urbanism: Radicalizing politics and economy beyond policy and programs. *International Journal of Urban and Regional Research* 32(3): 719–729.

Bennett J. (2010). *Vibrant Matter: A Political Ecology of Things.* Durham, NC: Duke University Press.

Berger, A. (2008). Karl Polanyi's and Karl William Kapp's Substantive Economics: Important Insights from the Kapp–Polanyi Correspondence. *Review of Social Economy* 66(3): 381–396.

Berglund, C. (2006). The assessment of households' recycling costs: The role of personal motives. *Ecological Economics* 56(4): 560–569.

Bertram, M., Graedel, T.E., Rechberger, H., and Spatari, S. (2002). The contemporary European copper cycle: Waste management. *Ecological Economics* 42(1–2): 43–57.

Bertram, M., Graedel, T.E., Rechberger, H., and Spatari, S. (2002). The contemporary European copper cycle: waste management. *Ecological Economics* 42(1-2): 43-57.

Bhan G. (2009). 'This is no longer the city I once knew': Evictions, the urban poor and the right to the city in millennial Delhi. *Environment and Urbanization* 21(1): 127–142.

Bhatt, P.N. (2004). *Monitoring of Marine Pollution at Alang–Sosiya Seacoast with Respect to Oil and Grease.* Final Progress Report, Dept. of Analytical Chemistry. Bhavnagar University, Gujarat, India.

Bianciardi, C., Tiezzi, E., and Ulgiati, S. (1996). Response. The 'recycle of matter' debate. Physical principles versus practical impossibility. *Ecological Economics* 19: 195–196.

Bisson, K. (2002). Attitudes to waste. In K. Bisson and J. Proops (Eds.), *Waste in Ecological Economics.* (pp. 31–54). Cheltenham: Edward Elgar.

Bisson, K., and Proops, J. (Eds.) (2002). *Waste in Ecological Economics.* Cheltenham: Edward Elgar.

Blaikie, P.M., and Brookfield, H., Eds. (1987). *Land degradation and society.* London and New York: Methuen.

Bohara, A.K., Caplan, A.J., and Grijalva, T. (2007). The effect of experience and quantity-based pricing on the valuation of a curbside recycling program. *Ecological Economics* 64(2): 433–443.

Brenner, R. (2006). What is, and what is not, imperialism? *Historical Materialism* 14(4): 79–105.

Bridge, G. (2011). The economy of nature: From political ecology to the social construction of nature. In A. Leyshon R. Lee, and L. McDowell, *The SAGE Handbook of Economic Geography* (pp. 216–230). SAGE Publications Ltd.

Bryant, R.L. (1998). Power, knowledge and political ecology in the third world: a review. *Progress in Physical Geography: Earth and Environment*, 22(1): 79–94.

Bryant, R.L., and Bailey, S. (1997). *Third World Political Ecology*. London: Routledge.

Bullard, R.D. (1993). *Confronting Environmental Racism: Voices from the Grassroots*. Boston, MA: South End Press.

Castan Broto V., Allen A., and Rapoport E. (2012). Interdisciplinary perspectives on urban metabolism. *Journal of Industrial Ecology* 16(6): 851–861.

Central Pollution Control Board (CPCB). (2006). *Assessment of Status of Municipal Solid Waste Management in Metro Cities and State Capitals*. Delhi: CPCB Series, CUPS/65.

Chatterjee P. (2011). *Lineages of Political Society: Studies in Postcolonial Democracy*. Ranikhet: Permanent Black.

Chaturvedi, B., and Gidwani, V. (2011). The right to waste: Informal sector recyclers and struggles for social justice in post-reform urban India. In W. Ahmed, A. Kundu, and R. Peet (Eds.), *India's New Economic Policy: A Critical Analysis* (pp. 125–153). London: Routledge.

Chaturvedi, B., Khan, I., and Sen, P. (2012). *Give Back Our Waste: What the Okhla Waste-to-Energy Plant Has Done to Local Wastepickers*. Delhi: Chintan http://www.chintan-india.org/documents/research_and_reports/chintan-report-give-back-our-waste.pdf (last accessed 5 May 2014) .

Chaudhari, S. (1999). *A study of port and Bhavnagar city*, PhD thesis, Bhavnagar University, Gujarat, India.

Chen, W., and Graedel, T.E. (2012). Dynamic analysis of aluminum stocks and flows in the United States: 1900–2009. *Ecological Economics* 81: 92–102.

Chintan (2009). *Cooling Agents: An Analysis of Greenhouse Gas Mitigation by the Informal Recycling Sector in India*. Available at: http://www.chintan-india.org/documents/research_and_reports/chintan_report_cooling_agents.pdf

Clapp, J. (1994). The toxic waste trade with less-industrialised countries: economic linkages and political alliances. *Third World Quarterly* 15(3): 505–518.

Costanza, R. (1989). What is ecological economics? *Ecological Economics* 1(1): 1–7.

Craig, P.P. (2001). Energy limits on recycling. *Ecological Economics* 36(3): 373–384.

D'Alisa, G., Demaria, F., and Kallis, G. (2015). *Degrowth: A Vocabulary for a New Era*. London: Routledge.

D'Alisa, G., Di Nola, M.F., and Giampietro, M. (2012). A multi-scale analysis of urban waste metabolism: Density of waste disposed in Campania. *Journal of Cleaner Production* 35: 59–70.

Demaria, F., and Schindler, S. (2015). Contesting urban metabolism: struggles over waste-to-energy in Delhi, India. *Antipode. A Radical Journal of Geography* 48 (2): 293–313.

Daniels, P.L., and Moore, S. (2001). Approaches for quantifying the metabolism of physical economies: Part I: Methodological overview. *Journal of Industrial Ecology* 5(4): 69–93.

Datta, A. (2013). *Illegal City: Space, Law and Gender in a Delhi Squatter Settlement*. Farnham: Ashgate.

Davies, A. (2006). *The Geographies of Garbage Governance: Interventions, Interactions, and Outcomes*. Farnham: Ashgate.

De Angelis, M. (2001). *Marx's theory of primitive accumulation: A suggested reinterpretation*. The Commoner 2: 1–22.

De Angelis, M. (2004). Separating the doing and the deed: Capital and the continuous character of enclosures. *Historical Materialism* 12(2): 57–87.

Decker, E.H., Elliott, S., Smith, F.A., Blake, D.R., and Rowland, F.S. (2000). Energy and material flow through the urban ecosystem. *Annual Review of Energy and the Environment* 25: 685–740.

Della Porta, D. and Diani, M. (2006). *Social Movements: An Introduction*, 2nd ed. Oxford: Blackwell.

Derickson, K.D. (2014). Urban geography I: Locating urban theory in the 'urban age'. *Progress in Human Geography*. doi: 10.1177/0309132514560961

Desai, A., and Vyas, P. (1997). *Preliminary Studies on Microbial Ecology of Ship-breaking Yard at Alang, Gujarat*. Gujarat Ecology Commission, Ecological Restoration and Planning for Alang–Sosiya Ship-Breaking Yard, Gujarat.

Deshpande, P. C., Tilwankar, A K., and Asolekar, A. A. (2012). A novel approach to estimating potential maximum heavy metal exposure to ship recycling yard workers in Alang, India. *Science of the Total Environment* 438: 304–311.

Dholakia, A.D. (1997). *Studies on Coastal Fauna*. Gujarat Ecology Commission, Ecological Restoration and Planning for Alang–Sosiya Ship-Breaking Yard, Gujarat.

Dodds, S. (1997). Towards a 'science of sustainability': Improving the way ecological economics understands human well-being. *Ecological Economics* 23 (2): 95–111.

Doshi, S. (2013). The politics of the evicted: Redevelopment, subjectivity, and difference in Mumbai's slum frontier. *Antipode* 45(4): 844–865.

Dubey, M.K. (2005). *A study on the role of banks in the development of ship breaking industry at Alang & Sosiya and its resultant impact on the economy of Bhavnagar District*. PhD Thesis, Bhavnagar University.

Dupont, V.D.N. (2010). The dream of Delhi as a global city. *International Journal of Urban and Regional Research* 35(3): 533–554.

EEA (European Environment Agency). (2000). *Household and Municipal Waste: Comparability of Data in EEA Member Countries*. Copenhagen: EEA.

Ernstson, H. (2012). Re-translating nature in post-apartheid Cape Town: The material semiotics of people and plants at Bottom Road. In R. Heeks (Ed.), *Actor-Network Theory for Development*: Working Paper Series (pp. 0–35, Working Paper 4). Manchester: Institute for Development Policy and Management, SED, University of Manchester.

Escobar, A. (2008). *Territories of Difference: Place, Movements, Life, Redes*. Durham, NC: Duke University Press.

European Commission, Directorate General Environment. (2007). *Ship Dismantling and Precleaning of Ships*. Brussels: European Commission. Available at: ec.europa.eu/environment/waste/ships/pdf/ship_dismantling_report.pdf (Accessed on 16 January 2023).

Eurostat. (2001). *Economy-wide Material Flow Accounts and Derived Indicators: A Methodological Guide*. Luxembourg: EU.

Farias, I., and Bender, T. (Eds.) (2010). *Urban Assemblages: How Actor-Network Theory Changes Urban Studies*. New York: Routledge.

Federici, S. (2004). *Caliban and the Witch: Women, the Body and Primitive Accumulation*. New York: Autonomedia.

Fischer-Kowalski, M. (1997). Society's metabolism: On the childhood and adolescence of a rising conceptual star. In M. Redclift and G. Woodgate (Eds.), *The International Handbook of Environmental Sociology* (pp. 119–137). Cheltenham: Edward Elgar.

Fischer-Kowalski, M. (1998). Society's metabolism: The intellectual history of material flow analysis. Part 1. 1860–1970. *Industrial Ecology* 2(1): 61–78.

Fischer-Kowalski, M., and Haberl, H. (1993). Metabolism and colonization: Modes of production and the physical exchange between societies and nature. *Innovation: The European Journal of Social Science Research* 6(4): 415–442.

Fischer-Kowalski, M., and Haberl, H. (2015). Social metabolism: A metric for biophysical growth and degrowth. In J. Martinez Alier and R. Muradian (Eds.), *Handbook of Ecological Economics* (pp. 100–138). Cheltenham: Edward Elgar.

Fischer-Kowalski, M., and Hüttler, W. (1999). Society's metabolism: The intellectual history of material flow analysis, Part II, 1970–1998. *Journal of Industrial Ecology* 2(4): 107–136.

Fischer-Kowalski, M., Krausmann, F., Giljum, S., Lutter, S., Mayer, A., Bringezu, S., et al. (2011). Methodology and indicators of economy-wide material flow accounting. *Journal of Industrial Ecology* 15(6): 855–876.

Folke, C. (1999). Ecological principles and environmental economic analysis. In J.C.J.M. van den Bergh (Ed.), *Handbook of Environmental and Resource Economics*, pp. 895–911. Cheltenham: Edward Elgar.

Forsyth, T. (2008). Political ecology and the epistemology of social justice. *Geoforum* 39(2): 756–764.

Foster, J.B. (1999). Marx's theory of metabolic rift: classical foundations for environmental sociology. *The American Journal of Sociology* 105(2): 366–405.

Gadgil, M., and Guha, R. (1995). *Ecology and Equity*. London and New York: Routledge.

Gandy, M. (2002). *Concrete and Clay: Reworking Nature in New York City*. Cambridge, MA: MIT Press.

Geddes, P. (1885). *An Analysis of the Principles of Economics*. London: Williams and Northgate.

Georgescu-Roegen, N. (1971). *The Entropy Law and the Economic Process*. Cambridge, MA.: Harvard University Press.

Georgescu-Roegen, N. (1975). Energy and economic myths. *Southern Economic Journal* 41: 347–381.

Ghazipur Anti-Incinerator Committee. (2012). *Residents and Wastepickers Protest Against Waste-to-Energy Incinerator in Ghazipur*. Press release 24 March.

Ghertner, A. (2011). Gentrifying the state, gentrifying participation: Elite governance programs in Delhi. *International Journal of Urban and Regional Research* 35(3): 504–532.

Ghosh, A. (2000). *Solid Waste Management in Delhi*, Report 14, Institute of Social Sciences (ISS).

Giampietro, M., and Mayumi, K. (2009). *The Biofuel Delusion: The Fallacy of Large Scale Agro-Biofuels Production*. Oxford, UK: Earthscan.

Giampietro, M., Mayumi, K., and Sorma, A.H. (2012). *The Metabolic Pattern of Society*. New York: Routledge.

Giljum, S., and Eisenmenger, N. (2004). North–South trade and the distribution of environmental goods and burdens: a biophysical perspective. *The Journal of Environment & Development* 13 (1), 73–100.

Gidwani, V. (2013). Value struggles: Waste work and urban ecology in Delhi. In A. Rademacher and K.C. Sivaramakrishnan (Eds.), *Ecologies of Urbanism in India: Metropolitan Civility and Sustainability* (pp. 169–200). Hong Kong: Hong Kong University Press.

Gidwani, V., and Reddy, R.N. (2011). The afterlives of 'waste': Notes from India for a minor history of capitalist surplus. *Antipode* 43(5): 1625–1658.

Gill, K. (2010). *Of Poverty and Plastic*. New Delhi: Oxford University Press.

Glassman (2006). Primitive accumulation, accumulation by dispossession, accumulation by 'extra-economic' means. *Progress in Human Geography* 30(5): 608–625.

Global Alliance of Waste Pickers. (2012). *First Global Strategic Workshop of Waste Pickers: Inclusive Solid Waste Management*. Globalrec: Pune, India. Available at: http://globalrec.org/wp-content/uploads/2012/04/report_waste-pickers-workshop_pune2012.pdf (last accessed 19 October 2022).

Goldman, M. (2011). Speculative urbanism and the making of the next world city. *International Journal of Urban and Regional Research* 35(3): 555–581.

GrassRoots Recycling Network. (2000). *Wasting and Recycling in the United States*. Available at: http://www.grrn.org/assets/pdfs/wasting/WRUS.pdf (last accessed 15 January 2016).

Gregory, D., Johnston, R., Pratt, G., Watts, M.J., and Whatmore, S. (2009). *The Dictionary of Human Geography*. Chichester: Wiley-Balckwell.

Guha, R. and Martinez Alier, J. (1997). *Varieties of Environmentalism: Essays North and South*. London: Routledge.

Gujarat Ecology Commission (GEC). (1997). *Ecological Restoration and Planning for Alang–Sosiya Ship-Breaking Yard, Gujarat*. Gandhinagar: Gujarat Maritime Board.

Haas, W., Krausmann, F., Wiedenhofer, D., and Heinz, M. (2015). How circular is the global economy? An assessment of material flows, waste production, and recycling in the European Union and the world in 2005. *Journal of Industrial Ecology* 19(5): 765–777.

Haas, W., Krausmann, F., Wiedenhofer, D., Lauk, C., and Mayer, A. (2020). Spaceship earth's odyssey to a circular economy - a century long perspective. *Resource, Conservation, Recycling* 163: 105076.

Hall, D. (2012). Rethinking primitive accumulation: Theoretical tensions and rural Southeast Asian complexities. *Antipode* 44(4): 1188–1208.

Hall, S. (1982). The rediscovery of ideology: return to the repressed in media studies. In: Gurevitch, M., Bennett, T., Curon, J., Woolacott, J. (Eds.), *Culture, Society and Media*. New York: Methuen.

Hanrahan, D., Srivastava, S., and Ramakrishna, A. (2006). *Municipal Solid Waste in India—Overview and Challenges*. World Bank Environment Unit South Asia Region.

Harris, A. (2013). Assembling global Mumbai through transport infrastructure. *City* 17(3): 343–360.

Harriss-White, B., and Sinha, A. (2007). *Trade Liberalization and India's Informal Economy*. Oxford: Oxford University Press.

Harvey, D. (2003). *The New Imperialism*. Oxford: Oxford University Press.

Harvey, D. (2005). *A Brief History of Neoliberalism*. Oxford: Oxford University Press.

Hayami Y., Dikshit, A.K., and Mishra S.N. (2006). Waste pickers and collectors in Delhi: Poverty and environment in an urban informal sector. *Journal of Development Studies* 41(1):42–69.

High Powered Committee (HPC). (2003). *Report on hazardous waste management*. Supreme Court of India, New Delhi.

Hoornweg, D., Bhada-Tata, P., and Kennedy, C. (2013). Environment: Waste production must peak this century. *Nature* 502: 615–617.

Hillyer, H. H. (2012). The hard reality of breaking up: the global transboundary movement of ocean vessel demolition and waste. *Vermont Journal of Environmental Law* 13: 754–795.

Hornborg, A., McNeill, J., Martinez Alier, J. (Eds.). (2007). *Rethinking Environmental History: World-system History and Global Environmental Change*. Altamira Press, Lanham.

Hornborg, A. (2009). Zero-sum world: Challenges in conceptualizing environmental load displacement and ecologically unequal exchange in the world-system. *International Journal of Comparative Sociology* 50(3–4): 237–262

Hossain, M.M., and Islam, M.M. (2006). *Ship Breaking Activities and Its Impact on the Coastal Zone of Chittagong, Bangladesh: Towards Sustainable Management*. YPSA (Young Power in Social Action), Chittagong.

Gerber, J-F., and Scheidel, A. (2018). In Search of Substantive Economics: Comparing Today's Two Major Socio-metabolic Approaches to the Economy – MEFA and MuSIASEM, *Ecological Economics* 144: 186-194.

Healy, H., Martínez-Alier, J., Temper, L., Walter, M., and Gerber, J.F. (2013). *Ecological Economics from the Ground Up*. London: Routledge.

Heynen, N.C. (2014). Urban political ecology I: The urban century. *Progress in Human Geography* 38(4): 598–604.

Heynen, N.C., Kaika, M., and Swyngedouw, E. (Eds.) (2006). *In the Nature of Cities: Urban Political Ecology and the Politics of Urban Metabolism*. London: Routledge.

The Hindu. (2011). *Jindal's Okhla waste-to-energy plant broke law, says Jairam*. 1 April http://www.thehindu.com/todays-paper/tp-national/tp-newdelhi/jindals-okhla-wastetoenergy-plant-broke-law-says-jairam/article1589906.ece (last accessed 5 July 2015). Chennai: The Hindu Group.

The Hindu. (2012). *Protest against waste-to-energy incinerator*. 25 March http://www.thehindu.com/todays-paper/tp-national/tp-newdelhi/protest-against-wastetoenergy-incinerator/article3221985.ece (last accessed 21 November 2014). Chennai: The Hindu Group.

Holifield, R. (2009). Actor-network theory as a critical approach to environmental justice: A case against synthesis with urban political ecology. *Antipode* 41(4): 637–658.

Hoornweg, D., Lam, P., and Chaudhry, M. (2005). *Waste Management in China: Issues and Recommendations*. Urban Development Working Papers No. 9. East Asia Infrastructure Department. Washington: World Bank.

Ijgosse, J. (2012). *Paying Waste Pickers for Environmental Services: A Critical Examination of Options Proposed in Brazil*. WIEGO. Available at: http://wiego.org/publications/paying-waste-pickers-environmental-services-critical-examination-options-proposed-brazi

International Federation for Human Rights (FIDH). (2002). *Where do the "floating dustbins" end up? Labour rights in Shipbreaking Yards in South Asia. The Case of Chittagong (Bangladesh) and Alang (India)*. FIDH, Report No. 348/2, Paris.

International Labour Organization (ILO). (2003). *Report of the Seventeenth International Conference of Labour Statisticians*. Geneva, 24 November–3 December 2003. Geneva: ILO.

International Labour Organization (ILO). (2004). *Safety and Health in Shipbreaking: Guidelines for Asian Countries and Turkey*. Geneva: ILO.

International Labour Organization (ILO). (2012). Statistical update on employment in the informal economy. http://laborsta.ilo.org/applv8/data/INFORMAL_ECONOMY/2012-06-Statistical%20update%20-%20v2.pdf (last accessed 10 November 2017).

International Labour Organization (ILO). (2013). *Promoting Green Jobs Through the Inclusion of Informal Waste Pickers in Chile*. ILO Factsheet. Available at: https://www.ilo.org/wcmsp5/groups/public/---ed_emp/---emp_ent/documents/publication/wcms_216961.pdf (last accessed 25 January 2023)

International Maritime Organization (IMO). (2003). *Guidelines on Ship Recycling*. London: IMO.

International Metalworkers' Federation (IMF), 2006. *Status of Shipbreaking Workers in India — A Survey*. IMF, Delhi.

Kaika, M. (2006). Dams as symbols of modernization: The urbanization of nature between geographical imagination and materiality. *Annals of the Association of American Geographers* 96(2): 276–301.

Kaika, M. and Swyngedouw, E. (2000). Fetishizing the modern city: The phantasmagoria of urban technological networks. *International Journal of Urban and Regional Research* 24(1): 120–138.

Kallis, G., Gómez-Baggethun, E., and Zografos, C. (2013). To value or not to value? That is not the question. *Ecological Economics* 94: 97–105.

Kannan, K., Tanabe, S., Iwata, H., Tatsukawa, R. (1995). Butyltins in muscle and liver of fish collected from certain Asian and Oceanian countries. *Environmental Pollution* 90 (3), 279–290.

Kapp, K.W. (1950). *The Social Costs of Private Enterprise*. Cambridge, MA: Harvard University Press.

Kapp, K.W. (1963). *The Social Costs of Private Enterprise*. New York: Schocken.

Kapp, K.W. (2011). *The Foundations of Institutional Economics*. Edited by S. Berger and R. Steppacher. London et al.: Routledge.

Kaza, S., Yao, L.C., Bhada-Tata, P., and Van Woerden, F. (2018). *What a Waste 2.0: A Global Snapshot of Solid Waste Management to 2050*. Washington, DC: The World Bank.

Keil, R. and Graham, J. (1998). Reasserting nature: Constructing urban environments after Fordism. In B. Braun and N. Castree (Eds.), *Remaking Reality: Nature at the Millenium* (pp. 43–63). London: Routledge.

Kennedy, C., Cuddihy, J., and Engel-Yan, J. (2007). The changing metabolism of cities. *Journal of Industrial Ecology* 11(2): 43–59.

Khan, I., Chowdhury, H., Alam, F., and Kumar, A. (2012). Sustainable design of ship breaking industry in developing countries. *Asian Journal of Water, Environment and Pollution* 9(1): 1–11.

Krausmann, F., Lauk, C., Haas, W., and Wiedenhofer, D. (2018) From resource extraction to outflows of wastes and emissions: the socioeconomic metabolism of the global economy, 1900–2015. *Global Environmental Change* 52: 131–140.

Krishna, G. (2013). Chinese incinerator is poisoning food chain of residents and birds of Delhi's Okhla. *Toxic Watch*. http://www.toxicswatch.org/2013/11/chinese-incinerator-is-poisoning-food.html (last accessed 21 November 2014).

Kumar, S., Bhattacharyya, J.K., Vaidya, A.N., Chakrabarti, T., Devotta, S., and Akolkar, A.B. (2009). Assessment of the status of municipal solid waste management in metro cities, state capitals, class I cities, and class II towns in India: An insight. *Waste Management* 29(2): 883–895.

Islam, K.L., and Hossain, M.M. (1986). Effect of ship scrapping activities on the soil and sea environment in the coastal area of Chittagong, Bangladesh. *Marine Pollution Bulletin* 17 (10), 462–463.

Lancione, M. (2013). Homeless people and the city of abstract machines: Assemblage thinking and the performative approach to homelessness. *Area* 45(3): 358–364.

Lawhon, M. (2013b). Flows, friction and the sociomaterial metabolization of alcohol. *Antipode* 45(3): 681–701.

Lawhon, M., Ernstson, H., and Silver J. (2014). Provincializing urban political ecology: Towards a situated UPE through African urbanism. *Antipode* 46(2): 497–516.

Levien, M. (2012). The land question: Special economic zones and the political economy of dispossession in India. *The Journal of Peasant Studies* 39(3–4): 933–969.

Lipman, Z. (1998). *Trade in hazardous waste: environmental justice versus economic growth*. Melbourne: Proceedings of the Conference on Environmental Justice.

McFarlane, C. (2011a). On context: Assemblage, political economy, and structure. *City* 15(3–4): 375–388.

McFarlane, C. (2011b). Assemblage and critical urbanism. *City* 15(2): 204–224.

McFarlane, C. (2013). Metabolic inequalities in Mumbai. Beyond telescopic urbanism. *City* 17(4): 498–503.

Makri, A. and Devraj, R. (2015). *Delhi's Waste Site Story*. http://www.scidev.net/global/cities/multimedia/delhi-waste-site-photo-essay.html (last accessed 5 July 2015).

Majumdar, J. (1997). *Study of Recent Benthic Foraminifera for Evaluating Environmental Stress in and Around Alang Ship-Breaking Yard (Ghogha-Gopnath sector) Off Saurashtra Coast, Gujarat: A Case Report*. Gujarat Ecology Commission, Ecological Restoration and Planning for Alang–Sosiya Ship-Breaking Yard, Gujarat.

Mandal S.K. (2004). *Studies on the effect of ship scrapping industry waste on marine phytoplankton at Alang, Gujarat*. Ph.D Thesis, Bhavnagar University, India.

Marín-Beltrán, I., Demaria, F., Ofelio, C., Sera, L., Turiel, A., Ripple, W.J., et al. (2022). Scientists' warning against the society of waste. *Science of the Total Environment* 811: 151359.

Martinez Alier, J. (1987). *Ecological Economics. Energy, Environment and Society*. Oxford: Blackwell.

Martinez Alier, J. (2002). *The Environmentalism of the Poor: A Study of Ecological Conflicts and Valuation*. Cheltenham: Edward Elgar.

Martinez Alier, J. (2021). The circularity gap and the growth of world movements for environmental justice. Academia Letters, Article 334. https://doi.org/10.20935/AL334.

Martinez Alier, J. (2003). Mining conflicts, environmental justice and valuation. In *Just Sustainabilities: Development in an Unequal World* (pp. 201–228). Cheltenham: Earthscan.

Martinez-Alier, J. (2009). Social metabolism, ecological distribution conflicts, and languages of valuation. *Capitalism Nature Socialism* 20(1): 58–87.

Martinez Alier, J., Kallis, G., Veuthey, S., Walter, M., and Temper, L. (2010). Social metabolism, ecological distribution conflicts, and valuation languages. *Ecological Economics* 70(2): 153–158.

Martinez Alier, J., Munda, G., and O'Neill, J. (1998). Weak comparability of values as a foundation for ecological economics. *Ecological Economics* 26(3): 277–286.

Martinez Alier, J., and O'Connor, M. (1996). Ecological and economic distribution conflicts, pp 153–183. In R. Costanza, J. Martinez Alier, and O. Segura (Eds.), *Getting Down to Earth: Practical Applications of Ecological Economics*. Washington, D.C.: Island Press/ISEE.

Martinez Alier, J., and O'Connor, M. (1999). Distributional issues: An overview. In J. Van den Bergh (Ed.), *Handbook of Environmental and Resource Economics* (pp. 380–392). Cheltenham: Edward Elgar.

Martinez Alier, J., and Røpke, I. (2008). *Recent Developments in Ecological Economics*. Cheltenham: Edward Elgar.

Martinez Alier, J., and Schupmann, K. (1987). *Ecological Economics: Energy, Environment and Society*. Oxford: Basil Blackwell.

Martinez Alier, J., Temper, L., and Demaria, F. (2014). Social metabolism and environmental conflicts in India. *Indialogs* 1: 51–83.

Marx, K. (1957 [1867]). *Capital: Critique of Political Economy*. New York: International Publs.

Maslow, A.H. (1943). A theory of human motivation. *Psychological Review* 50(4): 370–396.

Mawdsley E. (2004). India's middle classes and the environment. *Development and Change* 35(1): 79–103.

Max-Neef, M. (1991). *Human Scale Development*. New York: Apex Press.

Municipal Corporation of Delhi (MCD). (2012). *Report on Delhi's MSW Management*. Delhi: Department of Environment Management Services.

Medina, M. (2007). *The World's Scavengers. Salvaging for Sustainable Consumption and Production*. Lanham, MD: Alta Mira Press.

Medina, M. (2008). *The Informal Recycling Sector in Developing Countries: Organizing Waste Pickers to Enhance Their Impact*. Gridlines; No. 44. Washington, D.C.: World Bank. https://openknowledge.worldbank.org/handle/10986/10586 (last accessed 19 October 2022).

Mehta, S.N.K. (1997). *Studies on Offshore Areas*. Gujarat Ecology Commission, Ecological Restoration and Planning for Alang–Sosiya Ship-Breaking Yard, Gujarat.

Metallurgical and Engineering Consultants (MECON). (1997). *Shipbreaking Industry: Present Status in India and its Impact on Environment*. Delhi: Union Steel Ministry.

McKee, D.L. (1996). Some reflections on the international waste trade and emerging nations. *International Journal of Social Economics* 23: 235–244.

Meehan, K.M. (2014). Tool-power: Water infrastructure as wellsprings of state power. *Geoforum* 57: 215–224.

Mitchell, D.T. (2011). *Carbon Democracy: Political Power in the Age of Oil*. New York: Verso.

Moen, A.E. (2008). Breaking basel: The elements of the basel convention and its application to toxic ships. *Marine Policy* 32: 1053–1062.

Moore, J.W. (2015). *Capitalism in the Web of Life: Ecology and the Accumulation of Capital*. New York: Verso.

Moore, J.W. (2000). Sugar and the expansion of the early modern world-economy: Commodity frontiers, ecological transformation, and industrialization. *Review: A Journal of the Fernand Braudel Center* 23: 409–433.

Mumford, W. (1938). *The Culture of Cities*. New York: Harvest.

Munda, G. (1995). *Multi-Ccriteria Evaluation in a Fuzzy Environment: Theory and Applications in Ecological Economics*. Heidelberg: Physica-Verlag.

Munda, G. (2008). *Social Multi-Criteria Evaluation for a Sustainable Economy*. New York: Springer.

Nakamura, S. (1999). An interindustry approach to analyzing economic and environmental effects of the recycling of waste. *Ecological Economics* 28(1): 133–145.

Nakamura, S. and Kondo, Y. (2006). A waste input–output life-cycle cost analysis of the recycling of end-of-life electrical home appliances. *Ecological Economics* 57(3): 494–506.

Nandi, J. (2015). Delhi CM Kejriwal promises to shut Okhla waste plant. *Times of India*, 27 February http://timesofindia.indiatimes.com/city/delhi/Delhi-CM-Kejri wal-promises-to-shut-Okhla-waste-plant/articleshow/46389323.cms (last accessed 6 July 2015).

National Environmental Engineering Research Institute (NEERI) (2005). *Assessment of Status of Municipal Solid Waste Management in Metro Cities, State Capitals, Class I Cities and Class II Towns*. Delhi: CPCB.

Negi, R. (2010). Neoliberalism, environmentalism and urban politics in Delhi. In W. Ahmed, A. Kundu, and R. Peet (Eds.), *New Economic Policy in India: A Critical Analysis* (pp. 179–198). London: Routledge.

Neumann, R.P. (1998). *Imposing Wilderness: Struggles over Livelihood and Nature Preservation in Africa*. Berkeley, CA: University of California.

Newell, J.P., and Cousins, J.J. (2014). The boundaries of urban metabolism: Towards a political–industrial ecology. *Progress in Human Geography* 39(6): 702–728.

Neşer, G., Ünsalana, D., Tekoğula, N., and Stuer-Lauridsenb, F. (2008). The shipbreaking industry in Turkey: environmental, safety and health issues. *Journal of Cleaner Production* 16 (3): 350–358.

Neşer, G., Kontas, A., Ünsalan, D., Altay, O., Darılmaz, E., Uluturhan, E., Uluturhan, E., Küçüksezgin, F., Tekogˇulc, N., and Yercan, F. (2012). Polycyclic aromatic and aliphatic hydrocarbons pollution at the coast of Aliagˇa (Turkey) ship recycling zone. *Marine Pollution Bulletin* 64: 1055–1059.

Occupational Safety and Health Administration (OSHA). (2001). *Ship Breaking Fact Sheet*. U.S. Department of Labor, OSHA. www.osha.gov.

Pathak, S.J., (1997). *Impact of Alang Ship-Breaking Activity on Water-Sediment Quality of the Intertidal Ecosystem at Alang–Sosiya Complex and Surrounding Areas*. Gujarat Ecology Commission, Ecological Restoration and Planning for Alang–Sosiya Ship-Breaking Yard, Gujarat.

Pearson, C.S. (1987). *Multinational Corporations, Environment and the Third World*. Durham, NC: Duke University Press.

Peet, R. and Watts, M.J. (Eds.) (1996). *Liberation Ecologies: Environment, Development, Social Movements*. London: Routledge.

Pellow, D.N. (2007). *Resisting Global Toxics: Transnational Movements for Environmental Justice*. Cambridge, MA: MIT Press.

Peluso, N., and Watts, M. (Eds.) (2001). *Violent Environments*. Ithaca, NY: Cornell University Press.

Perrault, T. (2012). Dispossession by accumulation? Mining, water and the nature of enclosure on the Bolivian Altiplano. *Antipode* 45(5): 1050–1069.

Pieterse, E. (2008). *City Futures: Confronting the Crisis of Urban Development*. London: Zed Books.

Pigou, A.C. (1920). *The Economics of Welfare*. London: Macmillan.

Polanyi, K. (1944). *The Great Transformation*. New York and Toronto: Rinehart & Company.

Powell, J., Turner, K., Peters, M., and Strobl, B. (2002). Economics of waste. In K. Bisson and J. Proops (Eds.), *Waste in Ecological Economics* (pp. 180-211). Cheltenham: Edward Elgar.

Proops, J. (2002). Nuclear waste. In K. Bisson and J. Proops (Eds.), *Waste in Ecological Economics* (pp. 212-235). Cheltenham: Edward Elgar.

Prudham, S. (2007). The Fictions of autonomous invention: Accumulation by dispossession, commodification and life patents in Canada. *Antipode* 39(3): 406–429.

Rademacher, A. and Sivaramakrishnan, K.C. (Eds.). (2013). *Ecologies of Urbanism in India: Metropolitan Civility and Sustainability*. Hong Kong: Hong Kong University Press.

Ranganathan, M. (2015). Storm drains as assemblages: The political ecology of flood risk in post-colonial Bangalore. *Antipode*.

Reddy, S.M., Basha, S., Sravan Kumar, V.G., Joshi, H.V., and Ghosh, P.K. (2003). Quantification and classification of ship scrapping waste at Alang–Sosiya, India. *Marine Pollution Bulletin* 46, 1609–1614.

Reddy, M.S., Joshi, H.V., Basha, S., and Sravan Kumar, V.G. (2004a). An assessment for energy potential of solid waste generated from a ship-scrapping yard at Alang. *Journal of Solid Waste Technology & Management* 30, 90–99.

Reddy, M.S., Basha, S., Kumar, Sravan, Joshi, H.V., and Ramachandraiah, G. (2004b). Distribution enrichment and accumulation of heavy metals in coastal sediments of Alang–Sosiya ship scrapping yard, India. *Marine Pollution Bulletin* 48, 1055–1059.

Reddy, M.S., Basha, S., Joshi, H.V., Sravan Kumar, V.G., Jha, B., and Ghosh, P.K. (2005a). Modeling the energy content of combustible ship-scrapping waste at Alang–Sosiya, India, using multiple regression analysis. *Waste Management* 25, 747–754.

Reddy, M.S., Basha, S., Joshi, H.V., and Ramachandraiah, G., (2005b). Seasonal distribution and contaminations levels of total PHCs, PAHs and heavy metals in coastal waters of the Alang–Sosiya ship scrapping yard, Gulf of Cambay, India. *Chemosphere* 61, 1587–1593.

Rediff News (2012). Toxic ash engulfs south Delhi's Okhla neighbourhood. http://www.rediff.com/news/report/photo-toxic-ash-engulfs-south-delhis-okhla-neighbourhood/20121227.htm (last accessed 21 November 2014).

Rice, J. (2009). The transnational organization of production and uneven environmental degradation and change in the world economy. *International Journal of Comparative Sociology* 50, 215–236.

Ricklefs, R.E., and Miller, G.L. (2000). *Ecology*. New York: W.H. Freeman.

Robbins, P. (2004). *Political Ecology: A Critical Introduction*. Oxford: Blackwell.

Roberts, A. (2008) Privatizing social reproduction: The primitive accumulation of water in an era of neoliberalism. *Antipode* 40(4): 535–560.

Røpke, I. (2004). The early history of modern ecological economics. *Ecological Economics* 50(3–4): 293–314.

Røpke, I. (2005). Trends in the development of ecological economics from the late 1980s to the early 2000s. *Ecological Economics* 55(2): 262–290.

Rousmaniere, P., and Raj, N. (2007). Shipbreaking in the developing world: problems and prospects. *International Journal of Occupational and Environmental Health* 13: 359–368.

Samson, M. (2020) Whose frontier is it anyway? Reclaimer "Integration" and the battle over Johannesburg's waste-based commodity frontier. *Capitalism Nature Socialism* 31(4): 60–75.

Samson, M. (2009). Wasted citizenship? Reclaimers and the privatised expansion of the public sphere. *Africa Development* 34(3-4): 1–25.

Scheidel, A., and Sorman, A.H. (2012). Energy transitions and the global land rush: Ultimate drivers and persistent consequences. *Global Environmental Change* 22(3): 588–595.

Scheidel, A., Temper, L., Demaria, F., and Martínez-Alier, J. (2018). Ecological distribution conflicts as forces for sustainability: an overview and conceptual framework. *Sustainability Science* 13(3): 585–598.

Schindler, S. (2014a). The making of 'world-class' Delhi: Relations between street hawkers and the new middle class. *Antipode* 46(2): 557–573.

Schindler, S. (2014b). A New Delhi everyday: Multiplicities of governance regimes in a transforming metropolis. *Urban Geography* 35(3): 402–419.

Schindler, S., Demaria, F., and Pandit, S.B. (2012). Delhi's waste conflict. *Economic and Political Weekly* 47(42): 18–21.

Schindler, S., and Demaria, F. (2020) 'Garbage is gold': Waste-based commodity frontiers, modes of valorization and ecological distribution conflicts. *Capitalism, Nature and Socialism* 31(4): 52–59.

Schmidt-Bleek, F. (1999). *The Factor 10/MIPS-Concept: Bridging Ecological, Economic, and Social Dimensions with Sustainability Indicators.* Tokyo and Berlin: ZEF Publication Series.

Scott Frey, R. (1998). The hazardous waste stream in the world system. In: Ciccantell, P.S., Bunker, S.G. (Eds.), *Space and Transport in the World-System.* Westport, CT: Greenwood.

Searle, L.G. (2014). Conflict and commensuration: Contested market making in India's private real Estate development sector. *International Journal of Urban and Regional Research* 38(1): 60–78.

Sethi, A. (2012). Incinerator gases choking Okhla. *Deccan Herald,* 12 July. http://www.deccanherald.com/content/263944/incinerator-gases-choking-okhla.html (last accessed 12 January 2014).

Shatkin, G. (Ed.). (2014). *Contesting the Indian City: Global Visions and the Politics of the Local.* Malden, MA: John Wiley & Sons.

Shaw, G.R., and Meehan, K. (2013). Force-full: Power, politics and object-oriented philosophy. *Area* 45(2): 216–222.

Silver, J. (2014). Incremental infrastructures: Material improvisation and social collaboration across post-colonial Accra. *Urban Geography* 35(6): 788–804.

Singh, S. (2001). *Domestically prohibited goods, trade in toxic waste and technology transfer: issues and developments.* Discussion paper. CUTS, Centre for International Trade, Economics & Environment, Jaipur (India).

Smit, S., and Musango, J.K. (2015). Towards connecting green economy with informal economy in South Africa: A review and way forward. *Ecological Economics* 116: 154–159.

Sneddon, C. (2007). Nature's materiality and the circuitous paths of accumulation: Dispossession of freshwater fisheries in Cambodia. *Antipode* 39(1): 167–193.

Snow, D., Rochford, B., Worden, S., and Benford, R. (1986). Frame alignment processes, micromobilization, and movement participation. *American Sociological Review* 51(4): 464–481.

Soderbaum, P. (2004). *Politics and Ideology in Ecological Economics.* Internet Encyclopedia of Ecological Economics.

Soni, A. (1997). *Ecology of Intertidal Macrofauna and Literature Review for Marine Biota.* Gujarat Ecology Commission, Ecological Restoration and Planning for Alang–Sosiya Ship-Breaking Yard, Gujarat.

Spash, C. (1999). The development of environmental thinking in economics. *Environmental Values* 8(4): 413–435.

Spash, C.L. (2010). 'The brave new world of carbon trading'. *New Political Economy* 15(2): 169–195.

Stuer-Lauridsen, F., Husum, H., Jensen, M.P., Odgaard, T., and Winther, K.M. (2004). *Oil Tanker Phase-out and the Ship Scrapping Industry: A Study on the Implications of the Accelerated Phase Out Scheme of Single Hull Tankers Proposed by the EU for the World Ship Scrapping and Recycling Industry.* Final Report, Brussels.

Swaney, J.A. (2006). Policy for social costs: Kapp vs. Neoclassical economics. In *Social Costs and Public Action in Modern Capitalism: Essays Inspired by Karl William Kapp's Theory of Social Costs.* London: Routledge.

Swaney, J.A., and Evers, M.A. (1989). The social cost concepts of K. William Kapp and Karl Polanyi. *Journal of Economic Issues* 23(1): 7–33.

Swyngedouw, E. (1996). The city as hybrid: On nature, society and cyborg urbanization. *Capitalism, Nature, Socialism* 7(2): 65–80.

Swyngedouw, E. (2004). *Social Power and the Urbanization of Water: Flows of Power.*
Oxford: Oxford University Press.

Swyngedouw, E., and Heynen, N.C. (2003). Urban political ecology, justice, and the
politics of scale. *Antipode* 35(5): 898–918.

Talyan, V., Dahiya, R.P., and Sreekrishnan, T.R. (2008). State of municipal solid waste
management in Delhi, the capital of India. *Waste Management* 28(7): 1276–1287.

Tewari, A., Joshi, H.V., Trivedi, R.H., Sravankumar, V.G., Ragunathan, C., Khambhaty,
Y., Kotiwar, O.S., and Mandal, S.K. (2001). Studies on the effect of shipscrapping
industry and its associated waste on the biomass production and biodiversity of
biota "in situ" condition at Alang. *Marine Pollution Bulletin* 42: 462–469.

Tchobanoglous, G. and Kreith, F. (2002). *Handbook of Solid Waste Management.*
New York: McGraw-Hill.

TNN (2015). Sisodia gets feel of Okhla plant's smoke and ash. 23 May http://timesofin
dia.indiatimes.com/city/delhi/Sisodia-gets-feel-of-Okhla-plants-smoke-and-ash/
articleshow/47392336.cms (last accessed 21 November 2014).

Trivedi, J.M. (1997). *Microbiological studies.* Gujarat Ecology Commission, Ecological
Restoration and Planning for Alang–Sosiya Ship-Breaking Yard, Gujarat.

Ulli-Beer, S., Andersen, D.F., and Richardson, G.P. (2007). Financing a competitive
recycling initiative in Switzerland. *Ecological Economics* 62(3–4): 727–739.

UN-Habitat (2009). *Solid Waste Management in the World's Cities.* UN-Habitat.
Available at https://unhabitat.org/solid-waste-management-in-the-worlds-cities-
water-and-sanitation-in-the-worlds-cities-2010-2 (last accessed 19 November
2021).

UNCTAD (United Nations Conference on Trade and Development). (2007). *Review
of Maritime Transport.* Geneva: United Nations.

UNCTAD (United Nations Conference on Trade and Development). (2011). *Review
of Maritime Transport.* Geneva: United Nations.

UNESCO. (2001). *Impacts and Challenges of a Large Coastal Industry. Alang–Sosiya
Ship-Breaking Yard, Gujarat, India.* Paris: UNESCO.

UNEP. (2013). *City-Level Decoupling: Urban Resource Flows and the Governance of
Infrastructure Transitions* http://www.unep.org/resourcepanel/Publications/City-
Level decoupling/tabid/106135/Default.aspx (last accessed 2 November 2013).
Nairobi: United Nations Environment Programme (UNEP).

Upadhyay, G.B. (2002). *The problems and prospects of ship breaking industry in India
with reference to Alang ship breaking yard.* PhD Thesis, Bhavnagar University.

Usui, T. (2008). Estimating the effect of unit-based pricing in the presence of
sample selection bias under Japanese Recycling Law. *Ecological Economics* 66(2–
3): 282–288.

Vallejo, M.C. (2010). Biophysical structure of the Ecuadorian economy, foreign trade,
and policy implications. *Ecological economics* 70(2): 159–169.

van de Klundert, A., and Anschutz, J. (2001). *Integrated Sustainable Waste
Management- the Concept.* Tools for Decision-makers. Experiences from the
Urban Waste Expertise Programme (1995–2001). WASTE.

Veuthey, S., and Gerber, J.F. (2012). Accumulation by dispossession in coastal Ecuador: Shrimp farming, local resistance and the gender structure of mobilizations. *Global Environmental Change* 22(3): 611–622.

Villamayor, S., and Muradian, R. (Eds.) (2023). *The Barcelona School of Ecological Economics and Political Ecology.* Cheltenham, UK: Edward Elgar.

Visvanathan, S. (1997). *A Carnival for Science: Essays on Science, Technology and Development.* Delhi: Oxford University Press.

Watson V. (2003). Conflicting rationalities: Implications for planning theory and ethics. *Planning Theory and Practice* 4(4): 395–407.

Wayne Hess, R., Rushworth, D., Hynes, V. M., and Peters, E. J. (2001). *Disposal options for ships.* National Defense Research Institute (U.S.), Rand Corporation.

Weisz, H. (2006). *Accounting for Raw Material Equivalents of Traded Goods. A Comparison of Input-Output Approaches in Physical, Monetary, and Mixed Units.* Social Ecology Working Paper 87, Vienna: IFF Social Ecology.

While A., Jonas, A.E.G., and Gibbs, D. (2010). From sustainable development to carbon control: Eco-state restructuring and the politics of urban and regional development. *Transactions of the Institute of British Geographers* 35(1): 76–93.

Wilkinson, D. (2002). Waste law. In K. Bisson and J. Proops (Eds.), *Waste in Ecological Economics.* (pp. 19–42). Cheltenham: Edward Elgar.

Wilson, D.C., Araba, A.O., Chinwah, K., and Cheeseman, C.R. (2009). Building recycling rates through the informal sector. *Waste Management* 29(2): 629–635.

Wilson, D.C., Velis, C., and Cheeseman, C. (2006). Role of informal sector recycling in waste management in developing countries. *Habitat International* 30(4): 797–808.

Winiwarter, V. (2002). History of waste. In K. Bisson and J. Proops (Eds.), *Waste in Ecological Economics* (pp. 42–66). Cheltenham: Edward Elgar.

Wolman, A. (1965). The metabolism of cities. *Scientific American* 213(3): 179–190.

Women in Informal Employment: Globalizing and Organizing (WIEGO). (2013). *Waste Pickers: The Right to Be Recognized as Workers.* Manchester, UK: WIEGO.

World Bank. (1999). *Municipal Solid Waste Incineration. World Bank Technical Guidance Report.* Washington, D.C: World Bank.

World Bank, Hoornweg, D., and Bhada-Tata, P. (2012). *What a Waste: A Global Review of Solid Waste Management. Urban Development Series*; Knowledge Papers no. 15. Washington, DC: World Bank.

Zografos, C., and Howarth, R.B. (2010). *Deliberative Ecological Economics.* Delhi: Oxford University Press.

Yin, R. (2003). *Case Study Research: Design and Methods.* Thousand Oaks, CA: Sage Publications.

ZHijie, F. (1988) Pollution from Chinese shipbreaking. *Marine Pollution Bulletin* 19(10): 501.

Postface: My Intellectual Project, and How This Book Fits into It

I want to contextualize this book in my broader intellectual project. Political ecology understands every ecological issue as a political one. It aims at politicizing environmental issues. To this end, there are fundamental questions to be addressed: Who has access to the environment? How and by whom is it managed? How are environmental goods and bads distributed? How is nature socially constructed? How and by whom are new socio-natures and spaces produced? Who benefits and who loses? Accordingly, along these lines, my research in general, and this book in particular, aims to inform theory on how environments are shaped, politicized, and contested. It investigates the interactions between ecological and social processes putting emphasis upon spatial dimensions, biophysical dynamics, power relations, economic institutions, cultural narratives, political structures, and intersectionality of race, gender, and class.

The primary questions motivating my intellectual project are these: (1) Why are natural resources and environmental impacts unequally distributed? And how does this occur? (2) Who is best placed to promote a more socially just and ecologically sustainable world? And how could this be achieved? In pursuit of answers to these questions I have developed a two-pronged research agenda. First, I have engaged with a critique of growth-based development that depoliticizes genuine political antagonisms between alternative visions, as well as investigates the resistance it faces; and second, I have inquired into the alternative imaginaries. This gives coherence to my intellectual project as it pursues the following interrelated research interests: (1) Mapping environmental justice and conflicts; (2) Political ecologies of waste (the focus of this book); (3) Degrowth; and (4) the Pluriverse. In terms of geographical areas, I have mainly focused on the Global South in general, and India in particular.

P.1 Mapping Environmental Justice and Conflicts

Over recent decades, communities asking for environmental justice have multiplied throughout the world and increasingly made their grievances and claims internationally. The spatial and symbolic expansion of such struggles is expressed both in rural and urban settings, North and South alike. In the framework of the project EnvJustice, funded by the European Research Council and led by Joan Martinez-Alier with myself as deputy coordinator, we have mapped over 3,000 environmental conflicts with the Environmental Justice Atlas (EJAtlas.org) that has become the world's largest such inventory. The EJAtlas offers a visual representation of spatial relations, aiming to document, understand, and analyse social conflicts that actively create new spaces and socio-natures. This has allowed us to go beyond case studies, and move towards a comparative and statistical political ecology. The 13 papers of our special issue in *Sustainability Science* address why and through what political, social, and economic processes are some denied the right to a safe environment, and how to support the necessary social and political transformation to enact environmental justice (Temper et al., 2018). In particular, our conceptual overview paper shows how ecological distribution conflicts are transformative forces for sustainability (Scheidel et al., 2018). While the papers of this special issue focused on specific issues, countries or regions, our paper on environmental conflicts and defenders in *Global Environmental Change* analyses the overall EJAtlas database using the lens of statistical political ecology. The aim is to outline a general theory of environmental conflicts: why, through whom, how, and when conflicts over the use of the environment may take an active role in shaping transitions toward sustainability.

I am also developing a research interest in climate justice. With my PhD students, we are investigating coal-related environmental conflicts in India (Brototi Roy), as well as carbon budget and unburnable fossil fuels reserves globally (Naw Thiri May Aye). Climate change is arguably the largest waste disposal conflict given the excessive production of carbon dioxide.

P.2 Political Ecologies of Waste

In my PhD thesis, I have investigated the 'social relations of recycling', that recyclers must enter into in order to survive, to produce, and to reproduce their means of life. I carried out two case studies with action research methods in India in collaboration with grassroots groups: shipbreaking in Alang (Demaria, 2010) and waste management in Delhi (Demaria and Schindler, 2015), that resulted in two articles for *Ecological Economics* and *Antipode*, respectively. This book is the culmination of this process. My research shows that actors involved in environmental conflicts not only struggle against the dispossession from their means of production (what Harvey has notably theorized as 'accumulation by dispossession'), but also against the shifting of social costs of enterprises to vulnerable communities (what I propose to call 'accumulation by contamination'). Notably, class, race, and gender relations, and their intersectionality play a fundamental role in these processes.

In the future, I intend to investigate the expansion of waste-based commodity frontiers. In particular, first, I want to carry out comparative studies of the different place-based strategies and struggles of waste pickers. I intend to analyse at least 100 cases of environmental conflicts in the Global South that we have collected in the EJAtlas to explain why waste is a site of social conflict in the Southern metropolis.[1] Second, I want to investigate recyclers in the Global North, a totally under-researched topic, starting with the case study of Barcelona (Spain).[2]

P.3 Geographies of Degrowth

The term *décroissance* (degrowth) signifies a process of political and social transformation that reduces a society's material and energy use while improving the quality of life. Recent scholarship has focused on the

---

[1] See the featured map 'Waste pickers under threat'. Available at: https://ejatlas.org/featured/wastepickers (Accessed on 6 November 2021).
[2] Preliminary results have been featured in an article published by *The Guardian* and titled 'Chariots of steel: Barcelona's hidden army of scrap recyclers'. Available at: https://www.theguard ian.com/global-development/2021/mar/23/chariots-steel-barcelonas-hidden-migrant-army-scrap-recyclers (Accessed on 6 November 2021).

ecological and social costs of economic growth, on policies that may secure prosperity without growth, and the study of grassroots alternatives pre-figuring a post-growth future.

Degrowth is a slogan launched by activists in the early 2000s and it quickly became an interpretative frame for a new social movement. The article in *Environmental Values* co-authored by myself with F. Schenider, F. Sekulova, and J. Martinez-Alier, 'What is Degrowth?', discusses the definition, origins, evolution, practices, and construction of degrowth. We argue that: 'Generally degrowth challenges the hegemony of economic growth and calls for a democratically led redistributive downscaling of production and consumption in industrialized countries as a means to achieve environmental sustainability, social justice and well-being' (Demaria et al., 2013: 209). The book *Degrowth: A Vocabulary for a New Era* (Routledge, 2014), co-edited with Giacomo D'Alisa and Giorgos Kallis, comprehensively covers the burgeoning literature on degrowth. It presents and explains the different lines of thought, imaginaries, and proposed courses of action that together complete the degrowth puzzle. Translated into more than 10 languages, this book has become the international reference on the subject.

While early scholarly contributions were generally focused on problem diagnostics, that is, 'Why degrowth?', more recent debates have focused on prognosis, that is, 'What needs to be done? How? By and for whom?'. I intend to contribute to these more recent debates about the politics of degrowth. For instance, our special issue in *Sustainability Science* set the tone for some of the opportunities and challenges involved in the transformation that socially sustainable degrowth entails while challenging contemporary economic development narratives (Asara et al., 2015). In a paper for a special issue on Citizens vs Markets in the *Journal of Civil Society*, we discussed 'subjects of change', making the distinction between civil and uncivil actors for degrowth (D'Alisa et al., 2013). Related to this debate on who promotes sustainability, in the editorial of our special issue with 13 articles in *Ecological Economics* on relationships between degrowth and environmental justice, we conclude that an alliance between the two is not only possible but necessary (Akbulut et al., 2019).

The relative lack of engagement by geographers with degrowth is striking. This motivated us to edit a special issue on the geographies of degrowth in *Environment and Planning E* (with Giorgos Kallis and Karen

Bakker). This did not aim to define limits to growth or blueprints for degrowth, but rather to analyse how geographers may contribute to the study and understanding of innovative social processes that emerge as growth trajectories slow down or even collapse (Demaria et al., 2019). Last, we published the book *The Case for Degrowth* (Polity Press, 2020; with Giorgos Kallis, Susan Paulson, and Giacomo D'Alisa). This book is unlike any other on degrowth, in that it is the first to try to address the hard question of 'how to' in the current political conjuncture. Most books on degrowth stay on the diagnosis and on prescriptions—this book thinks hard about the grassroots and institutional politics that can realize a transformation akin to degrowth. In this sense, it is not redundant to the many books and articles already arguing that growth is harmful and doomed. Our book differs from those by also offering encouraging ways forward in daily practices and values, in communal organizing, in government policies, and in political mobilization. Although written before the outbreak of Covid-19, it offers strategies to the 'reconstruction' and the 'day after' from a degrowth perspective.

In the future, I want to investigate the geographical aspects of degrowth-relevant processes. I am interested in how degrowth ideas are socially produced, performed, and organized spatially at different scales, what sorts of places and territories these ideas produce, and how new spatial subjectivities may be constructed.

P.4 Geographies of the Pluriverse

My work contributes to a cultural and political ecological critique of (sustainable) development, and the search for alternatives to it, as outlined in an article for the journal *Development* (Kothari et al., 2014). It is inspired, first, by a notion of post-development that challenges the homogenization of cultures because of the widespread adoption of technologies, consumption, and production models experienced in the Global North; and second, by a political ecological critique of productivism and economism. The intention is to outline a vision of politics beyond today's imaginary of a unilinear future. Criticism of growth-based development, a Western cultural construct imposed upon the rest of the world, opens up a matrix of alternatives, worldviews and practices relating to the collective search for an ecologically wise and socially just world. My research hints at the pluriverse: 'a world where many worlds fit', as the Zapatista of Chiapas say. I draw on my work to show how environmental justice and degrowth contribute to building counter-hegemonic narratives (Akbulut et al., 2019), in alliance with equivalent alternative frameworks emerging from the Global South such as Buen Vivir from Latin America, ecological Swaraj from India, and Ubuntu from South Africa (Kothari et al., 2014). Along these lines, I have proposed a post-development research agenda towards the pluriverse in the journal *Third World Quarterly* (Demaria and Kothari, 2017). I intend to continue exploring the relationships among and potential for convergences of different alternatives to development.

The first step has been to establish an inventory. In fact, what has been missing is a broad transcultural compilation of concrete concepts, worldviews, and practices from around the world, challenging the modernist ontology of universalism in favour of a multiplicity of possible worlds. This is what we attempt with *Pluriverse: A Post-Development Dictionary* (2019), co-edited with Ashish Kothari, Ariel Salleh, Arturo Escobar, and Alberto Acosta. It is a stimulating collection of over 100 essays on transformative alternatives to the currently dominant processes of globalized development, including its structural roots in modernity, capitalism, state domination, and masculinist values. First and foremost, we had to attempt defining what we mean by alternatives to development, and how the transformative solutions can be distinguished from the false ones, proposed by the establishment to 'greenwash' development. The book follows the structure of an encyclopaedia, with short 1000-word entries for each of the key terms. The entries are written by widely known authors such as Katherine Gibson, Silvia Federici, Vandana Shiva, Serge Latouche, Wolfgang Sachs, and Nnimmo Bassey.

Likewise, with the intention of starting a debate about possible convergences, a further article on the discursive synergies for a 'Great Transformation', explores potentially fertile complementarities among trendy discourses challenging conventional notions of (un)sustainable development—Human Development, Degrowth, and Buen Vivir—and outlines pathways for their realization (Beling et al., 2018).

In future research, I would like to expand this inventory, advance the definition of what are transformative alternatives, show how they are different from techno-fixes, and also explore how they can be articulated.

For instance, what do they have in common and how do they differ? What potential for tensions and complementarities is there, given that the mixed socio-ecological communities they emerge from are rooted in specific geographies? How can we deal with those worlds that do not want to relate—ethno-nationalist and imperializing worlds—without going against the principles of the pluriverse? Is it possible to do so without resorting to universal criteria? These issues require further investigation. Some of these are addressed in our special issue in the journal *Sustainability Science* titled 'Alternatives to sustainable development: What can we learn from pluriverse in practice?' (Kaul et al., 2022).

P.5 A Global Political Economy of Environment and Development

In brief, my research contributes to a global political economy of environment and development. My work underlines the need for a politicization of socio-environmental debates, whereby political refers to the struggle over the kinds of worlds that people want to create and the types of ecologies they want to live in. I put the focus on who gains and who loses in ecological processes. First, I attempt to demonstrate how environmental justice groups and movements coming out of environmental conflicts play a fundamental role in redefining and promoting sustainability. Second, I want to show how counter-hegemonic discourses and praxis re-politicize the debate about what kind of society we want to live in and how to open up alternative avenues. Degrowth aims to re-politicize the debate on the relationships between sustainability, economy, and society by asking: If we are to guarantee a sustainable and just future for present and future generations, why should our economies grow? At the same time, the Pluriverse re-politicizes the debate over socio-ecological transformation by emphasizing its multi-dimensionality.

My research plan is ambitious, but it is meant to be a humble contribution to the struggles for social and environmental justice. As I have argued, the struggles of informal recyclers constitute an attempt to re-politicize waste metabolism beyond techno-managerial solutions by fostering counter-hegemonic discourses and praxis.

About the Author

I am an Associate Professor of Ecological Economics and Political Ecology at the University of Barcelona. I am also an associate researcher at the Institute of Environmental Science and Technology (ICTA) at the Autonomous University of Barcelona, a prestigious interdisciplinary centre of environmental research (ranked 8th in environmental studies by the Center for World University Rankings and awarded as a unit of research excellence by the Spanish Ministry of Economy). While working on this book I have been a visiting scholar at various research centres in India, China, the United States, UK, Netherlands, Croatia, Italy, Germany, and Argentina, such as Jawaharlal Nehru University, and the International Institute of Social Studies. I have a consolidated experience in international and national competitive research projects. For instance, I have been the deputy coordinator of the ERC project EnvJustice (led by Prof Joan Martinez-Alier) which maps and analyses the social conflicts between the environment and the economy (2016–2021; €2 mn).

Overall, I have published more than 25 articles in highly ranked journals in socio-environmental sciences like *Ecological Economics*, *Global Environmental Change*, and *Sustainability Science*; 25 book chapters; as well as edited five special issues, and two successful books, *Degrowth* (2014) and *Pluriverse* (2019). Moreover, I am co-author of the book *The Case for Degrowth* (Polity Press, 2020). My publications are regularly translated into other languages, most notably *Degrowth* (2014) into more than 10 languages.

I am an editor for the journal *Sustainability Science* that offers insights into interactions within and between nature and the rest of human society, and the complex mechanisms that sustain both. I am also an expert reviewer for the Intergovernmental Panel on Climate Change (IPCC).

I have given over 100 talks and presentations in more than 30 countries, mainly at scientific conferences, but also for the general public and policy makers, including at the House of Commons, Oxford University, and the European Commission. I am also active on academic social

networks with personal profiles at Academia.edu and ResearchGate
(with more than 105,000 and 95,000 views, respectively). Lastly, aiming
to ensure a wide outreach of my research, I regularly publish press articles in English, Spanish, French, and Italian, in publications such as The
Guardian, The Ecologist, The Conversation, Open Democracy, eldiario.
es (Spain) and Mediapart (France).

Index

For the benefit of digital users, indexed terms that span two pages (e.g., 52–53) may, on occasion, appear on only one of those pages.

Figures are indicated by *f* following the page number

202 INDEX

Milton Keynes UK
Ingram Content Group UK Ltd.
UKHW022215201023
430981UK00001B/1

9 780192 869050